# First Workshop on Bridging Human-Computer Interaction and Natural Language Processing 2021



Online
20 April 2021

ISBN: 978-1-7138-2961-4

**Printed from e-media with permission by:**

Curran Associates, Inc.
57 Morehouse Lane
Red Hook, NY 12571

**Some format issues inherent in the e-media version may also appear in this print version.**



Printed with permission by Curran Associates, Inc. (2021)

For permission requests, please contact the Association for Computational Linguistics at the address below.

Association for Computational Linguistics
209 N. Eighth Street
Stroudsburg, Pennsylvania 18360

Phone: 1-570-476-8006
Fax: 1-570-476-0860

acl@aclweb.org

**Additional copies of this publication are available from:**

Curran Associates, Inc.
57 Morehouse Lane
Red Hook, NY 12571 USA
Phone: 845-758-0400
Fax: 845-758-2633
Email: curran@proceedings.com
Web: www.proceedings.com

EACL 2021

# Bridging Human–Computer Interaction and Natural Language Processing

## Proceedings of the First Workshop

April 20, 2021

# Introduction

Welcome to the First Workshop on Bridging Human–Computer Interaction and Natural Language Processing!

The rapid advancement of natural language processing (NLP) research has led to a variety of applications spanning a wide range of domains. As NLP applications are being used by more people in their everyday lives, and are increasingly powered by data generated by people, it is more important than ever that NLP researchers and practitioners adopt and develop methods to incorporate people into their work in meaningful ways. Perspectives from human–computer interaction (HCI) can enable NLP researchers and practitioners to advance the field of NLP in ways that are aligned with people's needs, raising novel questions and research directions for both NLP and HCI.

The workshop brings together researchers and practitioners from both disciplines to discuss shared research interests, highlight work at the intersection of these fields, and identify challenges and opportunities for productive interdisciplinary collaborations.

We are delighted to present eighteen papers spanning reports of empirical work, research proposals, provocations, and surveys, along with seven non-archival papers to be presented at the workshop but not included in the proceedings. We would like to thank everyone who submitted their work to this workshop, as well as the program committee for their insightful feedback. We would also like to thank our invited speakers: Marti Hearst, Niloufar Salehi, and Burr Settles.

We hope you enjoy the workshop!

—Su Lin Blodgett, Michael Madaio, Brendan O'Connor, Hanna Wallach, and Qian Yang

**Organizers:**

Su Lin Blodgett, Microsoft Research

Michael Madaio, Microsoft Research

Brendan O'Connor, University of Massachusetts Amherst

Hanna Wallach, Microsoft Research

Qian Yang, Cornell University

**Program Committee:**

Heloisa Candello

Stevie Chancellor

Sindhu Ernala

Mitchell Gordon

Huda Khayrallah

Geza Kovacs

Narges Mahyar

David Mimno

Swati Mishra

Carolyn Rosé

Koustuv Saha

Joseph Seering

Qinlan Shen

Alison Smith-Renner

Adam Trischler

Austin Wright

Michael Yoder

Zhou Yu

Justine Zhang

**Invited Speakers:**

Marti Hearst, University of California Berkeley

Niloufar Salehi, University of California Berkeley

Burr Settles, Duolingo

# Table of Contents

# Non-Archival Papers

*Three Directions for the Design of Human-Centered Machine Translation*
Samantha Robertson, Wesley Hanwen Deng, Timnit Gebru, Margaret Mitchell, Daniel Liebling, Michal Lahav, Katherine Heller, Mark Díaz, Samy Bengio and Niloufar Salehi

*Humans predictably fail to detect fake self-presentations generated by AI*
Benjamin Carson, Maurice Jakesch and Mor Naaman

*What Human Rationales Tell Us about Machine Explanations*
Indira Sen, Mattia Samory, Fabian Floeck and Claudia Wagner

*An HCI+NLP Collaboration on Supporting Distributed Teamwork with Machine Translation*
Yongle Zhang, Dennis Owusu, Emily Gong, Shaan Chopra, Marine Carpuat and Ge Gao

*Influenced by Stochastic Parrots: Does AI-Assisted Writing Change Users' Views?*
Yujie Shao, Maurice Jakesch and Mor Naaman

*Spaced Repetition Meets Representation Learning*
Matthew Shu, Shi Feng and Jordan Boyd-Graber

*Wordcraft: a Human-AI Collaborative Editor for Story Writing*
Andy Coenen, Luke Davis, Daphne Ippolito, Emily Reif and Ann Yuan

# Towards Hybrid Human-Machine Workflow for Natural Language Generation

**Neslihan Iskender, Tim Polzehl, Sebastian Möller**
Technische Universität Berlin, Quality and Usability Lab
{neslihan.iskender, tim.polzehll, sebastian.moeller}@tu-berlin.de

## Abstract

In recent years, crowdsourcing has gained much attention from researchers to generate data for Natural Language Generation (NLG) tools or to evaluate them. However, the quality of crowdsourced data has been questioned repeatedly because of the complexity of NLG tasks and crowd workers' unknown skills. Moreover, crowdsourcing can also be costly and often not feasible for large-scale data generation or evaluation. To overcome these challenges and leverage the complementary strengths of humans and machine tools, we propose a hybrid human-machine workflow designed explicitly for NLG tasks with real-time quality control mechanisms under budget constraints. This hybrid methodology is a powerful tool for achieving high-quality data while preserving efficiency. By combining human and machine intelligence, the proposed workflow decides dynamically on the next step based on the data from previous steps and given constraints. Our goal is to provide not only the theoretical foundations of the hybrid workflow but also to provide its implementation as open-source in future work.

## 1 Introduction

With the rapid development of Internet technologies, crowdsourcing has become one of the primary resources to solve tasks such as image tagging, transcribing the text, or digitizing print documents that computers cannot yet solve and need human intelligence (Bernstein et al., 2010; Kittur et al., 2011; Tran-Thanh et al., 2015). Further, the cost and time advantages of crowdsourcing have raised the interest of many NLG researchers to generate corpus or to evaluate the quality of NLG outputs (Callison-Burch, 2009; Zaidan and Callison-Burch, 2011; Falke et al., 2017; Fan et al., 2018; Gao et al., 2018). Despite the increasing popularity of crowdsourcing, the quality of crowdsourced data has been many times questioned because of crowd worker's potential inaccuracy and the complexity of NLG tasks. As a solution, a variety of workflow approaches have been proposed with the aim of quality assurance, quality control, or cost optimization (Kamar et al., 2012; Kulkarni et al., 2012; Lin et al., 2012; Dai et al., 2013; Lofi and Maarry, 2014; Tran-Thanh et al., 2015; Goto et al., 2016; Retelny et al., 2017; Chen et al., 2019; Jiang et al., 2020).

However, all of these approaches are neither designed explicitly for the given NLG task nor integrate the NLG tools themselves into the workflow dynamically. Therefore, we propose an automatic hybrid human-machine workflow that decides on the next step (when to use humans and when to use an NLG tool) based on the given constraints and the previous workflow step, optimizing the cost/quality trade-off. With this hybrid dynamic methodology, we aim to collect high-quality data while preserving efficiency. Since this is a work-in-progress, we describe the logic and the theoretical aspects of the workflow in this paper and will provide its complete modeling and practical implementation as open-source in future work.

## 2 Related Work

Many crowdsourcing platforms provide support for repetitive independent micro-tasks, which can be completed in a short amount of time (Hélouët et al., 2020). However, the recent advances of Internet technologies require human intelligence for more complex tasks. As a solution, crowdsourcing workflows have been introduced to a variety of problems such as taxonomy creation (Chilton et al., 2013), entity resolution (Wang et al., 2012), and complex work (Kittur et al., 2011; Kulkarni et al., 2012). The main focus of these crowdsourcing workflows are cost/quality optimization, task allocation, modeling the incentive mechanism, or modeling the



*Proceedings of the First Workshop on Bridging Human–Computer Interaction and Natural Language Processing*, pages 1–7
April 20, 2021. 

crowd workers' skills (Kamar, 2016).

With artificial intelligence (AI) systems being an important part of our lives, combining crowdsourcing workflows with AI tools, *hybrid intelligence*, promise great potential for improving human-only workflows. Therefore, researchers have developed intelligent hybrid systems for real-time speech transcribing (Kushalnagar et al., 2012; Lasecki and Bigham, 2012; Lasecki et al., 2012, 2013, 2017), clustering data points (Gomes et al., 2011; Tamuz et al., 2011; Heikinheimo and Ukkonen, 2013), forecasting political or economic events (Baron et al., 2014; Mellers et al., 2015; Atanasov et al., 2017) or scheduling conference meetings (André et al., 2013; Kim et al., 2013; Bhardwaj et al., 2014; Chilton et al., 2014). These hybrid workflows have been proven to perform better than human-only and machine-only systems.

However, to this date, there is no hybrid human-machine workflow that combines the human and machine intelligence with quality control mechanisms for crowd workers and with a methodology for cost/quality optimization. Usage of crowdsourcing to NLG has been limited to single crowdsourcing studies for quality evaluation or data labeling for semantic parsing (Wang et al., 2015), information retrieval (Demartini, 2015), translation (Callison-Burch, 2009; Zaidan and Callison-Burch, 2011) and summarization (Falke et al., 2017; Fan et al., 2018; Gao et al., 2018; Iskender et al., 2020), but the hybrid intelligence approach has not been applied in these works. Therefore, we propose to combine the strength of the human-only workflows and NLG tools in the form of a hybrid human-machine workflow with quality control mechanisms. Such an integrative hybrid approach offers great promise for the development of practical applications by achieving high-quality data while preserving efficiency.

## 3 Hybrid Human-Machine Workflow for NLG

### 3.1 Research Aim

Our goal is to provide a hybrid human-machine workflow optimizing the cost/quality trade-off and its complete implementation using a workflow engine. First, we will integrate the existing state-of-the-art NLG tools into the workflow to create a hybrid human-machine workflow. Following this, we will model each step in the workflow to increase efficiency in terms of cost/quality trade-off. Based on the model and empirical data, the workflow will decide dynamically on the next step whether to use an NLG tool or humans. Additionally, we will implement this workflow using a workflow engine and provide its implementation as open-source. Such a workflow would be especially beneficial for NLG tools developed for low-resource languages, for which it is harder to acquire available data sets. In other languages, researchers usually need to create the data set from scratch for the specific NLG task with linguistic experts, which is extremely expensive and time-consuming for large-scale datasets.

### 3.2 Workflow Logic

Figure 1 illustrates the workflow logic. To explain it in detail, we use the summarization task as an example of NLG tasks and demonstrate each step in workflow for this task. The workflow starts with the following inputs to the system: new source document to be summarized, budget and time limit, and expected quality level. Based on these input factors (source text length and domain, budget and time limit), the algorithm in *D0: Creation Method* decides whether the summaries should be created by automatic tools, crowd workers, or experts.

In machine creation, the workflow logic chooses the most applicable summarization algorithm based on the source document characteristics such as language, length, domain, and the number of documents. If crowd creation is chosen, the input factors determine the crowdsourcing task design, such as the required qualification of crowd workers, payment, number of crowd workers and repetition patterns, and task duration. If the workflow decides for the expert creation, the created summary will be stored in the database, and the workflow will end because expert creation is the gold standard in NLG (van der Lee et al., 2019).

After crowd summary creation, there is a quality check for each summary to eliminate obvious cheaters and low-quality answers. This quality check is triggered after each crowd answer, and it works on a single answer basis. If the algorithm determines that the crowd worker is cheating (path *fail*), then the answer will be rejected, and the crowd worker will not be paid. The workflow will go back to *D0* state to decide again about the creation method. If the crowd worker is not cheating (path *success*) or machine summary is created, then the workflow goes to state *D1: Evaluation*

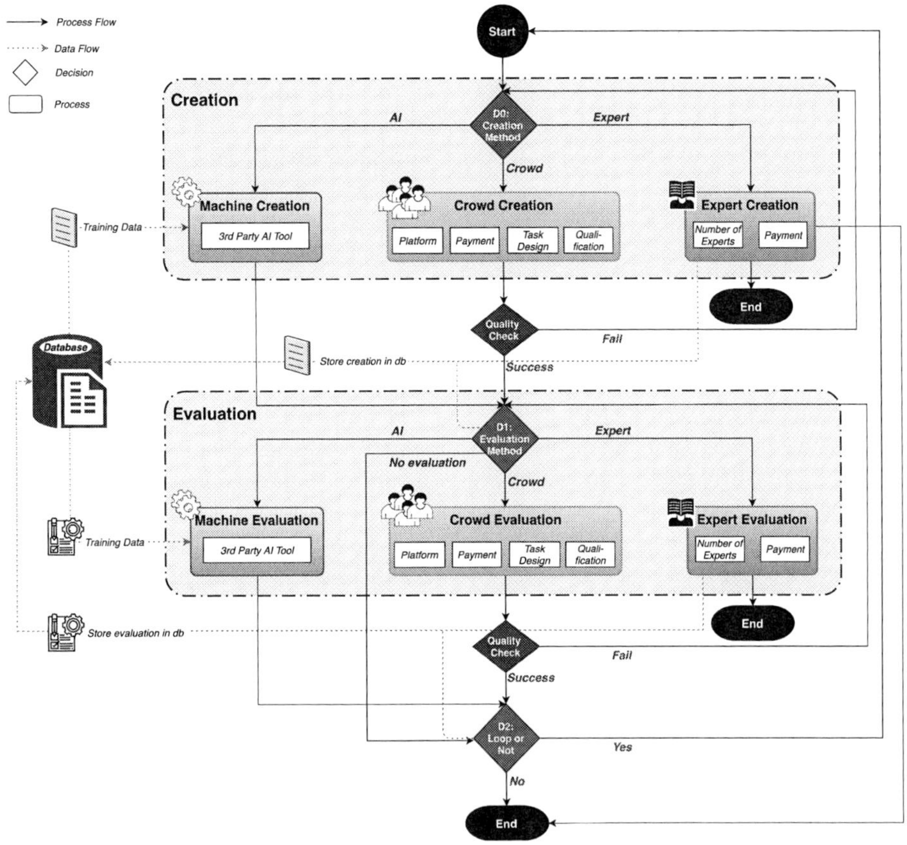


Figure 1: The Logic of the Hybrid Human-Machine Workflow for NLG

*Method* to decide about the evaluation method. In this state, all the summaries created in the creation part will be sent to the database to be stored. If the workflow decides that it cannot estimate the quality reliably at this early step, it may suggest triggering additional crowd-evaluation.

Analog to the creation part, in the evaluation part, the workflow establishes the most applicable summarization evaluation method based on the input factors from state *D0* and summary characteristics. If the machine creation is chosen, an automatic evaluation tool will evaluate the summary quality. If the algorithm decides for the crowd evaluation, the time, budget, source, and summary characteristics determine the task design, payment, requirements for crowd workers, and the number of crowd workers, and similar to creation, there is again cheater detection step after crowd evaluation. Lastly, in the case of expert evaluation, the evaluations will be directly stored in the database, and the workflow will be ended since the expert evaluation is the gold standard evaluation in NLG.

After successful crowd evaluation or machine evaluation, the workflow reaches the final decision step *D2: Loop or not*. Here, all the evaluation data will be sent to the database to be stored. Based on previous states' information, the workflow algorithm determines if the collected data is satisfying the requirements, e.g., cost and time limit, quality expectation, etc. In the following cases, the workflow will terminate: 1) if the given cost and time budgets are exceeded, or 2) if the quality of collected data satisfies the expected quality. Otherwise, the workflow will go back to *Start* state, and the whole process will be repeated, and results from the current loop serving as (additional) reference or for decisions of *D0*, *D1* and *D2*. After collecting sufficient number of summaries and summary evaluations, the stored data can be used for training summarization tools or improving the existing supervised summarization evaluation metrics.

### 3.3 Workflow Modeling

We plan to model the logic of the hybrid human-machine workflow as Markov Decision Process (MDP). MDP is defined as a discrete-time stochas-

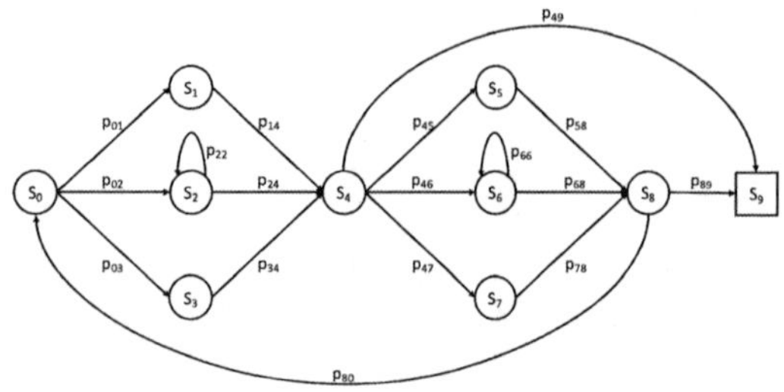


Figure 2: The Modeling of the Hybrid Human-Machine Workflow as a Markov Decision Process

tic control process providing a mathematical framework for modeling decision making in situations where outcomes are partly random and partly under the control of a decision-maker (Feinberg and Shwartz, 2012). The reason for choosing MDP is to model the uncertainty and randomness of workflow added by the humans in the process and subjectivity of NLG tasks. Dai et al. (2013) have already shown that MDPs are useful for optimizing crowdsourcing workflows in terms of cost and quality via dynamic programming.

Figure 2 shows the MDP representation of the hybrid human-machine workflow explained in section 3.2. An MDP is a four-tuple $\langle S, A, T, R \rangle$, where $S$ is a finite set of discrete states (the nodes in figure 2); $A$ is a finite set of all actions (the paths in figure 2); $T : S \times A \times S \rightarrow [0, 1]$ is the transition function; $R : S \times A \rightarrow R$ is the reward for taking an action in a state; $\pi : S \rightarrow A$ is the policy mapping states to actions; and $Q^* - value$ is the value of state action pair $(s, a)$.

The refinement of the transition function, the reward, and $Q^* - value$ will be part of future work. We plan to solve the MDP model by empirically collecting data from workflow applications for several NLG tasks and the Monte Carlo (MC) simulation algorithm repeatedly simulating the trials originating from the *Start*.

### 3.4 Workflow Implementation

The scientific workflows are generally represented as directed acyclic graphs (DAGs), which illustrate the computational tasks as nodes and the dependencies between them as edges (Liu et al., 2015). The task-driven approach, used by many workflow management engines such as Makeflow (Albrecht et al., 2012), and Pegasus (Deelman et al., 2015), is the traditional approach that relies on triggering tasks when the dependencies are satisfied. As next-generation task-based approach, Airbnb has developed an open-source workflow engine Apache Airflow[1] which can trigger tasks without satisfying dependencies. Another recent approach is triggering workflow by data input and output rather than task dependencies. Popular data-driven workflow engines are Nextflow (Di Tommaso et al., 2017) and Apache Hadoop YARN (Vavilapalli et al., 2013).

Mitchell et al. (2019) did a comparative analysis of common task- and data-driven workflow engines and showed that Apache Airflow suits both task- and data-driven systems with its modular structure and built-in operators. Apache Airflow is written on Python without any other requirement, so the workflow implementation is relatively easy and flexible. With its scheduling feature (each task in the workflow can be scheduled individually), the whole DAG can be triggered periodically, e.g., hourly or daily. Although it is not as robust as data-driven workflow engines, Apache Airflow allows data flow between tasks. Therefore, we plan to implement our hybrid human-machine workflow with Apache Airflow, supporting data flow by external databases.

## 4 Expected Contributions and Future Work

The current crowdsourcing platforms offer minimal guidance and support on how to interpret the collected data or how to assure quality. With this hybrid dynamic methodology, we aim to overcome this challenge by providing the logic, modeling, and implementation of a hybrid human-machine workflow for NLG with quality control and cost optimization methods. In this way, the data creation and evaluation can be accelerated for many languages leading to the enhancement of multilingual NLG tools. Since many NLG tasks usually require data creation and evaluation steps, the workflow can be adjusted easily to other NLG tasks such as translation, question-answering, or data-to-text.

As future work, after completing the modeling and implementation, we plan to run experiments with the proposed workflow to finalize the workflow decision algorithm and test it empirically. To foster the development of the proposed workflow, we welcome researchers in the NLG community to join our experiments, use the proposed workflow to collect data or evaluate their tool, improve the workflow based on empirical data and serve high-quality results for the researchers.

[1] `http://airflow.apache.org/`

## References


Michael Albrecht, Patrick Donnelly, Peter Bui, and Douglas Thain. 2012. Makeflow: A portable abstraction for data intensive computing on clusters, clouds, and grids. In *Proceedings of the 1st ACM SIGMOD Workshop on Scalable Workflow Execution Engines and Technologies*, SWEET '12, New York, NY, USA. Association for Computing Machinery.

Paul André, Haoqi Zhang, Juho Kim, Lydia Chilton, Steven Dow, and Robert Miller. 2013. Community clustering: Leveraging an academic crowd to form coherent conference sessions. *Proceedings of the AAAI Conference on Human Computation and Crowdsourcing*, 1(1).

Pavel Atanasov, Phillip Rescober, Eric Stone, Samuel A. Swift, Emile Servan-Schreiber, Philip Tetlock, Lyle Ungar, and Barbara Mellers. 2017. Distilling the wisdom of crowds: Prediction markets vs. prediction polls. *Manage. Sci.*, 63(3):691–706.

Jonathan Baron, Barbara A Mellers, Philip E Tetlock, Eric Stone, and Lyle H Ungar. 2014. Two reasons to make aggregated probability forecasts more extreme. *Decision Analysis*, 11(2):133–145.

Michael S. Bernstein, Greg Little, Robert C. Miller, Björn Hartmann, Mark S. Ackerman, David R. Karger, David Crowell, and Katrina Panovich. 2010. Soylent: A word processor with a crowd inside. In *Proceedings of the 23nd Annual ACM Symposium on User Interface Software and Technology*, UIST '10, page 313–322, New York, NY, USA. Association for Computing Machinery.

Anant Bhardwaj, Juho Kim, Steven Dow, David Karger, Sam Madden, Rob Miller, and Haoqi Zhang. 2014. Attendee-sourcing: Exploring the design space of community-informed conference scheduling. *Proceedings of the AAAI Conference on Human Computation and Crowdsourcing*, 2(1).

Chris Callison-Burch. 2009. Fast, cheap, and creative: Evaluating translation quality using Amazon's Mechanical Turk. In *Proceedings of the 2009 Conference on Empirical Methods in Natural Language Processing*, pages 286–295, Singapore. Association for Computational Linguistics.

Rong Chen, Bo Li, Hu Xing, and Yijing Wang. 2019. Crowdiy: How to design and adapt collaborative crowdsourcing workflows under budget constraints. In *International Conference on Web Engineering*, pages 203–210. Springer.

Lydia B. Chilton, Juho Kim, Paul André, Felicia Cordeiro, James A. Landay, Daniel S. Weld, Steven P. Dow, Robert C. Miller, and Haoqi Zhang. 2014. Frenzy: Collaborative data organization for creating conference sessions. In *Proceedings of the SIGCHI Conference on Human Factors in Computing Systems*, CHI '14, page 1255–1264, New York, NY, USA. Association for Computing Machinery.

Lydia B. Chilton, Greg Little, Darren Edge, Daniel S. Weld, and James A. Landay. 2013. *Cascade: Crowdsourcing Taxonomy Creation*, page 1999–2008. Association for Computing Machinery, New York, NY, USA.

Peng Dai, Christopher H. Lin, Mausam, and Daniel S. Weld. 2013. Pomdp-based control of workflows for crowdsourcing. *Artif. Intell.*, 202(1):52–85.

Ewa Deelman, Karan Vahi, Gideon Juve, Mats Rynge, Scott Callaghan, Philip J. Maechling, Rajiv Mayani, Weiwei Chen, Rafael Ferreira da Silva, Miron Livny, and Kent Wenger. 2015. Pegasus, a workflow management system for science automation. *Future Gener. Comput. Syst.*, 46(C):17–35.

Gianluca Demartini. 2015. Hybrid human–machine information systems: Challenges and opportunities. *Computer Networks*, 90:5 – 13. Crowdsourcing.

Paolo Di Tommaso, Maria Chatzou, Evan W Floden, Pablo Prieto Barja, Emilio Palumbo, and Cedric Notredame. 2017. Nextflow enables reproducible computational workflows. *Nature biotechnology*, 35(4):316–319.

Tobias Falke, Christian M. Meyer, and Iryna Gurevych. 2017. Concept-map-based multi-document summarization using concept coreference resolution and global importance optimization. In *Proceedings of the Eighth International Joint Conference on Natural Language Processing (Volume 1: Long Papers)*, pages 801–811, Taipei, Taiwan. Asian Federation of Natural Language Processing.

Angela Fan, David Grangier, and Michael Auli. 2018. Controllable abstractive summarization. In *Proceedings of the 2nd Workshop on Neural Machine Translation and Generation*, pages 45–54, Melbourne, Australia. Association for Computational Linguistics.

Eugene A Feinberg and Adam Shwartz. 2012. *Handbook of Markov decision processes: methods and applications*, volume 40. Springer Science & Business Media.

Yang Gao, Christian M. Meyer, and Iryna Gurevych. 2018. APRIL: Interactively learning to summarise by combining active preference learning and reinforcement learning. In *Proceedings of the 2018 Conference on Empirical Methods in Natural Language Processing*, pages 4120–4130, Brussels, Belgium. Association for Computational Linguistics.

Ryan Gomes, Peter Welinder, Andreas Krause, and Pietro Perona. 2011. Crowdclustering. In *Advances in Neural Information Processing Systems*, volume 24, pages 558–566. Curran Associates, Inc.

Shinsuke Goto, Toru Ishida, and Donghui Lin. 2016. Understanding crowdsourcing workflow: Modeling and optimizing iterative and parallel processes. *Proceedings of the AAAI Conference on Human Computation and Crowdsourcing*, 4(1).

Hannes Heikinheimo and Antti Ukkonen. 2013. The crowd-median algorithm. *Proceedings of the AAAI Conference on Human Computation and Crowdsourcing*, 1(1).

Loïc Hélouët, Zoltan Miklos, and Rituraj Singh. 2020. Cost and quality assurance in crowdsourcing workflows. Hal-02964736.

Neslihan Iskender, Tim Polzehl, and Sebastian Möller. 2020. Best practices for crowd-based evaluation of German summarization: Comparing crowd, expert and automatic evaluation. In *Proceedings of the First Workshop on Evaluation and Comparison of NLP Systems*, pages 164–175, Online. Association for Computational Linguistics.

Youxuan Jiang, Huaiyu Zhu, Jonathan K. Kummerfeld, Yunyao Li, and Walter Lasecki. 2020. A novel workflow for accurately and efficiently crowdsourcing predicate senses and argument labels. In *Findings of the Association for Computational Linguistics: EMNLP 2020*, pages 415–421, Online. Association for Computational Linguistics.

Ece Kamar. 2016. Directions in hybrid intelligence: Complementing ai systems with human intelligence. In *Proceedings of the Twenty-Fifth International Joint Conference on Artificial Intelligence*, IJCAI'16, page 4070–4073. AAAI Press.

Ece Kamar, Severin Hacker, and Eric Horvitz. 2012. Combining human and machine intelligence in large-scale crowdsourcing. In *Proceedings of the 11th International Conference on Autonomous Agents and Multiagent Systems - Volume 1*, AAMAS '12, page 467–474, Richland, SC. International Foundation for Autonomous Agents and Multiagent Systems.

Juho Kim, Haoqi Zhang, Paul André, Lydia B. Chilton, Wendy Mackay, Michel Beaudouin-Lafon, Robert C. Miller, and Steven P. Dow. 2013. Cobi: A community-informed conference scheduling tool. In *Proceedings of the 26th Annual ACM Symposium on User Interface Software and Technology*, UIST '13, page 173–182, New York, NY, USA. Association for Computing Machinery.

Aniket Kittur, Boris Smus, Susheel Khamkar, and Robert E. Kraut. 2011. Crowdforge: Crowdsourcing complex work. UIST '11, page 43–52, New York, NY, USA. Association for Computing Machinery.

Anand Kulkarni, Matthew Can, and Björn Hartmann. 2012. Collaboratively crowdsourcing workflows with turkomatic. In *Proceedings of the ACM 2012 Conference on Computer Supported Cooperative Work*, CSCW '12, page 1003–1012, New York, NY, USA. Association for Computing Machinery.

Raja S. Kushalnagar, Walter S. Lasecki, and Jeffrey P. Bigham. 2012. A readability evaluation of real-time crowd captions in the classroom. In *Proceedings of the 14th International ACM SIGACCESS Conference on Computers and Accessibility*, ASSETS '12, page 71–78, New York, NY, USA. Association for Computing Machinery.

Walter Lasecki, Christopher Miller, Adam Sadilek, Andrew Abumoussa, Donato Borrello, Raja Kushalnagar, and Jeffrey Bigham. 2012. Real-time captioning by groups of non-experts. In *Proceedings of the 25th Annual ACM Symposium on User Interface Software and Technology*, UIST '12, page 23–34, New York, NY, USA. Association for Computing Machinery.

Walter S. Lasecki and Jeffrey P. Bigham. 2012. Online quality control for real-time crowd captioning. In *Proceedings of the 14th International ACM SIGACCESS Conference on Computers and Accessibility*, ASSETS '12, page 143–150, New York, NY, USA. Association for Computing Machinery.

Walter S. Lasecki, Christopher D. Miller, and Jeffrey P. Bigham. 2013. *Warping Time for More Effective Real-Time Crowdsourcing*, page 2033–2036. Association for Computing Machinery, New York, NY, USA.

Walter S. Lasecki, Christopher D. Miller, Iftekhar Naim, Raja Kushalnagar, Adam Sadilek, Daniel Gildea, and Jeffrey P. Bigham. 2017. Scribe: Deep integration of human and machine intelligence to caption speech in real time. *Commun. ACM*, 60(9):93–100.

Chris van der Lee, Albert Gatt, Emiel van Miltenburg, Sander Wubben, and Emiel Krahmer. 2019. Best practices for the human evaluation of automatically generated text. In *Proceedings of the 12th International Conference on Natural Language Generation*, pages 355–368, Tokyo, Japan. Association for Computational Linguistics.

Christopher Lin, Mausam Mausam, and Daniel Weld. 2012. Dynamically switching between synergistic workflows for crowdsourcing. *Proceedings of the AAAI Conference on Artificial Intelligence*, 26(1).

Ji Liu, Esther Pacitti, Patrick Valduriez, and Marta Mattoso. 2015. A survey of data-intensive scientific workflow management. *Journal of Grid Computing*, 13(4):457–493.

C. Lofi and K. E. Maarry. 2014. Design patterns for hybrid algorithmic-crowdsourcing workflows. In *2014 IEEE 16th Conference on Business Informatics*, volume 1, pages 1–8.

Barbara Mellers, Eric Stone, Terry Murray, Angela Minster, Nick Rohrbaugh, Michael Bishop, Eva Chen, Joshua Baker, Yuan Hou, Michael Horowitz, et al. 2015. Identifying and cultivating superforecasters as a method of improving probabilistic predictions. *Perspectives on Psychological Science*, 10(3):267–281.

R. Mitchell, L. Pottier, S. Jacobs, R. F. d. Silva, M. Rynge, K. Vahi, and E. Deelman. 2019. Exploration of workflow management systems emerging features from users perspectives. In *2019 IEEE*

*International Conference on Big Data (Big Data)*, pages 4537–4544.

Daniela Retelny, Michael S. Bernstein, and Melissa A. Valentine. 2017. No workflow can ever be enough: How crowdsourcing workflows constrain complex work. *Proc. ACM Hum.-Comput. Interact.*, 1(CSCW).

Omer Tamuz, Ce Liu, Serge Belongie, Ohad Shamir, and Adam Tauman Kalai. 2011. Adaptively learning the crowd kernel. In *Proceedings of the 28th International Conference on International Conference on Machine Learning*, ICML'11, page 673–680, Madison, WI, USA. Omnipress.

Long Tran-Thanh, Trung Dong Huynh, Avi Rosenfeld, Sarvapali Ramchurn, and Nicholas Jennings. 2015. Crowdsourcing complex workflows under budget constraints. *Proceedings of the AAAI Conference on Artificial Intelligence*, 29(1).

Vinod Kumar Vavilapalli, Arun C. Murthy, Chris Douglas, Sharad Agarwal, Mahadev Konar, Robert Evans, Thomas Graves, Jason Lowe, Hitesh Shah, Siddharth Seth, Bikas Saha, Carlo Curino, Owen O'Malley, Sanjay Radia, Benjamin Reed, and Eric Baldeschwieler. 2013. Apache hadoop yarn: Yet another resource negotiator. In *Proceedings of the 4th Annual Symposium on Cloud Computing*, SOCC '13, New York, NY, USA. Association for Computing Machinery.

Jiannan Wang, Tim Kraska, Michael J. Franklin, and Jianhua Feng. 2012. Crowder: Crowdsourcing entity resolution. *Proc. VLDB Endow.*, 5(11):1483–1494.

Yushi Wang, Jonathan Berant, and Percy Liang. 2015. Building a semantic parser overnight. In *Proceedings of the 53rd Annual Meeting of the Association for Computational Linguistics and the 7th International Joint Conference on Natural Language Processing (Volume 1: Long Papers)*, pages 1332–1342, Beijing, China. Association for Computational Linguistics.

Omar F. Zaidan and Chris Callison-Burch. 2011. Crowdsourcing translation: Professional quality from non-professionals. In *Proceedings of the 49th Annual Meeting of the Association for Computational Linguistics: Human Language Technologies*, pages 1220–1229, Portland, Oregon, USA. Association for Computational Linguistics.

# Spellchecking for Children in Web Search: a Natural Language Interface Case-study

**Casey Kennington**
Computer Science
Boise State University
caseykennington@boisestate.edu

**Jerry Alan Fails**
Computer Science
Boise State University
jerryfails@boisestate.edu

**Katherine Landau Wright**
Literacy, Language and Culture
Boise State University
katherinewright@boisestate.edu

**Maria Soledad Pera**
Computer Science
Boise State University
solepera@boisestate.edu

## Abstract

Given the more widespread nature of natural language interfaces, it is increasingly important to understand who are accessing those interfaces, and how those interfaces are being used. In this paper, we explore spellchecking in the context of web search with children as the target audience. In particular, via a systematic literature review of work that illustrate challenges and limitations, we show that, while widely used, popular search tools are ill-designed for children. We then use spellcheckers as a case study to highlight the need for an interdisciplinary approach that brings together natural language processing, education, human-computer interaction to address a known information retrieval problem: query misspelling. We conclude that it is imperative that those for whom the interfaces are designed have a voice in the design process.

## 1 Introduction

The most popular web search engine, Google, logs roughly 3.5 billion searches per day.[1] Like many other commercial search engines, Google's primary interface is very simple: a search box (i.e., a single line text-box) and two buttons. The expected input is a natural language query using text as the primary modality; after the search is initiated, Google provides a ranked list of websites, presented also in text form. But how well does this well-used, simple natural language interface (NLI) serve everyone, including children whose natural language and user interface understandings is qualitatively different from that of adults? Gutnick and Green and Holloway (2014) documented that by age 8 two-thirds of children will use the Web on a daily basis, but mainstream search engines offer weak support for children's inquiry approaches. While these *emergent searchers* quickly develop the technical ability to use search engines and may frequently conduct online inquiry tasks, they still might not find relevant information – or information that matches their search intent (Anuyah et al., 2019; Bilal and Huang, 2019). These challenges go beyond just applying "safe search" filters to results; children struggle with the natural language *input* aspect of the interface for several well-studied reasons:[2]

**Keyword Choice.** Children find it difficult to formulate succinct, meaningful keyword queries (Broch, 2000; Duarte Torres et al., 2012). Search terms are generally nouns, a search convention that children have not yet grasped (Bilal and Ellis, 2011), which causes children to struggle to find keywords that express their information needs (Aspray and Bernat, 2000). This sometimes leads children to favor longer, grammatical natural language queries despite the difficulty they have in typing (Druin et al., 2009).

**Over/under-specified Queries.** Young children favor thematic categorizations, which may lead them to over/under-specify queries. Though typing is challenging, some children may over express their search intent and enter a complete sentence to initiate the search process or enter multiple keywords, not all related to their desired result (Kammerer and Bohnacker, 2012; Schacter et al., 1998).

**Spelling.** Emergent searchers are generally in either the Within Word Pattern or Syllables & Affixes stages of spelling development, meaning they tend to rely on their knowledge of letter names (rather than letter sounds), struggle to appropriately represent vowel sounds (Bear et al., 2016), and spell words phonetically. All of this can lead to queries that search engines do not process correctly. For example, as Spink et al. (2010) found, a

[1] https://www.internetlivestats.com/google-search-statistics/

[2] Note that few of these studies are recent. This is partially due to the fact that public data sets and benchmarks are not available (children are a protected population), so there is less research in the area of child-oriented information retrieval.



*Proceedings of the First Workshop on Bridging Human–Computer Interaction and Natural Language Processing*, pages 8–13
April 20, 2021. 

child searching for information about endangered animals may type "ndanged anemls." In this example, the child uses the letter name "N" to represent "en", struggles to represent the short /i/ sound, and omits other vowels (Bear et al., 2016). Moreover, Druin et al. (2010), who investigated children's use of keyword search in homes, shared an example of a child slowly spelling D-O-L-F and pressing the enter key as he searched for "dolphins." In these examples, search engines could assume users meant to type "deranged" or the acronym or first name DOLF, missing completely the intent of the query.

**Homonyms & Taxonomies.** Children are only becoming aware that written representations sometimes have different senses (Large et al., 2008). For example, a jaguar could be an animal or a car. While it might be easy for children to use related words ("dog" – "leash"), they can struggle with abstract categorizations ("dog" – "mammal") because of incomplete understanding of taxonomies and hierarchies (Nguyen and Murphy, 2003). For example, they may enter "lion," when looking for books about animals, or may enter "fairies," when they are interested in fantasy.

In addition to the challenges with input, children also struggle in different ways with the search *results*, which are displayed as text in a ranked order:

**Query Reformulation and Prompts.** Children have difficulty reformulating a query if their initial attempt does not lead to relevant information (Gossen et al., 2014; Kammerer and Bohnacker, 2012). In fact, they are more likely to input one query and read through all retrieved results instead of optimizing their time using new queries (Gossen et al., 2014). Additionally, children do not always take advantage of the query suggestions that search engines provide (Druin et al., 2009).

**Connection of Results with Query.** Children are not trained to identify suitable resources from among those that their favored search engines retrieve (Bilal and Ellis, 2011), nor are they trained to understand the direct connection between their queries and retrieved results (Karatassis, 2017).

**Quality & Comprehension of Results.** Children step through retrieved resources, though children rarely judge those resources for quality (Graham and Metaxas, 2003; Walker, 2013). The average readability level of the (snippets of) resources retrieved by search engines is the 10th-grade level (typically children 15-16 in the United States) (Azpiazu et al., 2016; Anuyah et al., 2019). This level is far beyond that appropriate for emergent searchers. As such, children may not be able to comprehend retrieved resources, thus making these results irrelevant (Bilal and Ellis, 2011; Graham and Metaxas, 2003; Walker, 2013).

As indicated above, the *input* and *results* elements of the search task for children have components that relate directly to natural language processing. However, these elements cannot be addressed individually and purely from a traditional natural language processing perspective. Additionally, the obvious must be stated: *children are not simply small adults*, which has implications for all interfaces that children use that frequently are designed for (and by) adults. Addressing these search challenges for children requires an interdisciplinary approach that sits at the crossroads of information retrieval (IR–the search task) and human-computer interaction (HCI–the interface), both with focus on children as users, as well as natural language processing (NLP–the medium) and education (Ed–developmental understanding of the user).

In this paper, we use Spelling as a case study for applying this interdisciplinary approach to illustrate that an interface as commonplace as web search and a basic operation such as automatic spellchecking are not yet effective tools when children are the users, and applying an interdisciplinary approach can result in important research and technological advances that impact users.

## 2 Case Study: Spellcheckers for Children in Web Search Settings

Children make many errors as they learn how to spell, which need to be addressed if search tools are to effectively respond to children's information needs. Spelling words incorrectly has potentially harmful implications for children because a word that is auto-corrected by an adult-designed spellchecker can completely change the meaning of the search query, thus affecting search success. In this section, we focus our attention on spellchecking. We first discuss assumptions about spellcheckers and sketch an interdisciplinary approach to resolving issues with spellcheckers for children. Lastly, we give examples of recent work on an effective spellchecker for children.

**Assumptions Inherent from the Task** Query spelling is a "crucial component of modern search engines" (Li, 2020), as misspelled queries can lead to the retrieval of results that do not respond to the nformation needs of the users, or even no results at all if the misspelling cannot be mapped to common vocabulary. Within this context, IR and HCI researchers have allocated resources to understanding and addressing the issue of spelling in search (Spink et al., 2010; Druin et al., 2010). Still, the majority of the literature in this area responds to the needs and interactions of traditional search engine users, i.e., adults (Chang and Deng; Duan and Hsu, 2011; Li et al., 2012; Gupta et al., 2019). In this case, there is an implicit assumption that these user groups would understand the conventions of using the interface of a search system where text is the primary modality of expressing a user's search intent. Strategies adopted by IR researchers to address spelling problems – often users' typos or misused words/phrases (Li, 2020) – depend on lookup dictionaries or existing adult query-logs. These corrections happen after the query is complete (e.g., "Did you mean..." feature in Google). These assumptions and challenges are confounded when the user is a child; they do not usually understand the interface conventions and may be confused by corrected spelling mistakes that use a dictionary lookup only after submitting a query. This is a problem as children may not realize that a correction occurred, nor identify that the results are skewed because they do not reflect the original intent of their queries. For example, if a child begins to type "ndanged" but the spell-checker corrects to "danger" instead of "endangered," the reformulated query clearly does not reflect the child's original intent. This poses a concern, especially in light of the fact that young searchers can have misconceptions about the search tools themselves – children expect results, but do not question the relevance of those results (Halavais, 2017; Anuyah et al., 2019). Of note, in the previous example, the child relies upon knowledge of the name of the letter "N" and not the sound the letter makes (Bear et al., 2016) a perspective that spellcheckers (designed for adults) generally miss.

### 2.1 Sketch of an Interdisciplinary Approach

As evidenced from our discussion above, tackling misspellings in children's query is not something that the IR community can undertake *alone*. Spellcheckers are not just the underlying technical mechanism that identifies the spelling mistakes, they are at the forefront, fostering interactions with the interface. Moreover, spelling correction and learning is an educational endeavor that can be addressed by combining NLP, HCI, and Ed. NLP is needed because the primary medium is text, albeit often not grammatical, and searching often happens across multiple turns, which is similar to interactive, spoken dialogue – a sub-field of NLP. We should treat spellchecking with children as an interactive, multi-turn process. Ed is needed because the interactive, multi-turn process and the spellchecker itself should apply a more principled model of spelling correction based upon educational research in spelling development so spelling mistakes can inform the system how to act, which is where HCI is needed. For example, spelling suggestions could be displayed, highlighting spelling differences, to draw the child's attention to the specific spelling mistake made, and providing an option to alter their input (i.e., in potential query reformulations). This naturally makes the process more interactive, drawing the query over several turns between the user and the system, and informs the child that query reformulation is a part of the search process. HCI expertise leverages researched principles and guidelines in addition to participatory design practices (Fails et al., 2013) to help design intuitive displays which can provide scaffolding in the form of visual cues to guide child users to describe their search intent accurately.

### 2.2 Recent work on Interdisciplinary Modeling and Evaluation of Child-directed Spellcheckers

In Downs et al. (2019), we examined what children actually expect from spellcheckers in search tools. We did so via *participatory design* (specifically using the Cooperative Inquiry method (Druin, 1999; Fails et al., 2013)) in order to involve children in designing the spellchecker. The main take-away from this research was the need for visual cues to act as scaffolding for the children to use as they learn to navigate the spellchecker's interface to identify and correct spelling mistakes. What otherwise appears to be a solved task for NLP is far from solved when children are the users. These efforts informed the modeling of the spellchecker *KidSpell* we introduced in Downs et al. (2020a). KidSpell is highly influenced by established Educational research in spelling development which led to the design of a phonetic-based spellchecker because children tend to make mistakes with the phonetic mappings of sounds to alphabet symbols. The authors evaluated

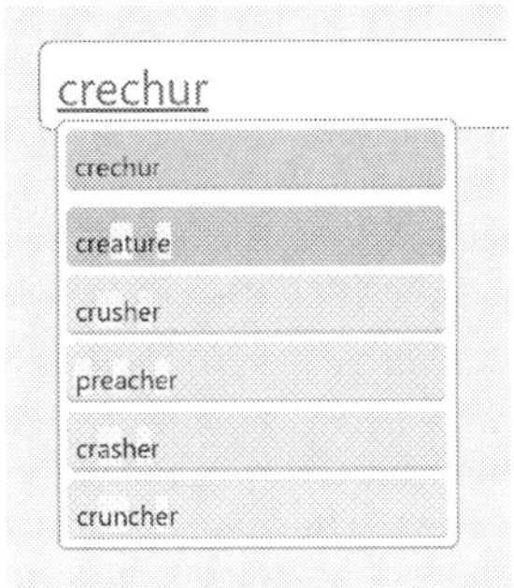


Figure 1: Example of the KidSpell child-directed spellchecker from Downs et al. (2020a).

their spellchecker on mistakes made in the context of handwritten writing samples (that were digitally transcribed) as well as spelling mistakes made during web search tasks. The phonetic spellchecker worked better for children than the current state-of-the-art spellcheckers used by adults (including Bing's spellchecker[3], and Aspell[4]), despite being a more parsimonious, rule-base approach. An example of the spellchecker in use is depicted in Figure 1, with visual cues showing the parts of the word that differ phonetically from what the child spelled.

The development and advancement of KidSpell included a multi-faceted approach that included algorithmic advances and user-interface enhancements (Downs et al., 2019, 2020a,b). Algorithm advances (applying NLP research) included evaluating input, identifying misspellings, and generating ranked spelling suggestions. With regards to the user interface, research included multiple participatory design sessions with an intergenerational design team consisting of children ages 6-11 and adult researchers (applying HCI research). The team collaboratively designed various approaches that could convey to children when a word was misspelled and enable them to better select the intended word from the suggested spelling corrections.[5] We then investigated the effectiveness of various cues within a web-search task (applying HCI and IR research). One cue was images that prototypically represented the word in question (e.g., if a child typed *dinsoer* and the spellchecker suggested *dinosaur*, then hovering over *dinosaur* with the mouse would display an image of a dinosaur, as depicted in Figure 2. Another cue we evaluated was speech synthesis; for the *dinosaur* example, hovering over it would play a synthesized voice reading the word over the speakers. We also looked at the combination of the two and showed that both cues had impact, but synthesized speech especially helped guide the children to select the correctly spelled word.

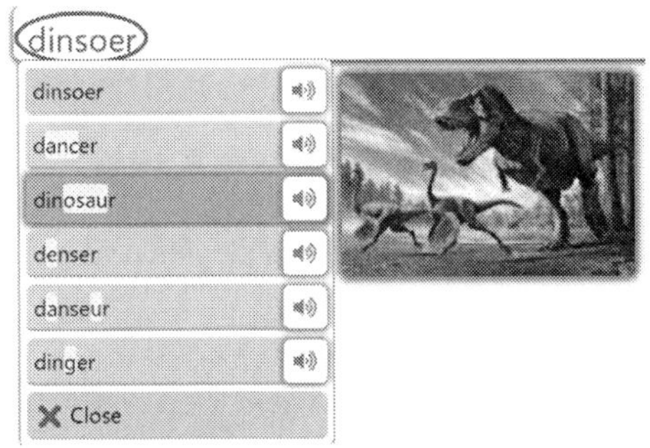


Figure 2: Example of the KidSpell child-directed spellchecker using both visual and synthesized voice cues. Taken from Downs et al. (2020b).

## 3 Conclusions: Lessons for NLP & HCI

Spellchecking (for English) appears to be low-hanging fruit in NLP, but it is clearly not a solved problem for children. In the context of search within IR, spellchecking is necessary for the best search results, but the search task and interface are not well-suited for children. In this paper, we sketched an interdisciplinary approach that combines knowledge from the fields of Education, NLP, and HCI in an IR task and reviewed recent literature that shows how critical the interdisciplinary approach is for solving spellchecking for children in web search settings.

As is the case with spellcheckers, search for children cannot be assumed to be solved because it is already widely adopted and useful for adults. The interface, the input medium, and the audience all need to be taken into account. We can learn an important lesson here from the field of HCI that has far-reaching implications: the best way to design an interface that is suitable to a target audience is to involve them in the design and evaluation process. This is becoming more critical as research from the NLP field turns into practical products that face users; NLIs are not always *natural*; they need to be designed with and for the users that they will serve.

[3] https://www.microsoft.com/en-us/bing/apis/bing-spell-check-api

[4] http://aspell.net/

[5] The spellchecker is active on http://cast.boisestate.edu.

## Acknowledgements

This research was partially supported by NSF Award 1565937 as well as NSF Award 1763649. We appreciate the anonymous reviewers' comments and feedback.

## References

Oghenemaro Anuyah, Ashlee Milton, Michael Green, and Maria Soledad Pera. 2019. An empirical analysis of search engines' response to web search queries associated with the classroom setting. *Aslib Journal of Information Management.*

William Aspray and Andrew Bernat. 2000. Recruitment and retention of underrepresented minority graduate students in computer science. In *Report on a Workshop by the Coalition to Diversity Computing.*

Ion Madrazo Azpiazu, Nevena Dragovic, and Maria Soledad Pera. 2016. Finding, understanding and learning: Making information discovery tasks useful for children and teachers. In *ACM SIGIR Workshop on Search as Learning.*

DR Bear, M Invernizzi, S Templeton, and F Johnston. 2016. Words their way: Word study for phonics, vocabulary, and spelling instruction, 2nd.

Dania Bilal and Rebekah Ellis. 2011. Evaluating leading web search engines on children's queries. In *International Conference on Human-Computer Interaction*, pages 549–558. Springer.

Dania Bilal and Li-Min Huang. 2019. Readability and word complexity of serps snippets and web pages on children's search queries. *Aslib Journal of Information Management.*

Elana Broch. 2000. Children's search engines from an information search process perspective. *School Library Media Research*, 3.

Yi Chang and Hongbo Deng. *Query Understanding for Search Engines.* Springer.

Brody Downs, Oghenemaro Anuyah, Aprajita Shukla, Jerry Alan Fails, Maria Soledad Pera, Katherine Wright, and Casey Kennington. 2020a. Kidspell: A child-oriented, rule-based, phonetic spellchecker. In *Proceedings of The 12th Language Resources and Evaluation Conference*, pages 6937–6946.

Brody Downs, Tyler French, Katherine Landau Wright, Maria Soledad Pera, Casey Kennington, and Jerry Alan Fails. 2019. Children and search tools: Evaluation remains unclear. In *KidRec Workshop co-located with ACM IDC 2019.*

Brody Downs, Aprajita Shukla, Mikey Krentz, Maria Soledad Pera, Katherine Landau Wright, Casey Kennington, and Jerry Fails. 2020b. Guiding the selection of child spellchecker suggestions using audio and visual cues. In *Proceedings of the Interaction Design and Children Conference*, pages 398–408.

Allison Druin. 1999. Cooperative Inquiry: New Technologies for Children. page 8.

Allison Druin, Elizabeth Foss, Leshell Hatley, Evan Golub, Mona Leigh Guha, Jerry Fails, and Hilary Hutchinson. 2009. How Children Search the Internet with Keyword Interfaces. In *Proceedings of the 8th International Conference on Interaction Design and Children*, IDC '09, pages 89–96, New York, NY, USA. ACM. Event-place: Como, Italy.

Allison Druin, Elizabeth Foss, Hilary Hutchinson, Evan Golub, and Leshell Hatley. 2010. Children's Roles Using Keyword Search Interfaces at Home. In *Proceedings of the SIGCHI Conference on Human Factors in Computing Systems*, CHI '10, pages 413–422, New York, NY, USA. ACM. Event-place: Atlanta, Georgia, USA.

Huizhong Duan and Bo-June Hsu. 2011. Online spelling correction for query completion. In *Proceedings of the 20th international conference on World wide web*, pages 117–126.

Sergio Duarte Torres, Djoerd Hiemstra, Ingmar Weber, and Pavel Serdyukov. 2012. Query recommendation for children. In *Proceedings of the 21st ACM international conference on Information and knowledge management*, pages 2010–2014.

Jerry Alan Fails, Mona Leigh Guha, and Allison Druin. 2013. Methods and Techniques for Involving Children in the Design of New Technology for Children. *Foundations and Trends® in Human–Computer Interaction*, 6(2):85–166.

Tatiana Gossen, Juliane Höbel, and Andreas Nürnberger. 2014. A Comparative Study About Children's and Adults' Perception of Targeted Web Search Engines. In *Proceedings of the SIGCHI Conference on Human Factors in Computing Systems*, CHI '14, pages 1821–1824, New York, NY, USA. ACM.

Leah Graham and Panagiotis Takis Metaxas. 2003. " of course it's true; i saw it on the internet!" critical thinking in the internet era. *Communications of the ACM*, 46(5):70–75.

Lelia Green and Donell Holloway. 2014. Zero to eight: Very young children and the domestication of touch screen technologies in australia.

Jai Gupta, Zhen Qin, Michael Bendersky, and Donald Metzler. 2019. Personalized online spell correction for personal search. In *The World Wide Web Conference*, pages 2785–2791.

Aviva Lucas Gutnick. Always connected: The new digital media habits of young children. In *In New York: The Joan Ganz Cooney Center at Sesame Workshop.*

Alexander Halavais. 2017. *Search engine society*. John Wiley & Sons.

Yvonne Kammerer and Maja Bohnacker. 2012. Children's web search with Google: the effectiveness of natural language queries. In *Proceedings of the 11th International Conference on Interaction Design and Children*, IDC '12, pages 184–187, Bremen, Germany. Association for Computing Machinery.

Ioannis Karatassis. 2017. Websail: Computer-based methods for enhancing web search literacy. In *Proceedings of the Conference on Conference Human Information Interaction and Retrieval, CHIIR*, pages 403–405.

Andrew Large, Valerie Nesset, and Jamshid Beheshti. 2008. Children as information seekers: what researchers tell us. *New Review of Children's Literature and Librarianship*, 14(2):121–140.

Yanen Li. 2020. Query spelling correction. In *Query Understanding for Search Engines*, pages 103–127. Springer.

Yanen Li, Huizhong Duan, and ChengXiang Zhai. 2012. A generalized hidden markov model with discriminative training for query spelling correction. In *Proceedings of the 35th international ACM SIGIR conference on Research and development in information retrieval*, pages 611–620.

Simone P Nguyen and Gregory L Murphy. 2003. An apple is more than just a fruit: Cross-classification in children's concepts. *Child development*, 74(6):1783–1806.

John Schacter, Gregory KWK Chung, and Aimée Dorr. 1998. Children's internet searching on complex problems: Performance and process analyses. *Journal of the American society for Information Science*, 49(9):840–849.

Amanda Spink, Susan Danby, Kerry Mallan, and Carly Butler. 2010. Exploring young children's web searching and technoliteracy. *Journal of documentation*, 66(2):191–206.

Henry M Walker. 2013. Homework assignments and internet sources. *ACM Inroads*, 4(4):16–17.

# Capturing Covertly Toxic Speech via Crowdsourcing

**Jorge Nario**
Google
nario@google.com

**Alyssa Lees**
Jigsaw
alyssalees@google.com

**Ian D. Kivlichan**
Jigsaw
kivlichan@google.com

**Daniel Borkan**
Jigsaw
dborkan@google.com

**Nitesh Goyal**
Jigsaw
teshg@google.com

## Abstract

We study the task of labeling covert or veiled toxicity in online conversations. Prior research has highlighted the difficulty in creating language models that recognize nuanced toxicity such as microaggressions. Our investigations further underscore the difficulty in parsing such labels reliably from raters via crowdsourcing. We introduce an initial dataset, COVERTTOXICITY, which aims to identify and categorize such comments from a refined rater template. Finally, we fine-tune a comment-domain BERT model to classify covertly offensive comments and compare against existing baselines.

## 1 Introduction

***Warning:*** *this paper contains content that may be offensive or upsetting.*

Tools identifying toxic content are essential for moderation of problematic online conversations (Jigsaw, 2018). Generally, "toxic" is an umbrella label for various types of disrespectful comments, including but not limited to identity attacks, profanity and threats, that could encourage a user to leave a conversation. Besides, "toxicity", other terms like "hate-speech", and "online violence" have also been used to refer to similar problems (Chandrasekharan et al., 2017) - yet no single conclusive definition exists. In this work, we chose to use "toxicity" because our research suggests that "toxicity" is an easy concept for annotators to understand, meaning we can gather opinions from a diverse range of people, allowing us to capture the inherent subjectivity of the concept. In other words, it was easier for more people to agree on what constituted "toxic" speech—comments likely to make someone leave a conversation—than it was for people to agree on other terms to describe problematic comments.[1]

[1]https://jigsaw.google.com/the-current/toxicity/

Previous works have published baseline toxicity detection datasets (Borkan et al., 2019; Wulczyn et al., 2016) along with models for detecting such content (Jigsaw, 2017; Zampieri et al., 2019; Schmidt and Wiegand, 2017; Pavlopoulos et al., 2020; Georgakopoulos et al., 2018).

However, (Han and Tsvetkov, 2020) recently established that covert or veiled toxicity is overwhelmingly misclassified by leading models. Perspective, a free API that uses machine learning to score comments for toxicity, is widely used to aid content moderators on online platforms (Jigsaw, 2017). As example, the deeply offensive comment masked as humor "What's the difference between boy scouts and Jews? Boy scouts come back from camp." is assigned a toxicity probability score of 0.31 by Perspective. Such comments can be as harmful to participants as more overt toxicity (Nadal et al., 2014).

Covert toxicity is an umbrella term which includes types of toxicity that may not be immediately obvious. Covertly toxic comments may use obfuscation, code words, suggestive emojis, dark humor, or sarcasm. It also includes subtle aggression, such as the user comment "'slurp slurp", says Chang', which contains a stereotype regarding Asian individuals. Microaggressions may be unintentional but can have profound psychological repercussions in aggregate (Sue et al., 2007a; Jackson, 2011; Sue et al., 2007b; Stryker and Burke, 2000).

In this work, we seek to close the gap in toxicity models. Our two main contributions include:

- A custom crowd-sourcing instruction template to identify covert toxicity
- A benchmark dataset for identifying covert toxicity.
- An enhanced toxicity model with improved performance in covert/veiled toxicity.



*Proceedings of the First Workshop on Bridging Human–Computer Interaction and Natural Language Processing*, pages 14–20
April 20, 2021. 

## 2 Related Work

Ogbonnaya-Ogburu et al. (2020) provides a call for race-conscious efforts within the human-computer interaction community. For example, Dosono and Semaan (2019) argues that Asian American Pacific Islander online community members need support. Further Aroyo et al. (2019) points out that the perceived toxicity of a comment is influenced by a variety of factors not limited to cultural background, rater bias, context and cognitive bias.

In particular, some of these efforts include explorations of microaggressions in social media posts (Breitfeller et al., 2019; Dosono and Semaan, 2019) with disadvantaged groups, surfacing contextual hate speech or words (Taylor et al., 2017) that have alternate meanings or veiled toxicity like codewords, adversarially generated or novel forms of offense (Jain et al., 2018), and exploring humor used as a tool for propagating hate (Billig, 2001).

Small datasets exist (Breitfeller et al., 2019) specifically for exploring microaggressions in online conversations. The Social Bias Inference Corpus (SBIC), a dataset of social media posts with structured annotations of thousands of demographic groups (Sap et al., 2019) is another example. To filter such datasets for veiled toxicity, Han and Tsvetkov (2020) proposed a procedure using probing examples.

Our paper builds on previous work with a strategy for consistently rating covertly toxic content, a shared dataset for training, and a baseline covert toxicity model.

## 3 Covert Toxicity

In order to formulate a covertly toxic dataset, we first extracted a set of candidate comments from the **CivilCommentsIdentities** dataset (Borkan et al., 2019) as described in Section 4.1. We manually labeled a random sample of these comments, seeking those which could have a negative impact on online conversations, but were frequently missed by raters. From this sample, we defined broad categories of *covert toxicity types*. See Figure 1 for an example.

- **Microaggression** Subtle discrimination towards an identity group
- **Obfuscation** Hidden toxicity via intentional misspellings, coded words, or implied references
- **Emoticons/Emojis** Toxic usage of non-text symbols
- **Sarcasm/Humor** Offensive content in the context of a joke
- **Masked Harm** Implied harm or threats masked by seemingly inoffensive language

### 3.1 Crowdsourcing Data Collection

We iterated on versions of an instruction templates to assist raters in identifying covertly toxic language with high precision. Previous work by Hube (2020) on biases and crowdworker annotations, illuminated relevant findings for the templates:

- Ask crowdworkers to reflect and put themselves in the shoes of participant
- Encourage crowdworkers to critically think about the task prior to engagement.

As such, two priming questions, see Table 3.1, were added in the final template. Note to improve rater comprehension we refer to covert and overt toxicity as implicit and explicit, respectively.See Figure 1 for an example.

| Overtly Offensive Rule |
|---|
| Overt offenses occur when text has some words that are clearly toxic and requires no hidden meaning interpretation.<br>**Can you think of a word/phrase that is clearly spelled or mis-spelled using toxic vocabulary, or is threatening?** |
| Covertly Offensive Rule |
| Covert offenses occur when text has some words that might have hidden meanings or relevance to a community.<br>**Can you think of a community or members of a community that might be targeted by use of words/phrases or might find text derogatory without explicitly calling out on them?** |

The addition of priming questions significantly improved rater performance. In an initial iteration, a test question of the overtly toxic comment "Peter is an idiot", had a 43% miss rate by raters. The miss rate dropped to 5% with priming questions.

However, raters still frequently missed comments containing stereotypes, identity attacks and veiled threats. As such, we reconfigured the template instructions (see Figure 1) to include a table outlining different types of toxicity with examples. Desired rater accuracy again improved.

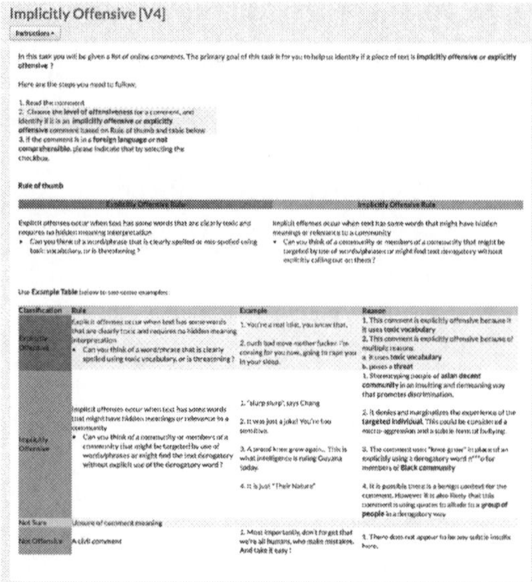


(a) A. Instructions for identifying implicitly (covertly) toxic comments versus explicit toxicity

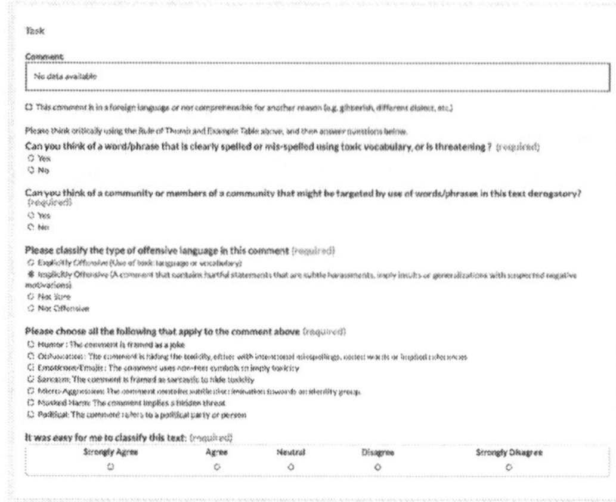

(b) B. Template for labeling covert toxicity

Figure 1: Rater Instructions and Template

| Rater Classification | Count | % |
|---|---|---|
| Not Sure | 4457 | 1.4 |
| Overtly Offensive | 34094 | 10.8 |
| Covertly Offensive | 120314 | 38.1 |
| Not Offensive | 157259 | 49.7 |

Table 1: COVERTTOXICITY rater scores.

## 4 Datasets

The COVERTTOXICITY[2] dataset consists of *covertly offensive* rater labels using the described template on a subset of CivilCommentsIdentities data (Borkan et al., 2019).

### 4.1 Training Data

The CivilComments dataset is a publicly available corpus of ~1.8 million crowd rated comments labeled for toxicity (Borkan et al., 2019). The CivilComments dataset is derived from the Civil Comments platform plugin, deprecated at the end of 2017, for independent news sites. The plugin utilized a peer-review submission process that required commenters to rate the randomly-selected comments before their own was posted for review. The CivilCommentsIdentities dataset is a subset of ~400K comments, additionally rated for specific identity terms (e.g. gender, religion, or sexual orientation).

A limitation of using this dataset is that the comments are directly targeted towards news related content. As such, this work should not be generalized for other types of online forums, such as 4Chan, which may contain vastly different content and context.

For the COVERTTOXICITY dataset, we applied the methodology of (Han and Tsvetkov, 2020) to the CivilCommentsIdentities set: comments with identity attack annotations and low Perspective API toxicity scores (Jigsaw, 2017) were marked as candidates for covert toxicity.

The CivilCommentsIdentities toxicity label is the fraction of raters who voted for the label. Han and Tsvetkov (2020) noted that comments with veiled toxicity were more likely to have dissent amongst crowd raters and empirically we observed the same. As such, we filtered the dataset using the toxicity label rater fraction, explicitly such that $0 < P(\text{toxicity}) \leq 0.4$. Additionally, we only considered comments with at least one identity label from raters.

The final COVERTTOXICITY training and test subsets consist of ~48000 and ~2000 candidate comments, respectively.

[2] https://www.tensorflow.org/datasets/catalog/civil_comments

### 4.2 Evaluation Datasets

Given the subjective nature of this task, evaluation was performed via two approximate tests sets.

- **COVERTTOXICITY** COVERTTOXICITY test set of ~2000 comments with continuous rater fractions as covertly toxic label.
- **SBIC Microaggressions Dataset** The Social Bias Inference Corpus (SBIC) consists of over 150k social media posts annotated for toxicity and implied offense over thousands of demographic groups (Sap et al., 2019). We again follow the the protocol used by Han and Tsvetkov (2020) for creating a synthetically binary label test set. The test set is the subset of SBIC that scored $P(\text{toxicity}) < 0.5$. A positive **covertly toxic** is applied if the comment includes at least one type of identity attack in the annotations and negative otherwise. This yielded an evaluation set with ~3100 marked covertly offensive and ~9000 marked not covert (and presumed not offensive given the low toxicity scores).

## 5 Results

Table 1 includes the breakdown of rater scores for COVERTTOXICITY, with 38% labeled as covertly offensive. The table results align with our expectations. The original comments were filtered for low (explicit) toxicity scores and as such a sizeable portion were confirmed as not offensive.

Raters marked humor (33.2%) and obfuscation (25.7%) as the predominant categories of covertly offensive comments. Humor and sarcasm are difficult for language models to detect in general. However, obfuscation, where offensive words are hidden with different spellings, symbols or other means is an easier target for improvement.

Comments with higher covertly offensive rating fractions (i.e. rater agreement), were more likely to be categorized as containing obfuscation, and less likely to be categorized as containing humor or emoticons/emoji. Additionally, obfuscation and comment length are anti-correlated in our dataset.

For example, the New Moon with Face emoji in 'But that's just "Their Nature". 🌚 ' is likely added to further target people of color. The comment should absolutely be labeled as toxic. However, such symbols remain challenging for raters to recognize and as such are not flagged. We include plots summarizing raters reported categories and self-reported confidence in figure 2.

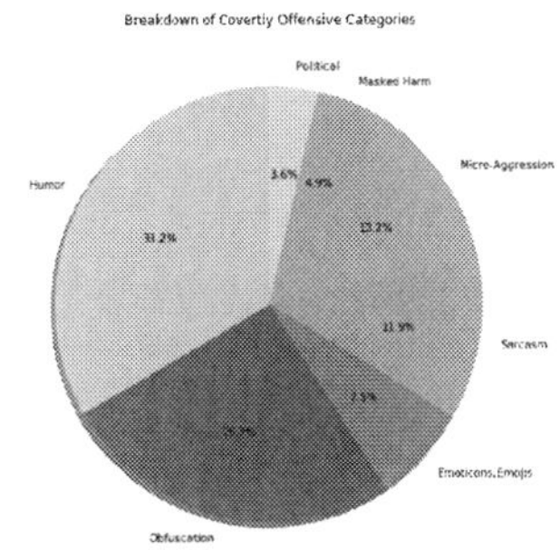


(a) Rater generated categories

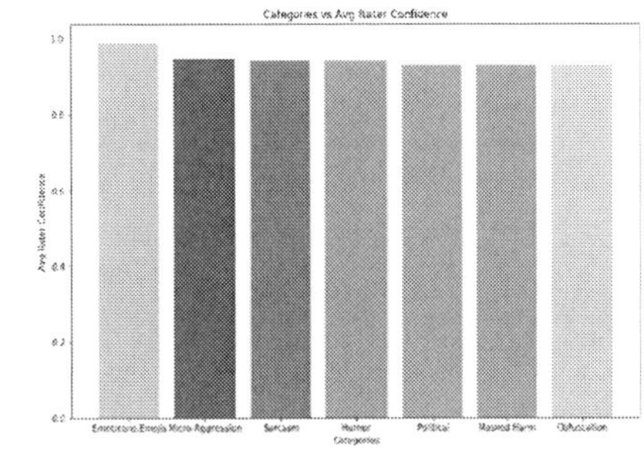


(b) Average rater confidence per category

Figure 2: Rater Covert Toxicity Categories for the CivilCommentsIdentities set.

### 5.1 Model Evaluation

We evaluate the efficacy of modeling with the COVERTTOXICITY dataset using a fine-tuned BERT model (Devlin et al., 2018). We used a pre-trained Comment-Domain BERT model (Lees et al., 2020) as checkpoint and jointly fine-tuned the **covertly toxic** and **toxic** labels. The entire CivilCommentsIdentities dataset was used for training toxicity with zero-weights assigned for missing covertly toxic labels. We employed cross-entropy loss with the two labels weighted by prevalence. The model is labeled as **Covert-BERT** in experiments below. A baseline model fine-tuned solely on the 'toxicity' label in CivilCommentsIdentities is marked as **Toxic-BERT**.

Toxic-Bert scored an average model probability for toxicity of 0.21 on comments with a majority of raters voting covertly toxic in the COVERTTOXICITY test set. In contrast, on these same comments, Covert-BERT achieved a 0.44 average model probability of toxicity. Figure 3 illustrates the shift in model probabilities for covert comments in Covert-BERT, suggesting the model is more adept at identifying covertly toxic comments.

However, the eval ROC-AUC on the held-out

| Comment | Toxicity | Perspective | Toxic-BERT | Covert-BERT |
|---|---|---|---|---|
| You're an engineering major? Wow, totally wouldn't have seen you as an engineer... I always picture them as men. | covert | 0.282 | 0.185 | **0.705** |
| If minorities in this country were truly oppressed you wouldn't have so many people desperately pretending to be one. | covert | 0.160 | 0.205 | **0.680** |
| Why do Ethiopians like paralyzed children? Because their food can't run now. | covert | 0.191 | 0.261 | **0.657** |
| I wonder who will be in the WWE hall of fame in 2018. | not toxic | 0.081 | 0.016 | 0.285 |
| you are an idiot | overt | **0.98** | 0.928 | 0.478 |

Table 2: Scored comments from micro-aggressions SBIC subset

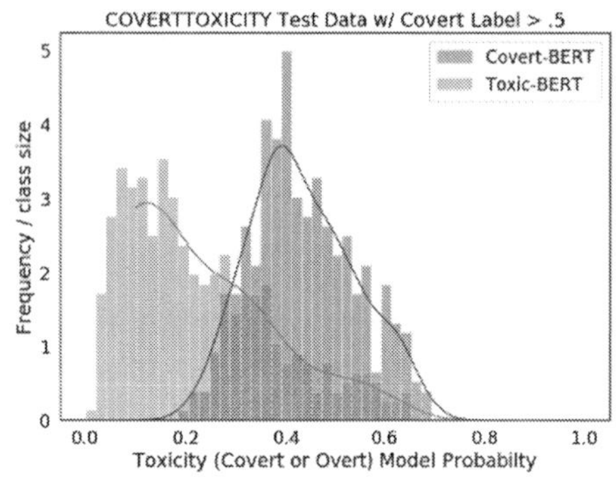


Figure 3: Shift in Covert-BERT model probabilities on covert label in COVERTTOXICITY dataset.

COVERTTOXICITY test set for the covert label established with majority rater consensus of covert toxicitiy ($\geq 0.5$) remained poor at 0.59. This is in contrast to Toxic-BERT with ROC-AUC of 0.52 for the same covertly toxic labels.

The Covert-BERT model shows more promise on the synthetic covert label subset of microaggressions from the SBIC dataset. The model showed substantially improvements in average model probability of toxicity for covert labels, ROC-AUC for covert toxicity, and recall as shown in Table 3. Similarly, Figure 4 illustrates the distribution of Covert-BERT model probabilities across covert and non covert synthetic labels. The Covert-BERT model appears better suited for extracting covert-toxicity among microaggression specific data, as demonstrated with sample rated comments in Table 2.

| Model | Avg Cov | AUC | R@0.3 | R@0.5 |
|---|---|---|---|---|
| T-BERT | 0.231 | 0.673 | 0.29 | 0.04 |
| C-BERT | **0.381** | **0.781** | **0.62** | **0.18** |

Table 3: Model evaluation on subset of SBIC. Avg Cov and Recall are the average covert model probability and recall across positive covert labels, respectively.

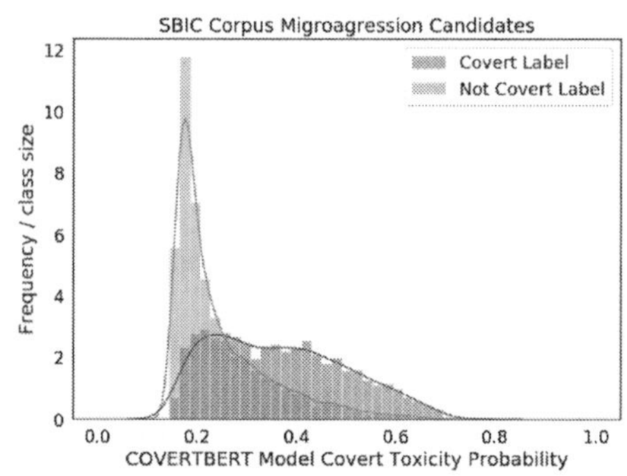


Figure 4: Distribution of COVERT-BERT model probabilities for SBIC microaggressions set.

## 6 Conclusion

We iterate on rater feedback to create an initial baseline dataset, COVERTTOXICITY, that encapsulates a variety of often mislabeled online toxicity. While progress is still needed in extracting coherent rater signals and modelling, our initial work demonstrates the possibility of capturing veiled toxic language with machine learning models.

## References


Lora Aroyo, Lucas Dixon, Nithum Thain, Olivia Redfield, and Rachel Rosen. 2019. *Crowdsourcing Subjective Tasks: The Case Study of Understanding Toxicity in Online Discussions*, page 1100–1105. Association for Computing Machinery, New York, NY, USA.

Michael Billig. 2001. Humour and hatred: The racist jokes of the ku klux klan. *Discourse & Society – DISCOURSE SOCIETY*, 12:267–289.

Daniel Borkan, Lucas Dixon, Jeffrey Sorensen, Nithum Thain, and Lucy Vasserman. 2019. Nuanced metrics for measuring unintended bias with real data for text classification. *CoRR*, abs/1903.04561.

Luke Breitfeller, Emily Ahn, David Jurgens, and Yulia Tsvetkov. 2019. Finding microaggressions in the wild: A case for locating elusive phenomena in social media posts. In *Proceedings of the 2019 Conference on Empirical Methods in Natural Language Processing and the 9th International Joint Conference on Natural Language Processing (EMNLP-IJCNLP)*, pages 1664–1674, Hong Kong, China. Association for Computational Linguistics.

Eshwar Chandrasekharan, Umashanthi Pavalanathan, Anirudh Srinivasan, Adam Glynn, Jacob Eisenstein, and Eric Gilbert. 2017. You can't stay here: The efficacy of reddit's 2015 ban examined through hate speech. *Proc. ACM Hum.-Comput. Interact.*, 1(CSCW).

Jacob Devlin, Ming-Wei Chang, Kenton Lee, and Kristina Toutanova. 2018. BERT: pre-training of deep bidirectional transformers for language understanding. *CoRR*, abs/1810.04805.

Bryan Dosono and Bryan Semaan. 2019. Moderation practices as emotional labor in sustaining online communities: The case of aapi identity work on reddit. In *Proceedings of the 2019 CHI Conference on Human Factors in Computing Systems*, CHI '19, page 1–13, New York, NY, USA. Association for Computing Machinery.

Spiros V. Georgakopoulos, Sotiris K. Tasoulis, Aristidis G. Vrahatis, and Vassilis P. Plagianakos. 2018. Convolutional neural networks for toxic comment classification. In *Proceedings of the 10th Hellenic Conference on Artificial Intelligence*, SETN '18, New York, NY, USA. Association for Computing Machinery.

Xiaochuang Han and Yulia Tsvetkov. 2020. Fortifying toxic speech detectors against veiled toxicity. In *Proceedings of the 2020 Conference on Empirical Methods in Natural Language Processing (EMNLP)*, pages 7732–7739, Online. Association for Computational Linguistics.

Christoph Hube. 2020. *Methods for detecting and mitigating linguistic bias in text corpora*. Ph.D. thesis, Hannover: Institutionelles Repositorium der Leibniz Universität Hannover.

Kelly Jackson. 2011. Derald wing sue, microaggressions in everyday life: Race, gender, and sexual orientation. *Social Service Review*, 85:519–521.

E. Jain, S. Brown, J. Chen, E. Neaton, M. Baidas, Z. Dong, H. Gu, and N. S. Artan. 2018. Adversarial text generation for google's perspective api. In *2018 International Conference on Computational Science and Computational Intelligence (CSCI)*, pages 1136–1141.

Google Jigsaw. 2017. Perspective api. `https://www.perspectiveapi.com/`. Accessed: 2021-02-02.

Google Jigsaw. 2018. Nyt moderators. `https://blog.google/technology/ai/new-york-times-using-ai-host-better-conversations/`. Accessed: 2021-02-02.

Alyssa Whitlock Lees, Ian Kivlichan, and Jeffrey Scott Sorensen. 2020. Jigsaw @ ami and haspeede2: Fine-tuning a pre-trainedcomment-domain bert model. In *Proceedings of Seventh Evaluation Campaign of Natural Language Processing and Speech Tools for Italian. Final Workshop (EVALITA 2020)*, Online.

Kevin Nadal, Katie Griffin, Yinglee Wong, Sahran Hamit, and Morgan Rasmus. 2014. The impact of racial microaggressions on mental health counseling implications for clients of color. *Journal of counseling and development: JCD*, 92:57–66.

Ihudiya Finda Ogbonnaya-Ogburu, Angela D.R. Smith, Alexandra To, and Kentaro Toyama. 2020. Critical race theory for hci. In *Proceedings of the 2020 CHI Conference on Human Factors in Computing Systems*, CHI '20, page 1–16, New York, NY, USA. Association for Computing Machinery.

John Pavlopoulos, Jeffrey Sorensen, Lucas Dixon, Nithum Thain, and Ion Androutsopoulos. 2020. Toxicity detection: Does context really matter?

Maarten Sap, Saadia Gabriel, Lianhui Qin, Dan Jurafsky, Noah A. Smith, and Yejin Choi. 2019. Social bias frames: Reasoning about social and power implications of language. *CoRR*, abs/1911.03891.

Anna Schmidt and Michael Wiegand. 2017. A survey on hate speech detection using natural language processing. In *Proceedings of the Fifth International Workshop on Natural Language Processing for Social Media*, pages 1–10, Valencia, Spain. Association for Computational Linguistics.

Sheldon Stryker and Peter Burke. 2000. The past, present, and future of an identity theory. *Social Psychology Quarterly*, 63:284.

D. W. Sue, Christina M. Capodilupo, Gina C. Torino, Jennifer M Bucceri, Aisha M. B. Holder, Kevin L Nadal, and Marta Esquilin. 2007a. Racial microaggressions in everyday life: implications for clinical practice. *The American psychologist*, 62 4:271–86.

Derald Sue, Jennifer Bucceri, Annie Lin, Kevin Nadal, and Gina Torino. 2007b. Racial microaggressions and the asian american experience. *Cultural diversity & ethnic minority psychology*, 13:72–81.

Jherez Taylor, Melvyn Peignon, and Yi-Shin Chen. 2017. Surfacing contextual hate speech words within social media. *CoRR*, abs/1711.10093.

Ellery Wulczyn, Nithum Thain, and Lucas Dixon. 2016. Ex machina: Personal attacks seen at scale. *CoRR*, abs/1610.08914.

Marcos Zampieri, Shervin Malmasi, Preslav Nakov, Sara Rosenthal, Noura Farra, and Ritesh Kumar. 2019. SemEval-2019 task 6: Identifying and categorizing offensive language in social media (OffensEval). In *Proceedings of the 13th International Workshop on Semantic Evaluation*, pages 75–86, Minneapolis, Minnesota, USA. Association for Computational Linguistics.

# Towards Human-Centered Summarization: A Case Study on Financial News

Tatiana Passali[1], Alexios Gidiotis[1], Efstathios Chatzikyriakidis[2], and Grigorios Tsoumakas[1,2]

[1]School of Computer Science, Aristotle University of Thessaloniki
{scpassali,gidiotis,greg}@csd.auth.gr

[2]Medoid AI
{stathis.chatzikyriakidis,greg}@medoid.ai

## Abstract

Recent Deep Learning (DL) summarization models greatly outperform traditional summarization methodologies, generating high-quality summaries. Despite their success, there are still important open issues, such as the limited engagement and trust of users in the whole process. In order to overcome these issues, we reconsider the task of summarization from a human-centered perspective. We propose to integrate a user interface with an underlying DL model, instead of tackling summarization as an isolated task from the end user. We present a novel system, where the user can actively participate in the whole summarization process. We also enable the user to gather insights into the causative factors that drive the model's behavior, exploiting the self-attention mechanism. We focus on the financial domain, in order to demonstrate the efficiency of generic DL models for domain-specific applications. Our work takes a first step towards a model-interface co-design approach, where DL models evolve along user needs, paving the way towards human-computer text summarization interfaces.

## 1 Introduction

The ever increasing amount of online text documents, such as blog posts, newswire articles and academic publications, during the last decades, has created the urgent need for appropriate natural language understanding tools. Summarization, i.e., shortening an initial text document by keeping only the most important information, plays a key role in addressing this information overload.

A lot of sophisticated summarization models have been proposed in the past, with a recent focus on Deep Learning (DL) architectures. DL models (See et al., 2017; Kryściński et al., 2018; Celikyilmaz et al., 2018; Chen and Bansal, 2018; Liu and Lapata, 2019; Song et al., 2019; Zhang et al., 2020) achieve great results in the task of summarization, outperforming most of the previously used methods. Typical DL models involve sequence to sequence architectures with RNNs (Nallapati et al., 2016; See et al., 2017) often combined with attention mechanisms (Luong et al., 2015; Bahdanau et al., 2015), as well as Transformers (Vaswani et al., 2017; Lewis et al., 2020; Raffel et al., 2020a).

Despite the success of DL models, some significant challenges remain. The low interpretability of these models (Brunner et al., 2020; Vig and Belinkov, 2019; Serrano and Smith, 2019; Vashishth et al., 2019) is a major drawback that limits significantly the trust of users in the whole process.

In addition, existing pipelines do not adequately engage the human in the summarization process (Trivedi et al., 2018; Shapira et al., 2017), providing isolated and static predictions. The engagement of users and their feedback in the whole process can be a key factor in creating high-quality models and improving the quality of existing models (Stiennon et al., 2020; Ghandeharioun et al., 2019).

To overcome the above limitations, we revisit the task of neural summarization from a human-centered perspective and with a unifying view of user interfaces and underlying summarization models. More specifically, we present a system that allows the active involvement of the user, setting the basis for human-computer text summarization interfaces. Our system allows users to choose over different decoding strategies and control the number of alternative summaries that are generated. Users can give their feedback by combining parts of the different generated summaries as a target summary for the corresponding input. These summaries are recorded, and can then be used as additional training examples, which in turn will improve the performance of the model and customize it to the preferences of the users.



*Proceedings of the First Workshop on Bridging Human–Computer Interaction and Natural Language Processing*, pages 21–27
April 20, 2021. 

In addition, our system provides useful insights about the inner workings of the model, based on the self-attention mechanism of Transformers. Knowing which parts of the source document are most important for the generation of the final summary, can build up the trust between users and the machine.

We present a case study of the proposed system on the challenging, domain-specific task of financial articles summarization, to demonstrate the ability of the suggested approach to successfully employ generic DL models for domain-specific applications that often have different requirements. Indeed, domain-focused summarization models (Kan et al., 2001; Reeve et al., 2007) are generally more challenging, as they require deeper knowledge of the specific domain intricacies in order to generate salient summaries with logical entailment. To this end, we compiled a novel financial-focused dataset, which consists exclusively of financial articles from Bloomberg[1].

The rest of this paper is structured as follows. The main features of the proposed human-centered system are detailed in Section 2. The case study on financial news summarization is presented in Section 3. Finally, conclusions and interesting future research directions are discussed in Section 4.

## 2 HCI meets Summarization

In this section we will introduce the main features of our human-centered summarization system. We first present the approach used for interpreting the summaries generated by the model. Then we present the different decoding strategies we employ during inference. Finally, we explain how users can interact with our system.

### 2.1 Peeking into the Black Box

Our interface assumes the existence of a Transformer-based model with self-attention (Vaswani et al., 2017), which are the backbone of most modern summarization approaches. To provide insights into the produced summaries, we exploit the fact that the self-attention mechanism offers an implicit explanation about the factors that drive the behavior of the model. In particular, it helps the model identify input-output text dependencies by focusing on different parts of the input in order to generate the final sequence representation. This mechanism is typically combined with multiple attention heads. The attention weights of each head are concatenated with each other to compute the final weights.

Extracting the weights of each encoder layer separately, gives us useful insights about the model's behavior. In particular, we observe that different layers give us different types of insights regarding the way that the model perceives natural language. The first layers tend to focus on named entities and phrases taking a whole picture of the text, while the last layers attend additionally prepositions and articles in order to learn the language structure. In order to provide an overview of the model, we average all the self-attention layers along with all their attention heads, giving the user an overall picture regarding the model's learning process.

Assuming that a word which is attended by many words is more salient for the final decision of the model, we highlight the words according to their self-attention weights. Thus, high-weight words are strongly highlighted, while lower-weight words are faintly highlighted. This allows users to get a glimpse of where the model focuses on to generate the final summary.

### 2.2 Decoding Strategies

The selection of the right decoding strategy during inference can play a critical role in the whole process as it greatly affects the quality of a model's predictions (Holtzman et al., 2020), with different decoding strategies exhibiting different behaviors (Ippolito et al., 2019). Some decoding strategies, such as greedy search, suffer from redundancy issues (Shao et al., 2017), while others, such as beam search, might generate almost identical hypotheses among the different generated beams (Gimpel et al., 2013). Beam search is widely used in generative models, but there are also attempts that utilize other decoding mechanisms, such as top-k sampling (Fan et al., 2018b).

Our system allows for the active involvement of users into the underlying summarization process, by offering them the opportunity to select among the following decoding strategies:

- **Random sampling** selects randomly a token out of the word probability distribution. Often combined with a temperature parameter to control the entropy of the distribution (Ficler and Goldberg, 2017; Fan et al., 2018b; Caccia et al., 2020).

- **Top-$k$ sampling** limits the space of possible

[1]https://www.bloomberg.com

next tokens to the top-$k$ higher-ranked tokens of the distribution (Fan et al., 2018b) .

- **Top-$p$ or nucleus sampling** selects the next token from a subset of tokens with cumulative probability up from a predefined threshold $p$ (Holtzman et al., 2020). It can also be combined with top-$k$ sampling.
- **Greedy search** selects the token with the highest probability at each time step.
- **Beam search** selects not only the token with the highest probability at each time step, but also a number of tokens with the highest probability according to the beam width. The number of the final generated beams is equal to the beam width. Beam search with beam width set to 1 degenerates to greedy search.
- **Diverse beam search** follows the beam search algorithm, but also adds a diversity penalty to enhance the diversity between the top most probable generated beams (Vijayakumar et al., 2016).

### 2.3 User Interaction

The interaction of a user with our system consists of the following steps. It starts with the user entering the source text into a text box. Then users have the option to view the visualization of the attention weights, as well as choose a particular visualization color. Next users can select among the available decoding strategies, which also gives them the opportunity to change the default hyperparameters of each decoding strategy. Finally, they can click on a button to obtain the summaries. It is also possible for users to mix and match sentences from the alternative produced summaries, as well as enter their own text, in order to create a personalized summary. This summary can then be saved, and later be used for further fine-tuning of the model.

## 3 Case Study: Financial Summarization

In this section, we detail our experiments with the case study of financial summarization. We first describe the data collection process and the preprocessing steps we followed. Then we discuss the models that we constructed and their evaluation. Finally we discuss concrete examples of the user experience. The code and instructions for this case study of our system is publicly available[2].

[2]https://bit.ly/human-centered-summarization-notebook

Table 1: Dataset Statistics

| | Initial | Preprocessed |
|---|---|---|
| min. document length (words) | 20 | 79 |
| max. document length (words) | 3758 | 2537 |
| avg. document length (words) | 676 | 669 |
| avg. summary length (words) | 23 | 23 |
| # single-sentence summaries | 21 | 0 |
| # total documents | 2120 | 2096 |

### 3.1 Dataset

We compiled a novel collection of financial news articles along with human-written summaries using the Bloomberg Market and Financial News API by RapidAPI[3]. The articles concern different financial and business categories, such as stocks, markets, currency, rates, cryptocurrencies and industries.

We removed outlier documents, i.e., relatively small (up to 70 tokens) and very large (over 3,000 tokens) ones. As most of the summaries consist of two sentences, we also removed single-sentence summaries to maintain a consistent target structure. Table 1 presents some basic statistics about our dataset before and after this simple pre-processing pipeline.

### 3.2 Models

We use the recently proposed PEGASUS model (Zhang et al., 2020), which is based on the transformer encoder-decoder architecture. It features 16 layers for both the encoder and the decoder, each of them with 16 attention heads. PEGASUS is already pre-trained on two large corpora, C4 (Raffel et al., 2020b) and HugeNews, and fine-tuned on 12 different downstream datasets. The model uses SentencePiece, a subword tokenizer (Kudo and Richardson, 2018), which divides rare tokens into known subword units allowing for the efficient handling of unknown words.

We experimented with two models fine-tuned on two different newswire datasets respectively, namely Extreme Summarization (XSum) (Narayan et al., 2018) and CNN/Daily Mail (Hermann et al., 2015). We used the open-sourced weights of these models to initialize our summarizers, and then further fine-tuned them on the collected financial dataset.

We observed that both model variants quickly adapted to the new dataset, and after only a few

[3]https://rapidapi.com/marketplace

**Reference Summary:** Local bonds a good buy despite political noise, fund head says. Rising copper prices will underpin demand for government debt.
**Before Fine-tuning:** All images are copyrighted.
**After Fine-tuning:** Peru's president set to win impeachment vote Friday. Rising copper prices will underpin demand for local debt: Credicorp.

**Reference Summary:** Damac will not bring new supply to the market, chairman says. Dubai home prices have slumped 30% since 2014 amid supply glut.
**Before Fine-tuning:** Dubai's property market will be in for a bumpy ride in the next few years, according to one of the city's biggest developers.
**After Fine-tuning:** Damac's Sajwani wants builders to stop building. Dubai home prices have fallen more than 30% since 2014.

**Reference Summary:** Kotak Mutual Fund sold part of Future bond holding at discount. A court adjourned hearings this week on the feud until Nov. 19
**Before Fine-tuning:** India's retail sector may be in for a rude awakening.
**After Fine-tuning:** Kotak sells Future bonds at 25% discount. Dispute over the e-commerce group's sale to RIL is dragging on.

Figure 1: Examples of generated summaries before and after fine-tuning.

training epochs they were capable of generating salient, non-redundant financially-focused summaries, which target explicit economic and business issues. Examples of the generated summaries before and after fine-tuning are shown in Figure 1. Fine-tuning on our dataset, leads to an improvement in performance by approximately 10 ROUGE-1 (F1 score) points (Lin, 2004) for the XSum model, which is eventually used in our system. The evaluation results are shown in Table 2.

Table 2: Evaluation Results. We measure the F1 scores for ROUGE-1, ROUGE-2, ROUGE-L and ROUGE-S.

| | CNN/Daily Mail model | | | | XSum model | | | |
|---|---|---|---|---|---|---|---|---|
| Fine-tuning | R-1 | R-2 | R-L | R-S | R-1 | R-2 | R-L | R-S |
| No | 20.00 | 4.86 | 15.04 | 16.97 | 13.80 | 2.40 | 10.63 | 12.03 |
| Yes | 23.34 | 6.30 | 17.98 | 21.04 | **23.55** | **6.99** | **18.14** | **21.36** |

### 3.3 Samples from the User Experience

An example of the visualized self-attention weights is shown in Figure 2. The model focuses on basic named entities of the source text, which are indeed important for the final generation. We also observe that different layer depths provide different insights regarding the model's learning process as shown in Figure 3. For example, the first layers attempt to focus on every word of the input document in order to capture phrases and sentences, while the last layers pay close attention to prepositions and articles attempting to learn language structure.

An example of the output differentiation between different decoding strategies for the same input text is shown in Figure 4. The different summaries that are generated by the model, demonstrate the value of selecting an appropriate decoding strategy for the final generation.

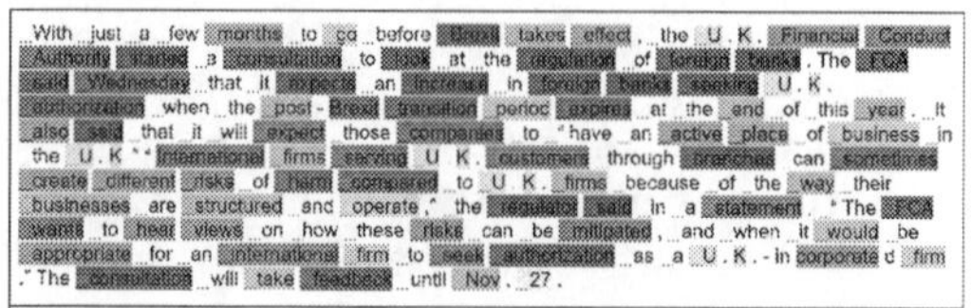

**Predicted Summary:** Regulator expects increase in foreign banks seeking U.K. authorization. FCA says it will expect foreign banks to have an 'active place of business'.

Figure 2: Visualization of the encoder self-attention weights. The underscore before a token indicates the start of the token according to the subword tokenizer.

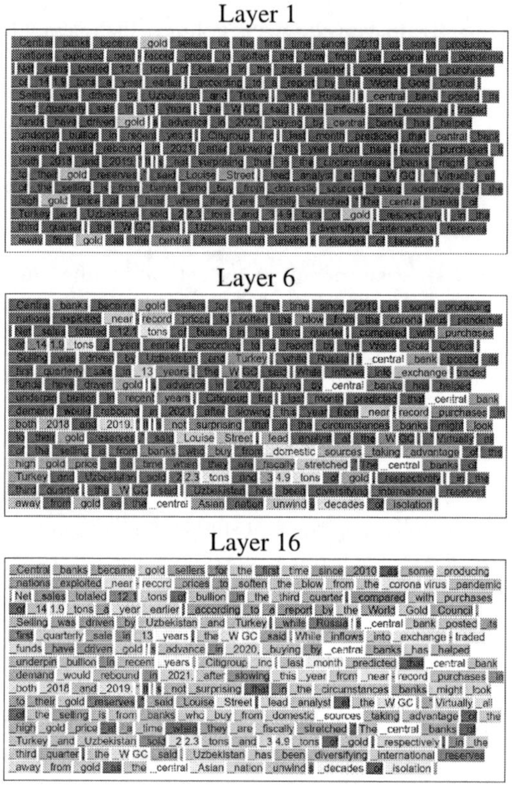


Figure 3: Self-attention weights of layers 1, 6 and 16.

## 4 Conclusions and Future Work

We presented a novel system for human-centered summarization that actively engages the user into

**Reference Summary:** Turkish and Uzbek central banks lead selling in third quarter. Overall gold demand fell 19% year-on-year: World Gold Council.

**Greedy Search:** Turkey, Russia sold gold in third quarter. Central banks bought gold at near-record pace in recent years.

**Beam Search:** Turkey, Russia sold gold in third quarter. Central banks bought gold in recent years to cushion blow from pandemic.

**Random Sampling:** Turkey, Russia sold gold in third quarter. Central banks bought gold at record pace in recent years.

**Top-*k* Sampling:** Turkey, Russia sold gold in third quarter. Central banks bought gold in recent years to cushion blow from pandemic.

**Top-*p* Sampling:** Turkey, Uzbekistan, Russia sold gold in third quarter. Central banks bought gold at near-record pace in recent years.

**Diverse Beam Search:**
**1.** Turkey, Russia sold gold in third quarter. Central banks bought gold in recent years to cushion blow from pandemic.
**2.** Turkey, Russia sold gold in third quarter. Central banks have been buying the metal to cushion blow from pandemic.
**3.** Central banks sold 12.1 tons of bullion in third quarter. Turkey, Russia posted first quarterly sales in 13 years.
**4.** Russia posts first quarterly sales since 2002. Turkey, Uzbekistan among nations to sell in third quarter.
**5.** Russia posts first quarterly sales since 2002. Turkey, Uzbekistan among nations to sell gold reserves.

Figure 4: Output for different decoding strategies.

the whole process of summarization, enabling personalized summaries and models. The users interact with the model, by entering a source text, selecting different decoding strategies, viewing a visualization of the model's attention and synthesizing a final summary from parts of multiple summaries, which can be used for further fine-tuning. We also presented a case study of our work, along with a novel dataset, on summarizing financial news. We observed that pre-trained PEGASUS models adapt quickly to our dataset, generating salient financially-focused summaries. Our work aims to inspire future research in human-centered techniques for neural summarization systems.

In future work, human involvement in the summarization process could be enhanced by using approaches that allow users to control different aspects of the generated summaries, such as length (Kikuchi et al., 2016; Liu et al., 2018; Takase and Okazaki, 2019; Fan et al., 2018a), style (Fan et al., 2018a) or generation based on a specific entity of the text (He et al., 2020; Fan et al., 2018a).

The interface we designed can be also further extended, allowing the user to evaluate the generated summaries, assessing different aspects of the text, such as salience, readability and coherence. Finally, more advanced approaches can be explored for leveraging the user submitted feedback in order to further improve the underlying model (Lertvittayakumjorn et al., 2020; Li et al., 2016).

## References


Dzmitry Bahdanau, Kyung Hyun Cho, and Yoshua Bengio. 2015. Neural machine translation by jointly learning to align and translate. In *Proceedings of the 2015 International Conference on Learning Representations*.

Gino Brunner, Yang Liu, Damian Pascual, Oliver Richter, Massimiliano Ciaramita, and Roger Wattenhofer. 2020. On identifiability in transformers. In *8th International Conference on Learning Representations, ICLR 2020, Addis Ababa, Ethiopia, April 26-30, 2020*. OpenReview.net.

Massimo Caccia, Lucas Caccia, William Fedus, Hugo Larochelle, Joelle Pineau, and Laurent Charlin. 2020. Language gans falling short. In *International Conference on Learning Representations*.

Asli Celikyilmaz, Antoine Bosselut, Xiaodong He, and Yejin Choi. 2018. Deep Communicating Agents for Abstractive Summarization. In *Proceedings of the 2018 Conference of the North American Chapter of the Association for Computational Linguistics: Human Language Technologies, Volume 1 (Long Papers)*, pages 1662–1675, New Orleans, Louisiana. Association for Computational Linguistics.

Yen Chun Chen and Mohit Bansal. 2018. Fast abstractive summarization with reinforce-selected sentence rewriting. In *ACL 2018 - 56th Annual Meeting of the Association for Computational Linguistics, Proceedings of the Conference (Long Papers)*.

Angela Fan, David Grangier, and Michael Auli. 2018a. Controllable abstractive summarization. In *Proceedings of the 2nd Workshop on Neural Machine Translation and Generation*, pages 45–54, Melbourne, Australia. Association for Computational Linguistics.

Angela Fan, Mike Lewis, and Yann Dauphin. 2018b. Hierarchical neural story generation. In *Proceedings of the 56th Annual Meeting of the Association for Computational Linguistics (Volume 1: Long Papers)*, pages 889–898, Melbourne, Australia. Association for Computational Linguistics.

Jessica Ficler and Yoav Goldberg. 2017. Controlling linguistic style aspects in neural language generation. In *Proceedings of the Workshop on Stylistic Variation*, pages 94–104, Copenhagen, Denmark. Association for Computational Linguistics.

Asma Ghandeharioun, Judy Hanwen Shen, Natasha Jaques, Craig Ferguson, Noah Jones, Àgata Lapedriza, and Rosalind W. Picard. 2019. Approximating interactive human evaluation with self-play for open-domain dialog systems. In *Advances in Neural Information Processing Systems 32: Annual Conference on Neural Information Processing Systems 2019, NeurIPS 2019, December 8-14, 2019, Vancouver, BC, Canada*, pages 13658–13669.

Kevin Gimpel, Dhruv Batra, Chris Dyer, and Gregory Shakhnarovich. 2013. A systematic exploration of diversity in machine translation. In *Proceedings of the 2013 Conference on Empirical Methods in Natural Language Processing*, pages 1100–1111.

Junxian He, Wojciech Kryściński, Bryan McCann, Nazneen Rajani, and Caiming Xiong. 2020. Ctrlsum: Towards generic controllable text summarization. *arXiv preprint arXiv:2012.04281*.

Karl Moritz Hermann, Tomas Kocisky, Edward Grefenstette, Lasse Espeholt, Will Kay, Mustafa Suleyman, and Phil Blunsom. 2015. Teaching machines to read and comprehend. *Advances in neural information processing systems*, 28:1693–1701.

Ari Holtzman, Jan Buys, Li Du, Maxwell Forbes, and Yejin Choi. 2020. The curious case of neural text degeneration. In *8th International Conference on Learning Representations, ICLR 2020, Addis Ababa, Ethiopia, April 26-30, 2020*. OpenReview.net.

Daphne Ippolito, Reno Kriz, João Sedoc, Maria Kustikova, and Chris Callison-Burch. 2019. Comparison of diverse decoding methods from conditional language models. In *Proceedings of the 57th Annual Meeting of the Association for Computational Linguistics*, pages 3752–3762, Florence, Italy. Association for Computational Linguistics.

Min-Yen Kan, Kathleen R McKeown, and Judith L Klavans. 2001. Domain-specific informative and indicative summarization for information retrieval. In *In: Workshop on text summarization (DUC 2001*. Citeseer.

Yuta Kikuchi, Graham Neubig, Ryohei Sasano, Hiroya Takamura, and Manabu Okumura. 2016. Controlling output length in neural encoder-decoders. In *Proceedings of the 2016 Conference on Empirical Methods in Natural Language Processing*, pages 1328–1338, Austin, Texas. Association for Computational Linguistics.

Wojciech Kryściński, Romain Paulus, Caiming Xiong, and Richard Socher. 2018. Improving abstraction in text summarization. In *Proceedings of the 2018 Conference on Empirical Methods in Natural Language Processing*, pages 1808–1817, Brussels, Belgium. Association for Computational Linguistics.

Taku Kudo and John Richardson. 2018. SentencePiece: A simple and language independent subword tokenizer and detokenizer for neural text processing. In *Proceedings of the 2018 Conference on Empirical Methods in Natural Language Processing: System Demonstrations*, pages 66–71, Brussels, Belgium. Association for Computational Linguistics.

Piyawat Lertvittayakumjorn, Lucia Specia, and Francesca Toni. 2020. FIND: human-in-the-loop debugging deep text classifiers. In *Proceedings of the 2020 Conference on Empirical Methods in Natural Language Processing, EMNLP 2020, Online, November 16-20, 2020*, pages 332–348. Association for Computational Linguistics.

Mike Lewis, Yinhan Liu, Naman Goyal, Marjan Ghazvininejad, Abdelrahman Mohamed, Omer Levy, Veselin Stoyanov, and Luke Zettlemoyer. 2020. BART: Denoising sequence-to-sequence pretraining for natural language generation, translation, and comprehension. In *Proceedings of the 58th Annual Meeting of the Association for Computational Linguistics*, pages 7871–7880, Online. Association for Computational Linguistics.

Jiwei Li, Alexander H. Miller, Sumit Chopra, Marc'Aurelio Ranzato, and Jason Weston. 2016. Dialogue learning with human-in-the-loop. *CoRR*, abs/1611.09823.

Chin-Yew Lin. 2004. Rouge: A package for automatic evaluation of summaries. In *Text summarization branches out*, pages 74–81.

Yang Liu and Mirella Lapata. 2019. Text Summarization with Pretrained Encoders. In *Proceedings of the 2019 Conference on Empirical Methods in Natural Language Processing and the 9th International Joint Conference on Natural Language Processing (EMNLP-IJCNLP)*, pages 3721–3731.

Yizhu Liu, Zhiyi Luo, and Kenny Zhu. 2018. Controlling length in abstractive summarization using a convolutional neural network. In *Proceedings of the 2018 Conference on Empirical Methods in Natural Language Processing*, pages 4110–4119, Brussels, Belgium. Association for Computational Linguistics.

Thang Luong, Hieu Pham, and Christopher D. Manning. 2015. Effective approaches to attention-based neural machine translation. In *Proceedings of the 2015 Conference on Empirical Methods in Natural Language Processing*, pages 1412–1421, Lisbon, Portugal. Association for Computational Linguistics.

Ramesh Nallapati, Bowen Zhou, Cicero dos Santos, Caglar Gülçehre, and Bing Xiang. 2016. Abstractive Text Summarization using Sequence-to-sequence RNNs and Beyond. In *Proceedings of The*

*20th SIGNLL Conference on Computational Natural Language Learning*, pages 280–290, Stroudsburg, PA, USA. Association for Computational Linguistics.

Shashi Narayan, Shay B Cohen, and Mirella Lapata. 2018. Don't give me the details, just the summary! topic-aware convolutional neural networks for extreme summarization. *arXiv preprint arXiv:1808.08745*.

Colin Raffel, Noam Shazeer, Adam Roberts, Katherine Lee, Sharan Narang, Michael Matena, Yanqi Zhou, Wei Li, and Peter J. Liu. 2020a. Exploring the limits of transfer learning with a unified text-to-text transformer. *J. Mach. Learn. Res.*, 21:140:1–140:67.

Colin Raffel, Noam Shazeer, Adam Roberts, Katherine Lee, Sharan Narang, Michael Matena, Yanqi Zhou, Wei Li, and Peter J. Liu. 2020b. Exploring the limits of transfer learning with a unified text-to-text transformer. *Journal of Machine Learning Research*, 21(140):1–67.

Lawrence H Reeve, Hyoil Han, and Ari D Brooks. 2007. The use of domain-specific concepts in biomedical text summarization. *Information Processing & Management*, 43(6):1765–1776.

Abigail See, Peter J Liu, and Christopher D Manning. 2017. Get To The Point: Summarization with Pointer-Generator Networks. In *Proceedings of the 2017 Annual Meeting of the Association for Computational Linguistics*, pages 1073–1083.

Sofia Serrano and Noah A. Smith. 2019. Is attention interpretable? In *Proceedings of the 57th Annual Meeting of the Association for Computational Linguistics*, pages 2931–2951, Florence, Italy. Association for Computational Linguistics.

Yuanlong Shao, Stephan Gouws, Denny Britz, Anna Goldie, Brian Strope, and Ray Kurzweil. 2017. Generating high-quality and informative conversation responses with sequence-to-sequence models. In *Proceedings of the 2017 Conference on Empirical Methods in Natural Language Processing*, pages 2210–2219, Copenhagen, Denmark. Association for Computational Linguistics.

Ori Shapira, Hadar Ronen, Meni Adler, Yael Amsterdamer, Judit Bar-Ilan, and Ido Dagan. 2017. Interactive abstractive summarization for event news tweets. In *Proceedings of the 2017 Conference on Empirical Methods in Natural Language Processing: System Demonstrations*, pages 109–114, Copenhagen, Denmark. Association for Computational Linguistics.

Shengli Song, Haitao Huang, and Tongxiao Ruan. 2019. Abstractive text summarization using lstm-cnn based deep learning. *Multimedia Tools and Applications*, 78.

Nisan Stiennon, Long Ouyang, Jeff Wu, Daniel M Ziegler, Ryan Lowe, Chelsea Voss, Alec Radford, Dario Amodei, and Paul Christiano. 2020. Learning to summarize from human feedback. *arXiv preprint arXiv:2009.01325*.

Sho Takase and Naoaki Okazaki. 2019. Positional encoding to control output sequence length. In *Proceedings of the 2019 Conference of the North American Chapter of the Association for Computational Linguistics: Human Language Technologies, Volume 1 (Long and Short Papers)*, pages 3999–4004, Minneapolis, Minnesota. Association for Computational Linguistics.

Gaurav Trivedi, Phuong Pham, Wendy W. Chapman, Rebecca Hwa, Janyce Wiebe, and Harry Hochheiser. 2018. Nlpreviz: an interactive tool for natural language processing on clinical text. *J. Am. Medical Informatics Assoc.*, 25(1):81–87.

Shikhar Vashishth, Shyam Upadhyay, Gaurav Singh Tomar, and Manaal Faruqui. 2019. Attention interpretability across nlp tasks. *arXiv*.

Ashish Vaswani, Noam Shazeer, Niki Parmar, Jakob Uszkoreit, Llion Jones, Aidan N Gomez, Łukasz Kaiser, and Illia Polosukhin. 2017. Attention is all you need. In *Advances in neural information processing systems*, pages 5998–6008.

Jesse Vig and Yonatan Belinkov. 2019. Analyzing the structure of attention in a transformer language model. In *Proceedings of the 2019 ACL Workshop BlackboxNLP: Analyzing and Interpreting Neural Networks for NLP*, pages 63–76, Florence, Italy. Association for Computational Linguistics.

Ashwin K Vijayakumar, Michael Cogswell, Ramprasath R Selvaraju, Qing Sun, Stefan Lee, David Crandall, and Dhruv Batra. 2016. Diverse beam search: Decoding diverse solutions from neural sequence models. *arXiv preprint arXiv:1610.02424*.

Jingqing Zhang, Yao Zhao, Mohammad Saleh, and Peter Liu. 2020. Pegasus: Pre-training with extracted gap-sentences for abstractive summarization. In *International Conference on Machine Learning*, pages 11328–11339. PMLR.

# Methods for the Design and Evaluation of HCI+NLP Systems

**Hendrik Heuer**
Institute for Information Management
University of Bremen
Bremen, Germany
hheuer@uni-bremen.de

**Daniel Buschek**
Department of Computer Science
University of Bayreuth
Bayreuth, Germany
daniel.buschek@uni-bayreuth.de

## Abstract

HCI and NLP traditionally focus on different evaluation methods. While HCI involves a small number of people directly and deeply, NLP traditionally relies on standardized benchmark evaluations that involve a larger number of people indirectly. We present five methodological proposals at the intersection of HCI and NLP and situate them in the context of ML-based NLP models. Our goal is to foster interdisciplinary collaboration and progress in both fields by emphasizing what the fields can learn from each other.

## 1 Introduction

NLP is the subset of AI that is focused on the scientific study of linguistic phenomena (Association for Computational Linguistics, 2021). Human-computer interaction (HCI) is "the study and practice of the design, implementation, use, and evaluation of interactive computing systems" (Rogers, 2012). Grudin described HCI and AI as two fields divided by a common focus (Grudin, 2009): While both are concerned with intelligent behavior, the two fields have different priorities, methods, and assessment approaches. In 2009, Grudin argued that while AI research traditionally focused on long-term projects running on expensive systems, HCI is focused on short-term projects running on commodity hardware. For successful HCI+NLP applications, a synthesis of both approaches is necessary. As a first step towards this goal, this article, informed by our sensibility as HCI researchers, provides five concrete methods from HCI to study the design, implementation, use, and evaluation of HCI+NLP systems.

One promising pathway for fostering interdisciplinary collaboration and progress in both fields is to ask what each field can learn from the methods of the other. On the one hand, while HCI directly and deeply involves the end-users of a system, NLP involves people as providers of training data or as judges of the output of the system. On the other hand, NLP has a rich history of standardised evaluation metrics with freely available datasets and comparable benchmarks. HCI methods that enable deep involvement are needed to better understand the perspective of people using NLP, or being affected by it, their experiences, as well as related challenges and benefits.

As a synthesis of this user focus and the standardized benchmarks, HCI+NLP systems could combine more standardized evaluation procedures and material (data, tasks, metrics) with user involvement. This could lead to better comparability and clearer measures of progress. This may also spur systematic work towards "grand challenges", that is, uniting HCI researchers under a common goal (Kostakos, 2015).

To facilitate a productive collaboration between HCI+NLP, clearly defined tasks that attract a large number of researchers would be helpful. These tasks could be accompanied with data to train models, as a methodological approach from NLP, and methodological recommendations on how to evaluate these systems, as a methodological approach from HCI. One task could e.g. define which questions should be posed to experiment participants. If the questions regarding the evaluation of an experiment are fixed, the results of different experiments could be more comparable. This would not only unite a variety of research results, but it could also increase the visibility of the researchers who participate. Complementary, NLP could benefit from asking further questions about use cases and usage contexts, and from subsequently evaluating contributions in situ, including use by the intended target group (or indirectly affected groups) of NLP.

In conclusion, both fields stand to gain an enriched set of methodological procedures, prac-



*Proceedings of the First Workshop on Bridging Human–Computer Interaction and Natural Language Processing*, pages 28–33
April 20, 2021. 

| Method | Description |
|---|---|
| 1. User-Centered NLP | user studies ensure that users understand the output and the explanations of the NLP system |
| 2. Co-Creating NLP | deep involvement from the start enables users to actively shape a system and the problem that the system is solving |
| 3. Experience Sampling | richer data collected by (active) users enables a deeper understanding of the context and the process in which certain data was created |
| 4. Crowdsourcing | an evaluation at scale with humans-in-the-loop ensures high system performance and could prevent biased results or discrimination |
| 5. User Models | simulating real users computationally can automate routine evaluation tasks to speed up the development |

Table 1: The five methodological proposals for HCI+ML that we present in this paper.

tices, and tools. In the following, we propose five HCI+NLP methods that we consider useful in advancing research in both fields. Table 1 provides a short description of each of the five HCI+NLP methods that this paper highlights. With our non-exhaustive overview, we hope to inspire interdisciplinary discussions and collaborations, ultimately leading to better interactive NLP systems – both "better" in terms of NLP capabilities and regarding usability, user experience, and relevance for people.

## 2 Methods For HCI+NLP

This section presents and discusses a set of concrete ideas and directions for developing evaluation methods at the intersection of HCI and NLP.

### 2.1 User-Centred NLP

Our experience as researchers at the intersection of HCI+AI taught us that systems that may work from an AI perspective, may not be helpful to users. One example of this is an unpublished machine learning-based fake news detection based on text style. Even though this worked in principle with F1-scores of 80 and higher, pilot studies showed that the style-based explanations are not meaningful to users. Even for educated participants, it may be an overextension to comprehend such explanations about an ML-based system. This relates to previous work that showed an explanatory gap between what is available to explain ML-based systems and what users need to understand such systems (Heuer, 2020). Far too frequently, NLP systems are built on assumptions about users, not based on insights about users. We argue that all ML systems aimed at users need to be evaluated with users. Following ISO 9241-210, user-centered design is an iterative process that involves repeatedly 1. specifying the context of use, 2. specifying requirements, 3. developing solutions, and 4. evaluating solutions, all in close collaboration with users (Normalizacyjnych, 2011).

Our review of prior work indicates that HCI and NLP follow different approaches regarding the requirements analysis and the evaluation of complex information systems. To the best of our knowledge, we did not find good examples for true interdisciplinary collaborations that contribute to both fields. While there are HCI contributions that leverage NLP technology, they rarely make a fundamental contribution towards computational linguistics, merely applying existing approaches. On the other hand, where NLP aims to make a contribution to an HCI-related field, this contribution is commonly presented without empirical evidence in the form of user studies. Our most fundamental and important contribution in this position paper is a call to recenter efforts in natural language processing around users. We argue that empirical studies with and of users are central to successful HCI+AL applications. A contribution on a system for recognizing fake news, for example, has to empirically show that the way the system predicts its results is helpful to users. Training an ML-based system with good intentions is not enough for real progress.

### 2.2 Co-Creating NLP Systems

While user-centered design is already a great improvement from developing systems based on assumptions, HCI has moved beyond it, involving users much deeper. With so-called Co-Creation, users are not just objects that are studied to build better systems, but subjects that actively shape the system. We, therefore, argue that HCI+NLP researchers should (co)-create services with users. Jarke (2021), among others, describes co-creation as a joint problem-making and problem-solving of researcher and user. This deep involvement of users enables novel ways of sharing expertise and control over design decisions.

Prior research showed how challenging it can be for users to understand complex, machine-learning-based systems like the recommendation system on YouTube (Alvarado et al., 2020). The field of HCI, therefore, recognized the importance of involving users in the design, implementation, and evaluation of interactive computing systems. While users are frequently the subject of investigation, recent trends in interaction design aim to involve users much earlier and deeper.

If users are deeply involved in the design and development of NLP systems, they can share their expertise on the task at hand. On the one hand, this can yield insights into UI and interaction design for the NLP system (Yang et al., 2019). On the other hand, it is relevant regarding the output. Sharing control is also crucial considering the potential biases enacted by such systems. Deep involvement of a diverse set of users could help prevent problematic applications of machine learning and prevent discrimination based on gender (Bolukbasi et al., 2016) or ethnicity (Buolamwini and Gebru, 2018).

### 2.3 Collecting Context-Rich Text Data with the Experience Sampling Method (ESM)

The need for very large text datasets in NLP has motivated and favored certain methods for data collection, such as scraping text from the web. These methods assume that text is "already there", i.e. they do not consider or facilitate its creation: For example, scraping Wikipedia neither supports Wikipedia authors, nor does it care if authors would want to have their texts included in such models, or not.

To advance future HCI+NLP applications, it could be helpful to create and deploy tools for more interactive data collection. One important method here is the *experience sampling method (ESM)* (Csikszentmihalyi and Larson, 2014; van Berkel et al., 2017), which is used widely in HCI and could be deployed for NLP as well. This method of data collection repeatedly asks short questions throughout participants' daily lives, and thus captures data in context: For instance, an ESM smartphone app could prompt users to describe their current environment, an experience they had today, or to "donate" input and language data (e.g. from messaging) in an anonymous way (Bemmann and Buschek, 2020; Buschek et al., 2018). This could be enriched with further context (e.g. location, date, time, weather, phone sensors) to answer novel research questions, such as how a language model for a chatbot can improve its text generation and understanding by making use of the location or other context data. One important example for such experience sampling is work on citizen sociolinguistics, which explores how citizens can participate (often through mobile technologies) in sociolinguistic inquiry (Rymes and Leone, 2014).

Although it would be challenging to collect massive amounts of text using this method, the ESM-based data collection could be used to complement data collected via scarping (e.g. via finetuning with ESM data). ESM also supports more personalized and context-rich language data and models, from specific communities or contexts. This might cater to novel research questions, e.g. on context-based and personalized language modeling. More generally, methods like ESM furthermore give the people that act as data sources more of a "say" in the data collection for NLP, for instance, via explicitly sharing data via an interactive ESM application, or via their rich daily contexts being better represented in metadata.

### 2.4 Involving the Crowd for Interactive Benchmark Evaluations

As described, NLP has a strong tradition in using and reusing benchmark datasets, which are beneficial for comparable and standardized evaluations. However, some aspects cannot be evaluated in this way. First, comparisons with human language understanding or generation are limited to the (few) humans that originally provided data for the limited set of examples that these people had been given. Yet language understanding and use change over time, and vary between people and their backgrounds and contexts. Second, "offline" evaluations without people cannot assess *interactive use* of NLP systems by people (e.g. chatting with a bot, writing with AI text suggestions). Therefore, at the intersection of HCI and NLP, one may ask: Is it possible to keep the benefits of (large) standardized benchmark evaluations while involving humans?

*Crowd-sourcing* may provide one approach to address this: HCI and NLP researchers should create evaluation tools that streamline large-scale evaluations with remote participants. Practically speaking, one would then still set a benchmark task running "with one click", yet this would trigger the creation, distribution, and collection of crowd-tasks. One example of this is "GENIE", a system and leaderboard for human-in-the-loop evaluation of text generation (Khashabi et al., 2021).

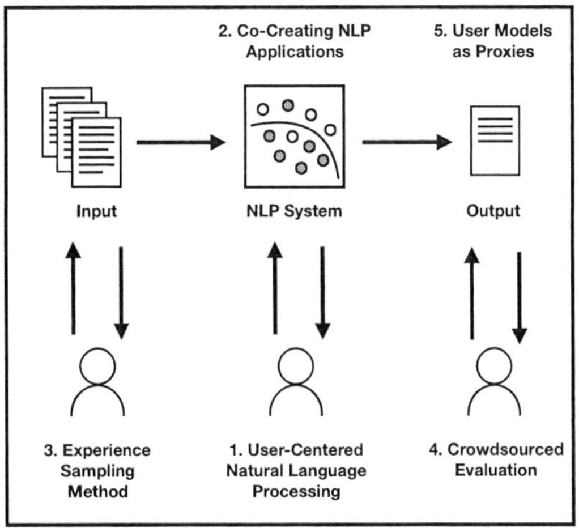


Figure 1: The model situates the five methodological proposals in the context of an NLP system.

### 2.5 Employing User Models as Proxies for Interactive Evaluations

In addition to involving users deeply and collecting context-rich data, relevant aspects of people's interaction behavior with interactive NLP systems may also be modeled explicitly. HCI, psychology, and related fields offer a variety of models, for example, relating to pointing at user interface targets or selecting elements from a list. Extending and improving those modeled aspects is particularly pursued in the emerging area of *Computational HCI* (Oulasvirta et al., 2018). Even though such models cannot replace humans, they may help evaluate certain aspects and parameter choices of an interactive NLP system in a standardized and rapid manner.

For instance, Todi et al. (2021) showed that approaches based on reinforcement learning can be used to automatically adapt related user interfaces. For interactive NLP, Buschek et al. (2021) investigated how different numbers of phrase suggestions from a neural language model impact user behavior while writing, collecting a dataset of 156 people's interactions. In the future, data such as this might be used, for example, to train a model that replicates users' selection strategies for text suggestions from an NLP system. Such a model might then be used in lieu of actual users to gauge general usage patterns for HCI+NLP systems, e.g. for interactive text generation.

## 3 Discussion

Figure 1 situates the different methods in the context of HCI+NLP systems. The figure illustrates that two approaches are focused on the model side and three methods are focused on the user side. Methods 1 and 2 are focused on the NLP system itself. The *1. User-Centered NLP* is at the heart of the model and focuses on users' understanding of the output and the explanations of the NLP system. While Method 2 is also strongly related to the user, we put it on the system side to highlight that when *2. Co-Creating an NLP system*, the goal is not just to evaluate the experience with an NLP system, but to enable users to actively shape the system. This does not only include what the system looks like but means involving users in the problem formulation stage and allowing them to shape what problem is being solved. Considering the input that an NLP system is trained on, Method *3. Experience Sampling* provides a simpler way of collecting metadata and more actively involving people in the collection of the dataset. Regarding the output of an NLP system, we showed the utility of *4. Crowdsourcing* the Evaluation of NLP systems, which puts users into the loop to evaluate existing NLP systems at scale. The advantage of this is that a large number of users can be involved in the evaluation of the system. Finally, Method 5 proposes simulating real users through other ML-based systems. These *5. User Models* can act as proxies for real users and allow a fast, automated evaluation of NLP systems at scale. We hope that this work informs novel approaches on how to standardize tools for large-scale interactive evaluations that will generate comparable and actionable benchmarks.

## 4 Conclusion

The five methods presented in Figure 1 cover the whole spectrum of HCI+NLP systems including the input, the NLP system, and the output of the system. Though each method has merits on its own, for successful future HCI+NLP applications, we believe that the whole will be greater than the sum of its parts. The design of future HCP+NLP applications should be centered around users (1) and involve them not only in the evaluation but also in the development and the problem formulation of an NLP system (2). Rich-meta data (3) that shapes the input of such a system are equally important as a thorough investigation of the output of the system, both by humans-in-the-loop (4) and by approaches based on computational methods that automate certain key aspects of such systems (5).

We hope that this overview of HCI and NLP methods is a useful starting point to engage interdisciplinary collaborations and to foster an exchange of what HCI and NLP have to offer each other methodologically. With this work, we hope to stimulate a discussion that brings HCI and NLP together and that advances the methodologies for technical and human-centered system design and evaluation in both fields.

## 5 Acknowledgments

This work was partially funded by the Deutsche Forschungsgemeinschaft (DFG, German Research Foundation) under project number 374666841, SFB 1342. This project is also partly funded by the Bavarian State Ministry of Science and the Arts and coordinated by the Bavarian Research Institute for Digital Transformation (bidt).

## References

Oscar Alvarado, Hendrik Heuer, Vero Vanden Abeele, Andreas Breiter, and Katrien Verbert. 2020. Middle-aged video consumers' beliefs about algorithmic recommendations on youtube. *Proc. ACM Hum.-Comput. Interact.*, 4(CSCW2).

Association for Computational Linguistics. 2021. What is the ACL and what is Computational Linguistics?

Florian Bemmann and Daniel Buschek. 2020. Languagelogger: A mobile keyboard application for studying language use in everyday text communication in the wild. *Proc. ACM Hum.-Comput. Interact.*, 4(EICS).

N. van Berkel, D. Ferreira, and V. Kostakos. 2017. The experience sampling method on mobile devices. *ACM Computing Surveys*, 50(6):93:1–93:40.

Tolga Bolukbasi, Kai-Wei Chang, James Zou, Venkatesh Saligrama, and Adam Kalai. 2016. Man is to computer programmer as woman is to homemaker? debiasing word embeddings. In *Proceedings of the 30th International Conference on Neural Information Processing Systems*, NIPS'16, page 4356–4364, Red Hook, NY, USA. Curran Associates Inc.

Joy Buolamwini and Timnit Gebru. 2018. Gender shades: Intersectional accuracy disparities in commercial gender classification. In *Proceedings of the 1st Conference on Fairness, Accountability and Transparency*, volume 81 of *Proceedings of Machine Learning Research*, pages 77–91, New York, NY, USA. PMLR.

Daniel Buschek, Benjamin Bisinger, and Florian Alt. 2018. *ResearchIME: A Mobile Keyboard Application for Studying Free Typing Behaviour in the Wild*, page 1–14. Association for Computing Machinery, New York, NY, USA.

Daniel Buschek, Martin Zürn, and Malin Eiband. 2021. The impact of multiple parallel phrase suggestions on email input and composition behaviour of native and non-native english writers. In *Proceedings of the SIGCHI Conference on Human Factors in Computing Systems*, CHI '21, New York, NY, USA. ACM. (forthcoming).

M. Csikszentmihalyi and R. Larson. 2014. Validity and Reliability of the Experience-Sampling Method. In M. Csikszentmihalyi, editor, *Flow and the Foundations of Positive Psychology: The Collected Works of Mihaly Csikszentmihalyi*, pages 35–54.

Jonathan Grudin. 2009. Ai and hci: Two fields divided by a common focus. *Ai Magazine*, 30(4):48–48.

Hendrik Heuer. 2020. *Users & Machine Learning-based Curation Systems*. Ph.D. thesis, University of Bremen.

Juliane Jarke. 2021. *Co-creating Digital Public Services for an Ageing Society: Evidence for User-centric Design*. Springer Nature.

Daniel Khashabi, Gabriel Stanovsky, Jonathan Bragg, Nicholas Lourie, Jungo Kasai, Yejin Choi, Noah A. Smith, and Daniel S. Weld. 2021. Genie: A leaderboard for human-in-the-loop evaluation of text generation.

Vassilis Kostakos. 2015. The big hole in hci research. *Interactions*, 22(2):48–51.

Polska. Polski Komitet Normalizacyjny. Wydział Wydawnictw Normalizacyjnych. 2011. *Ergonomics of Human-system Interaction - Part 210: Human-centred Design for Interactive Systems (ISO 9241-210:2010):*. pt. 210. Polski Komitet Normalizacyjny.

Antti Oulasvirta, Xiaojun Bi, and Andrew Howes. 2018. *Computational interaction*. Oxford University Press.

Yvonne Rogers. 2012. *HCI Theory: Classical, Modern, and Contemporary*, 1st edition. Morgan & Claypool Publishers.

Betsy Rymes and Andrea R Leone. 2014. Citizen sociolinguistics: A new media methodology for understanding language and social life. *Working Papers in Educational Linguistics (WPEL)*, 29(2):4.

Kashyap Todi, Luis A Leiva, Gilles Bailly, and Antti Oulasvirta. 2021. Adapting user interfaces with model-based reinforcement learning.

Qian Yang, Justin Cranshaw, Saleema Amershi, Shamsi T. Iqbal, and Jaime Teevan. 2019. Sketching nlp: A case study of exploring the right things to design with language intelligence. In *Proceedings of the 2019 CHI Conference on Human Factors in Computing Systems*, CHI '19, page 1–12, New York, NY, USA. Association for Computing Machinery.

# Context-sensitive evaluation of automatic speech recognition: considering user experience & language variation

**Nina Markl**
Institute for Language, Cognition and Computation
The University of Edinburgh
nina.markl@ed.ac.uk

**Catherine Lai**
Centre for Speech Technology Research
Linguistics and English Language
The University of Edinburgh
c.lai@ed.ac.uk

## Abstract

Commercial Automatic Speech Recognition (ASR) systems tend to show systemic predictive bias for marginalised speaker/user groups. We highlight the need for an interdisciplinary and context-sensitive approach to documenting this bias incorporating perspectives and methods from sociolinguistics, speech & language technology and human-computer interaction in the context of a case study. We argue evaluation of ASR systems should be disaggregated by speaker group, include qualitative error analysis, and consider user experience in a broader sociolinguistic and social context.

## 1 Introduction

Automatic Speech Recognition (ASR) has become a common tool in human-computer interaction, enabling, for example, voice user interfaces and (imperfect) automatic captioning of multimedia content. As with other language technologies (e.g. Sap et al., 2019; Blodgett and O'Connor, 2017), rapid improvements in performance have not been equal for different user groups. As Blodgett et al. (2020) show, discussions of this "bias" are often poorly defined, not grounded in explicit normative judgments and divorced from socio-historical contexts, origins and harms of the system behaviours. In this paper, we argue that researchers at the intersection of speech and language technologies (SLT), human-computer interaction (HCI), and sociolinguistics are well-placed to consider the experiences and social context of different speaker/user groups in critical quantitative and qualitative evaluations of ASR systems. Knowledge about language variation and its relation to society coupled with expertise from HCI allows us to understand how predictive biases reflect larger social structures and ideologies about language, and how they affect users.

After presenting prior work on language variation and ASR, a case study of self-recorded audio diaries collected for the Lothian Diary Project[1] highlights the need for a context-sensitive approach to ASR evaluation which we outline.

## 2 Language variation, bias and ASR

Blodgett et al. (2020)'s critique notwithstanding, predictive bias, defined here as error and outcome disparities for different user groups (Shah et al., 2020), has become a research focus in SLT and other machine learning fields as applications are extended to high-stakes contexts such as hiring, policing and banking where they have been shown to (re)produce structural inequalities (see e.g. Benjamin, 2019). Predictive bias also appears to be prevalent in commercial ASR systems for English[2].

Recent work describes stark racial bias in commercial American English ASR systems (including Google's Cloud Speech) (Koenecke et al., 2020), with much higher word error rates (WER)[3] for speakers of African American English (AAE) than white speakers of (Californian) American English. Notably, these types of error disparities appear to be driven by under-representation of AAE training data both for the acoustic modelling (Koenecke et al., 2020) and the language model used to decode sequences of phones into utterances (Martin and Tang, 2020). "Regional" variation has also been reported as a source of unequal performance, with particularly high error rates reported on YouTube's captions for speakers from Scotland and (the US state) Georgia (Tatman, 2017). Similar to more recent work, YouTube captions have been found to perform worse for African American speakers (Tatman and Kasten, 2017). These problems are

[1] https://lothianlockdown.org/

[2] The focus here is on English, but predictive bias is likely to affect stigmatised and unstandardised varieties vis-a-vis standardised varieties of other languages too.

[3] WER is an edit-distance measure capturing the number of deletions, substitutions and insertions required per word to match a reference transcript.



*Proceedings of the First Workshop on Bridging Human–Computer Interaction and Natural Language Processing*, pages 34–40
April 20, 2021. 

not limited to proprietary systems, as Mozilla's open source system DeepSpeech performs significantly worse for speakers of Indian English than "American English"[4] (Meyer et al., 2020), and also fails to transcribe AAE morpho-syntactic variation correctly (Martin and Tang, 2020). While some early research has suggested ASR performance differences based on (binary) speaker gender (Adda-Decker and Lamel, 2005; Benzeghiba et al., 2007; Tatman, 2017), it is unclear that gender by itself is a significant factor in recent systems (Tatman and Kasten, 2017; Meyer et al., 2020). Koenecke et al. (2020) suggest that the interaction of gender and race is significant, with differences between Black men and Black women being more significant than between white men and white women or men and women across race[5]. These results appear to be linked to speaker's speech styles (e.g. in Adda-Decker and Lamel, 2005) and use of dialect features (Koenecke et al., 2020), both of which have long been documented to pattern with gender (see Labov, 1990, for a classic paper) and could be correlated with gender in training and test sets. Other work in this space has focused on the potential of ASR to improve accessibility of audio media and digital technologies, looking at experiences of Deaf and hard of hearing users (Glasser, 2019) and dysarthric speakers (De Russis and Corno, 2019; Young and Mihailidis, 2010). For both groups commercial ASR systems perform quite poorly, though the severity and amount of errors varies by speaker. Research on predictive bias in commercial ASR for regional varieties of English beyond the United States and in the context of systems not exclusively trained on American English, as well as experiences of second language learners of English, and other groups who are potentially particularly reliant on ASR to access computing technologies such as elderly people, is sparse.

From a linguistic perspective, no language variety or speech style is inherently more difficult, incorrect, or inappropriate than any other. There are, however, powerful ideologies regarding the relative status of different varieties and styles which are rooted in broader socio-historical contexts and reflect the social status of the groups who speak them (Woolard and Schieffelin, 1994). In addition to being stigmatised in "traditional" contexts of power in society, varieties spoken by marginalised communities appear to be (not coincidentally) underrepresented in the data we use to build and evaluate speech technologies, leading to substantial predictive biases making speech technologies less accessible to already marginalised groups.

## 3 Lothian Diaries: A case study

The Lothian Diary project is an ongoing interdisciplinary research project inviting residents of the Lothians region of Scotland to contribute self-recorded audio and video diaries about their experiences of the COVID-19 pandemic. The more than 120 diaries collected so far are highly variable in recording quality, number of speakers and topics discussed, and participants are diverse[6] in terms of age, gender, linguistic background, ethnicity, socio-economic class and level of education. Edinburgh and the surrounding Lothians region are of particular interest for sociolinguistic research because of the capital region's status as a centre for higher education, finance and tourism. In addition to the variation within Scottish English[7] between different areas and different socio-economic groups within the city, there is also a wide range of other first and second language varieties of English, as well as other languages. The Lothian Diary project also includes many of these other varieties of English, rather than focusing on speakers with long residential histories in a particular area (as is often the case in sociolinguistic work) or first language speakers (as is usually the case in SLT evaluation). The recordings form a highly naturalistic and exceptionally varied data set. ASR is used here to facilitate social science research which requires accurate and complete transcriptions (achieved through manual correction).

So far, 13 diaries submitted by participants who agreed to have them made public, have been processed with the Google Cloud Speech-to-Text API[8] (GC STT). Diaries (16 kHz FLAC files) were processed in their entirety using the model used for long audio files which uses asynchronous speech recognition. WER was computed separately for

[4]Meyer et al. (2020)/Mozilla do not specify speaker race or region within the US.

[5]A finding which echoes work in other ML domains and other areas of SLT highlighting the way that multiple demographic axes linked to interacting structures of oppression (e.g. gender and race) cannot be considered separately (Buolamwini and Gebru, 2018; Jiang and Fellbaum, 2020)

[6]though not representative of the Scottish population

[7]"Scottish English" is used here as a broad term including the continuum between Scots and Scottish Standard English (see Stuart-Smith, 2004)

[8]`https://cloud.google.com/speech-to-text`

| ID | G | Variety | WER |
|---|---|---|---|
| RF | F | Scottish English | 46.4 |
| La | F | Scottish English | 35.7 |
| CE | F | Scottish English | 20.9 |
| AA | M | Scottish English | 29.8 |
| MR | M | Scottish English | 55.3 |
| DL | M | Scottish English/Scots | 88.9 |
| Li | F | Southern British English | 29.5 |
| JW | M | Canadian English* | 25.3 |
| L | F | L2 English (L1: Lithuanian) | 31.5 |
| S | F | L2 English (L1: Cantonese) | 27.7 |
| MG | F | L2 English (L1: Italian) | 35.3 |
| JL | M | L2 English (L1: Filipino) | 40.8 |
| A | M | L2 English (L1: Chinese) | 70.2 |

Table 1: Word Error Rates for different participants vary widely both across and within groups (lower is better). *Decoded using 'en-US' language option, for all others 'en-GB' was used

each speaker using `sclite`[9]. In the following section, we present a brief qualitative error analysis.

WER for individual speakers varies dramatically (see Table 1). Some of these errors appear to be related to accent differences. For example, Scottish speakers' pronunciations of *I* or *I've* are frequently mistranscribed as *ah* or *of* and other accent-based errors include: *cat* [kaʔ] > *car*, *living* > *leaving*, *hating our* > *heating are*. However, there is also significant variation within each accent group. GC STT fails to transcribe filled pauses (*uh, um*) and word fragments and occasionally deletes false starts and repetitions. Furthermore, errors appear to be more prevalent in the vicinity of hesitations and repetitions. As a result speakers who produce more hesitations and repetitions tend to have higher error rates, while people who appear to read from prepared notes tend to be more fluent and have lower error rates. The highest WER in this sample derives from a recording by a Scottish English speaker who produces many false starts, word fragments and a number of Scots words (which the system likely would not recognise under any circumstances). Words are also often substituted by a wrong (but often grammatically appropriate) inflectional form (e.g. past tense > present tense).

All of these errors are particularly challenging for the accurate and complete transcription of spontaneous and conversational speech, especially for social science research where researchers (users) might consider hesitations, false starts and filled pauses important as they convey pragmatic information. Considering impacts of this predictive bias, transcripts of speakers who produce more "fluent" speech are much more easily interpretable. Retrieving speech content and speech style of less fluent speakers as well as some second language speakers, on the other hand, requires more labour and time, potentially negating any benefits of ASR.

## 4 Proposed methods

To document predictive bias in ASR in a way that is mindful of 1) user experience, 2) socio-historical and (socio)linguistic context, 3) (potential) harms (re)produced by the system, and 4) technical aspects of ASR, we need to draw on methodologies and knowledge from HCI, sociolinguistics, research on fairness in AI, and SLT.

### 4.1 Intersectional benchmarks

ASR systems are usually evaluated in terms of their WER, for one or more unseen test sets (often including well-established benchmark sets). As seen in the case study above, word error rates vary strongly across individual recordings and speakers, and (benchmark) test sets (e.g. Barker et al., 2017) are becoming increasingly naturalistic and (potentially) diverse; a recent state-of-the-art system by Google (Chiu et al., 2018) was trained and tested on "representative" data drawn from Google's voice-search traffic. However, even assuming that the test sets are representative of the developer's users, it is 1) not clear that the intended or current user base is reflective of all use cases or potential users (especially if the system is sold to third parties as with GC STT), and 2) possible or even likely that significant variation in performance between user groups is hidden by reporting an average across all tested recordings. Importantly, as Black feminist scholarship has pointed out, multiple demographic axes linked to interlocking structures of oppression (e.g. race and gender) cannot be considered separately (Crenshaw, 1991). It is thus important that in addition to disaggregating by language variety to also consider, for example, gender to create an "intersectional" benchmark (see also Costanza-Chock, 2020). This approach has been successful in highlighting disproportionate predictive bias for particular subgroups in other ML domains (e.g. darker-skinned women in facial analysis: Buolamwini and

[9] https://github.com/usnistgov/SCTK

Gebru, 2018; Raji and Buolamwini, 2019), and SLT (Jiang and Fellbaum, 2020).

To apply an intersectional benchmark to a larger sample of the Lothian Diaries, we intend to match short audio snippets with the same reference transcript produced by different speaker groups to isolate pronunciation effects, and look systematically at potential differences in content and speech style (following Koenecke et al., 2020).

### 4.2 Qualitative error analysis

Intersectional benchmarks alone are not enough however, as WER does not account for the context or effect of an error. Understanding the context of errors is useful since errors are both more likely to occur and to be severe in particular phonetic, prosodic and lexical contexts. Like us (though working with a very different system and data), Goldwater et al. (2010) find that words before or after hesitations, repetitions and word fragments, turn-initial words and infrequent words are more likely to be misrecognised and that erroneous substitutions are often different forms of the same lexeme (e.g. *ask/asked*). While some of these errors can be easily disambiguated through context, others (e.g. *can/can't*) could be quite disruptive to communication. Word errors can also lead to domino effects, where one wrongly decoded word feeds into further erroneous predictions (Martin and Tang, 2020). While metrics which are more sensitive to the type and context of the error or directly model human evaluations have been proposed (Nanjo and Kawahara, 2005; Morris et al., 2004; Mishra et al., 2011; Kafle and Huenerfauth, 2020) they are not widely adopted and extensive qualitative error analysis is rare. A context-sensitive approach would be particularly interested in the type of error and its effect given the linguistic context.

### 4.3 User experience

Evaluations of SLT systems rarely reflect explicitly on how users interact with them[10]. However, because both (perceived) severity and impact as well as prevalence of errors depends on recording and task, understanding how people use ASR-based technologies in their daily life is important. Future work concerning predictive bias in ASR would benefit from incorporating HCI methodologies like interviews, ethnography and qualitative surveys to gain a deeper understanding of users' experiences. So far, researchers in HCI have been particularly interested in how people interact with voice user interfaces (e.g. Porcheron et al., 2018; Luger and Sellen, 2016), though little attention has been paid to the role of accent and dialect. Furthermore, especially given the context of the recent shift to increased remote work and education, applications of cloud-based speech recognition for personal or business use extend beyond voice user interfaces to automatic captioning of audio and video lectures and meetings. Domain-general and naturalistic recordings of continuous spontaneous speech pose a particular challenge to ASR systems, and insights into what types of errors users perceive to be particularly disruptive and common depending on their linguistic and demographic background should inform development and evaluation of ASR systems. For example, in the context of the Lothian Diary Project the goal of ASR is to produce transcriptions which can be used by linguists and other social science researchers to analyse both what participants are saying and how they are saying it. Every aspect of their speech, including disfluencies and repetitions as well as specific lexical choices (e.g. past tense vs present tense) are relevant to this analysis and should as such be preserved in a transcript. Furthermore, because most speech in this context is largely unplanned, higher error rates around disfluent or informal speech are particularly disruptive. When applying the proposed methodology to other use cases (e.g. automatic captioning of video lectures or business meetings) interviews with stakeholders can clarify what types of errors are particularly disruptive.

### 4.4 Considering context and impacts

Considering the broader societal context in which an ASR system is developed and implemented allows us to identify the specific harms it could inflict on users and (sometimes at least) see the underlying societal structures giving rise to predictive bias. Identifying risk and causes in turn allows us to mitigate harms (and, in future systems, bias). In the case of commercial ASR (in English), research suggests that predictive bias is a result of under-representation of varieties of marginalised speaker groups in proprietary training and test sets. For many open source and licensed corpora used to train and benchmark ASR systems, incomplete documentation makes it difficult to es-

[10]Though intended use is sometimes implicit in the choice of training and test data: e.g. Google's use of voice search data (Chiu et al., 2018)

timate representation; the commonly used Switchboard (Godfrey and Holliman, 1993) and TIMIT corpora (Garofolo et al., 1993) (both US English) and Mozilla's recent open-source Common Voice corpus[11], for example, do not record speaker race. The speaker characteristics of training sets depends on the broader societal context. For example, use of commercial speech recognition (e.g. in the case of Google's system) and participation in scientific studies (e.g. the licensed corpora) or crowd-source tasks (e.g. Mozilla Common Voice) differs across demographic groups (for example based on income and education). Imbalanced corpora are also tied to ideologies around whose ways of speaking are considered "legitimate", "correct" or "native".

Some of the more obvious specific harms of predictive bias include difficulties using voice user interfaces, which for some users are crucial assistive technology. As ASR spreads into high-stakes contexts such as hiring, substantial harms could be incurred if systems perform worse for already marginalised groups, effectively encoding "accentism" and linguistic prejudice in automatic systems. Even assuming no prediction bias across different speaker groups, the use of ASR in automatic analysis of video interviews to recommend or rank applicants (e.g. HireVue[12]) risks real harm in the case of even small recognition errors and potentially entrenches existing language ideologies around "professional", "fluent" or "competent" speech patterns. For example, *HireNet* (Hemamou et al., 2019) extracts information about prosody and speech fluency to predict "hireability" (as annotated by recruiters). Other harms include less usable automatic captions and potential downstream effects as described in our case study.

## 5 Conclusion

We have proposed an approach to ASR evaluation which considers the experiences of different user/speaker groups, sociolinguistic context and potential impacts of predictive bias. We argue that this interdisciplinary approach is necessary to significantly advance our understanding of ASR usability. We particularly invite perspectives from the fields of human-computer interaction in order evaluate speech and language technologies as systems situated in specific sociolinguistic and socio-technical contexts which perform specific tasks for specific (language) users.

[11]available here: `https://commonvoice.mozilla.org/en/datasets`

[12]`https://www.hirevue.com/`


## Acknowledgements

This work was supported in part by the UKRI Centre for Doctoral Training in Natural Language Processing, funded by the UKRI (grant EP/S022481/1) and the University of Edinburgh, School of Informatics and School of Philosophy, Psychology & Language Sciences.


## References


Martine Adda-Decker and Lori Lamel. 2005. Do speech recognizers prefer female speakers? *9th European Conference on Speech Communication and Technology*, (January 2005):2205–2208.

Jon P. Barker, Ricard Marxer, Emmanuel Vincent, and Shinji Watanabe. 2017. *The CHiME Challenges: Robust Speech Recognition in Everyday Environments*, pages 327–344. Springer International Publishing, Cham.

Ruha Benjamin. 2019. *Race after technology : abolitionist tools for the New Jim Code*. Polity Press, Newark.

M. Benzeghiba, R. De Mori, O. Deroo, S. Dupont, T. Erbes, D. Jouvet, L. Fissore, P. Laface, A. Mertins, C. Ris, R. Rose, V. Tyagi, and C. Wellekens. 2007. Automatic speech recognition and speech variability: A review. *Speech Communication*, 49(10-11):763–786.

Su Lin Blodgett, Solon Barocas, Hal Daumé III, and Hanna Wallach. 2020. Language (technology) is power: A critical survey of "bias" in NLP. In *Proceedings of the 58th Annual Meeting of the Association for Computational Linguistics*, pages 5454–5476, Online. Association for Computational Linguistics.

Su Lin Blodgett and Brendan O'Connor. 2017. Racial disparity in natural language processing: A case study of social media african-american english.

Joy Buolamwini and Timnit Gebru. 2018. Gender shades: Intersectional accuracy disparities in commercial gender classification. In *Proceedings of the 1st Conference on Fairness, Accountability and Transparency*, volume 81 of *Proceedings of Machine Learning Research*, pages 77–91, New York, NY, USA. PMLR.

C. Chiu, T. N. Sainath, Y. Wu, R. Prabhavalkar, P. Nguyen, Z. Chen, A. Kannan, R. J. Weiss, K. Rao, E. Gonina, N. Jaitly, B. Li, J. Chorowski, and M. Bacchiani. 2018. State-of-the-art speech recognition with sequence-to-sequence models. In *2018 IEEE International Conference on Acoustics, Speech and Signal Processing (ICASSP)*, pages 4774–4778.

Sasha Costanza-Chock. 2020. Design values: Hard-coding liberation? In *Design Justice*. MIT Press. Https://design-justice.pubpub.org/pub/3h2zq86d.

Kimberle Crenshaw. 1991. Mapping the Margins: Intersectionality, Identity Politics, and Violence against Women of Color. *Stanford Law Review*, 43(6):1241–1299.

Luigi De Russis and Fulvio Corno. 2019. On the impact of dysarthric speech on contemporary ASR cloud platforms. *Journal of Reliable Intelligent Environments*, 5(3):163–172.

John S. Garofolo, Lori F. Lamel, William M. Fisher, Jonathan G. Fiscus, David S. Pallett, Nancy L. Dahlgren, and Victor Zue. 1993. TIMIT Acoustic-Phonetic Continuous Speech Corpus LDC93S1.

Abraham Glasser. 2019. Automatic speech recognition services: Deaf and hard-of-hearing usability. In *Extended Abstracts of the 2019 CHI Conference on Human Factors in Computing Systems*, page 1–6, New York, NY, USA. Association for Computing Machinery.

John J. Godfrey and Edward Holliman. 1993. Switchboard-1 Release 2 LDC97S62.

Sharon Goldwater, Dan Jurafsky, and Christopher D. Manning. 2010. Which words are hard to recognize? prosodic, lexical, and disfluency factors that increase speech recognition error rates. *Speech Communication*, 52(3):181 - 200.

Léo Hemamou, Ghazi Felhi, Vincent Vandenbussche, Jean-Claude Martin, and Chloé Clavel. 2019. Hirenet: A hierarchical attention model for the automatic analysis of asynchronous video job interviews. *Proceedings of the AAAI Conference on Artificial Intelligence*, 33(01):573–581.

May Jiang and Christiane Fellbaum. 2020. Interdependencies of gender and race in contextualized word embeddings. In *Proceedings of the Second Workshop on Gender Bias in Natural Language Processing*, pages 17–25, Barcelona, Spain (Online). Association for Computational Linguistics.

Sushant Kafle and Matt Huenerfauth. 2020. Usability evaluation of captions for people who are deaf or hard of hearing. *ACM SIGACCESS Accessibility and Computing*, (122):1–1.

Allison Koenecke, Andrew Nam, Emily Lake, Joe Nudell, Minnie Quartey, Zion Mengesha, Connor Toups, John R. Rickford, Dan Jurafsky, and Sharad Goel. 2020. Racial disparities in automated speech recognition. *Proceedings of the National Academy of Sciences*, 117(14):7684–7689.

William Labov. 1990. The intersection of sex and social class in the course of linguistic change. *Language Variation and Change*, 2(2):205–254.

Ewa Luger and Abigail Sellen. 2016. "like having a really bad pa": The gulf between user expectation and experience of conversational agents. In *Proceedings of the 2016 CHI Conference on Human Factors in Computing Systems*, page 5286–5297, New York, NY, USA. Association for Computing Machinery.

Joshua L. Martin and Kevin Tang. 2020. Understanding Racial Disparities in Automatic Speech Recognition: The Case of Habitual "be". In *Proc. Interspeech 2020*, pages 626–630.

Josh Meyer, Lindy Rauchenstein, Joshua D. Eisenberg, and Nicholas Howell. 2020. Artie bias corpus: An open dataset for detecting demographic bias in speech applications. In *Proceedings of the 12th Language Resources and Evaluation Conference*, pages 6462–6468, Marseille, France. European Language Resources Association.

Taniya Mishra, Andrej Ljolje, Mazin Gilbert, Park Avenue, and Florham Park. 2011. Predicting Human Perceived Accuracy of ASR Systems. In *INTERSPEECH-2011*, August, pages 1945–1948.

Andrew C Morris, Viktoria Maier, and Phil Green. 2004. From WER and RIL to MER and WIL : improved evaluation measures for connected speech recognition. In *INTERSPEECH-2004*, pages 2765–2768.

H. Nanjo and T. Kawahara. 2005. A new asr evaluation measure and minimum bayes-risk decoding for open-domain speech understanding. In *Proceedings. (ICASSP '05). IEEE International Conference on Acoustics, Speech, and Signal Processing, 2005.*, volume 1, pages I/1053–I/1056 Vol. 1.

Martin Porcheron, Joel E. Fischer, Stuart Reeves, and Sarah Sharples. 2018. *Voice Interfaces in Everyday Life*, page 1–12. Association for Computing Machinery, New York, NY, USA.

Inioluwa Deborah Raji and Joy Buolamwini. 2019. Actionable Auditing. In *AIES '19: Proceedings of the 2019 AAAI/ACM Conference on AI, Ethics, and Society*, pages 429–435.

Maarten Sap, Dallas Card, Saadia Gabriel, Yejin Choi, and Noah A. Smith. 2019. The risk of racial bias in hate speech detection. In *Proceedings of the 57th Annual Meeting of the Association for Computational Linguistics*, pages 1668–1678, Florence, Italy. Association for Computational Linguistics.

Deven Santosh Shah, H. Andrew Schwartz, and Dirk Hovy. 2020. Predictive biases in natural language processing models: A conceptual framework and overview. In *Proceedings of the 58th Annual Meeting of the Association for Computational Linguistics*, pages 5248–5264, Online. Association for Computational Linguistics.

Jane Stuart-Smith. 2004. Scottish English. In Bernd Kortmann, Kate Burridge, Rajend Mesthrie, Edgar W. Schneider, and Clive Upton, editors, *A*

*Handbook of Varieties of English*, pages 47–67. Mouton de Gruyter, Berlin; Boston.

Rachael Tatman. 2017. Gender and dialect bias in YouTube's automatic captions. In *Proceedings of the First ACL Workshop on Ethics in Natural Language Processing*, pages 53–59, Valencia, Spain. Association for Computational Linguistics.

Rachael Tatman and Conner Kasten. 2017. Effects of talker dialect, gender race on accuracy of bing speech and youtube automatic captions. In *Proc. Interspeech 2017*, pages 934–938.

Kathryn A. Woolard and Bambi B. Schieffelin. 1994. Language ideology. *Annual Review of Anthropology*, 23:55–82.

Victoria Young and Alex Mihailidis. 2010. Difficulties in automatic speech recognition of dysarthric speakers and implications for speech-based applications used by the elderly: A literature review. *Assistive Technology*, 22(2):99–112. PMID: 20698428.

# Embodied Multimodal Agents to Bridge the Understanding Gap

**Nikhil Krishnaswamy**
Department of Computer Science
Colorado State University
Fort Collins, CO, USA
nkrishna@colostate.edu

**Nada Alalyani**
Department of Computer Science
Colorado State University
Fort Collins, CO, USA
n.alalyani@colostate.edu

## Abstract

In this paper we argue that embodied multimodal agents, i.e., avatars, can play an important role in moving natural language processing toward "deep understanding." Fully-featured interactive agents, model encounters between two "people," but a language-only agent has little environmental and situational awareness. Multimodal agents bring new opportunities for interpreting visuals, locational information, gestures, etc., which are more axes along which to communicate. We propose that multimodal agents, by facilitating an *embodied* form of human-computer interaction, provide additional structure that can be used to train models that move NLP systems closer to genuine "understanding" of grounded language, and we discuss ongoing studies using existing systems.

## 1 Introduction

As of the 2020s, high-profile NLP successes are being driven by large (and ever-growing) deep neural language models[1]. These models perform impressively according to common metrics on a variety of tasks such as text generation, question answering, summarization, machine translation, and more.

However, deep examinations of large language models show that they may exploit artifacts or heuristics in the data (McCoy et al., 2019; Niven and Kao, 2019). Similar observations have been made about computer vision systems (Zhu et al., 2016; Barbu et al., 2019). The black-box nature of much NLP leads to the argument that they are insufficient at demonstrating understanding of communicative intent and also cannot explain why or when these failures occur. (Bender and Koller, 2020).

[1] As of writing, the largest language model is the Switch Transformer by Google (Fedus et al., 2021), a trillion-parameter language model beating previous record-holder GPT-3 (Brown et al., 2020)

The *neurosymbolic* approach to AI has long argued for *structured representation* (Garcez et al., 2015; Besold et al., 2017), and similar arguments have also been made by deep learning luminaries e.g., Bengio (2017). Introducing preexisting structure into NLP facilitates higher-order reasoning, but a hybrid approach also does so at larger scales than purely symbolic systems, by using flexible deep-learning representations as input channels.

Multimodal NLP systems, particularly those with embodied agents, model encounters between two "people." A fully-featured interaction requires an encoding of structures that make language interpretable and "deeply understandable." This makes embodied multimodal interaction a uniquely useful tool to examine what NLP models in use meaningfully learn and "understand.". If one mode of expression (e.g., gesture) is insufficiently communicative, another (e.g., language) can be used to examine where it went wrong. Each additional modality provides an avenue through which to validate models of other modalities.

In this paper we review common components of embodied multimodal agent systems and their contributions to "deep understanding." We present ongoing experiments in agents who exhibit grounded understanding, using complex multimodal referring expressions as an example task.

## 2 Multimodal Conversational Systems

As AI systems become more integrated with everyday life, users at times harbor misapprehensions that they behave like humans. This dates as far back as ELIZA (Weizenbaum, 1966), whose users were convinced that ELIZA "understood" them despite Weizenbaum's insistence otherwise. The well-known SHRDLU displayed some situational understanding, but SHRDLU's deterministic perception was not sensor-driven (Winograd, 1972).



*Proceedings of the First Workshop on Bridging Human–Computer Interaction and Natural Language Processing*, pages 41–46
April 20, 2021. 

Quek et al. (2002) and Dumas et al. (2009), among many others, define *multimodal* interaction as interactions with multiple distinct input channels, e.g., spoken language and gestures, that complement and reinforce each other. This relates to "communicative intent" in that if one channel is ambiguous, the other(s) may clarify or add to the meaning. Multimodal interactions may increase understanding by making it easier to retrieve a communicative intent from a combination of inputs. This makes it critical in computer systems that display understanding.

Bolt's "Put-that-there" (1980) anticipated some critical issues, including the use of deixis for disambiguation. The subsequent community that evolved around multimodal integration (e.g., Kennington et al. (2013), Turk (2014)) gave rise to a number of *embodied conversation agents* (ECAs) (e.g., Cassel (2000)) deployed in different task domains, including education (Barmaki and Hughes, 2018), negotiations (Mell et al., 2018), and medical practitioner evaluation (Carnell et al., 2019).

Humans communicate contextually; they may gesture and refer to items in their co-perceived space. This co-perception and co-attention is "central to determining the meanings of communicative acts [...] in shared events" (Pustejovsky, 2018). A communicative act, $C_a$, can be modeled as a tuple of expressions from the modalities available to the agent, which convey complementary or redundant information. For example, if the modalities involved are $S$peech, $G$esture, $F$acial expression, ga$Z$e, and $A$ction, then $C_a = \langle S, G, F, Z, A \rangle$, of which any may be null or empty. Information in one channel may be supplemented by another channel, and they may disambiguate each other if properly aligned. For instance, if interpreted from the human's point of view, $C_a = \langle S = \text{"}left\text{"}, G = [Point_g \wedge Dir = \text{RIGHT}] \rangle$ (cf. Kendon (2004), Lascarides and Stone (2009)), this may signal a difference in the agents' relative frames of reference. This effect of embodiment is critical for deep understanding of situated language, vis-à-vis something as basic as directional terms.

An *embodied* agent can demonstrate aspects of their worldview, including how they ground and interpret utterances, gestures, or the consequences of actions, by acting themselves in their worlds. "Embodied worlds" may be virtual, physical, or mixed-reality. In the remainder of this paper we focus on virtual worlds.

To align various modalities in the state space accessed by the agent's dialogue system, we assume a "common ground" structure associated with a dialogue state. This state monad (Unger, 2011; Bekki and Masuko, 2014): $\mathbf{M}\alpha = State \rightarrow (\alpha \times State)$, corresponds to those computations that read and modify the state. **M** is a type constructor that consumes a state and returns a pair: $\langle value, modified\_state \rangle$.

A system operating under the aforementioned assumptions is "Diana" (McNeely-White et al., 2019). Diana's semantic knowledge of objects and actions is based on the VoxML modeling language (Pustejovsky and Krishnaswamy, 2016), and she asynchronously interprets spoken language and gesture to collaborate on construction tasks with humans. The human instructs Diana by deictically or linguistically referencing objects and indicating what to do with them multimodally. Diana's responses and *actions* make clear whether she understands what the user intended or not: a clear extraction of communicative intent from utterance, and a measure of "deep understanding."

However, Diana's capabilities are not fully symmetrical. The human may speak verbosely, but Diana's responses are brief: "OK," or the occasional disambiguatory question. To increase Diana's capacity for deep understanding, and symmetric retrieval of intent from utterance on the part of both Diana and the human, we are conducting experiments to fully develop the capabilities afforded by Diana's multimodal embodiment. These are outlined subsequently.

## 3 Ongoing Experiments

Referring expressions (REs) provide a defined and evaluable case study in the ability of an NLP system to extract communicative intent from an utterance. Either the agent correctly retrieves the object the human referenced or it does not; either the human can correct misunderstanding or they cannot.

Referring expressions exploit information about both object characteristics and locations. Linguistic referencing strategies can use high-level abstractions to distinguish an object in a given location from similar ones elsewhere, yet the location described may still be difficult to ground or interpret. When interacting person-to-person, humans deploy a variety of strategies to clearly indicate objects and locations in a discourse, including mixing and matching modalities on the fly and switching strategies to optimize both economy and clarity. Therefore, in an ongoing study to replicate this same capacity in interactive agents, we are exploring how to generate symmetrically-descriptive references of distinct objects in context.

Krishnaswamy and Pustejovsky (2019) presented the EMRE (Embodied Multimodal Referring Expressions) dataset. It contains 1,500 videos of a version of the Diana agent referencing multiple objects in sequence with a mix of language and gestures. The authors found that human evaluators found multimodal referring strategies most natural and preferred more descriptive language. However, they also found that the data gathered was not enough to train an effective generation model, so we build on this strategy to augment the available data to a sufficient level.

### 3.1 Multimodal Referring Expression Generation

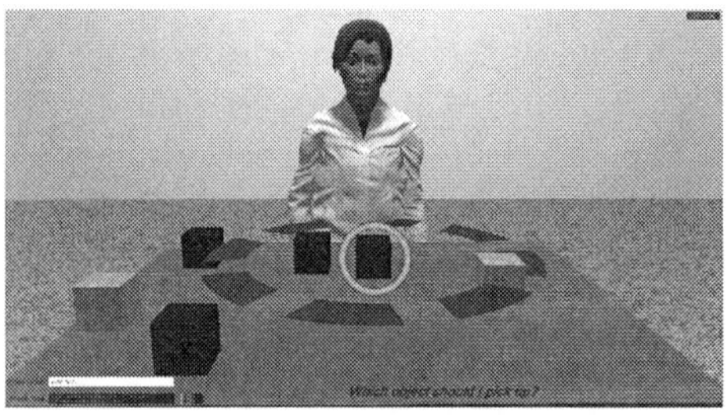

Figure 1: The pink circle indicates the target object. Diana asks "Which object should I pick up?" and waits for her partner to reference an object multimodally. The purple circle shows where the user is pointing.

We are deploying a web-based version of the Diana system, where participants are presented with a scene populated with randomly-placed objects, including objects that are identical in nominal attributes like color, as in the EMRE dataset. The human participant will be prompted analogously to what is shown in Fig. 1. The experimental system indicates one object of focus and Diana prompts the user to generate a referring expression with a question, e.g., "Which object should I pick up?" We then log information about how the human participant responds to the question, and about the scene (which act as contextual parameters). These include including the target object, distance from the agent, object coordinates, relations in the scene, previously referred-to objects; and about how the user responds, including complete utterance, modality(ies) used, attribute (identity) based description, demonstratives used, and relational descriptions used relative to other objects including those referred to at previous points in the dialogue.

Some of these parameters are identical to those in the EMRE dataset; others are included because we hypothesize that they will be useful to our proposed generation models (§3.1.2).

The multimodal inputs our system captures from the user are speech, transcribed via automated speech recognition, and mouse-based deictic gesture as a proxy for live pointing (see more details in §3.1.1). The modes of presentation available to Diana are: speech (generated via text-to-speech), pointing (via animated gesture), and visualized action (acting directly on virtual objects in the scene).

Participants in this study will be given explicit instructions as to the nature of the task, including that they should speak to Diana and can use the mouse to point to objects, to construct the conceit that Diana is a peer, such that the participants treat her like an appropriately collaborative agent. Depending on the crowdsourcing platform, we will also be able to filter the participants we solicit to make sure they have access to appropriate equipment, like a high-quality computer microphone.

Fig. 2 contains an example dialogue, which shows how Diana both extracts distinct objects from multimodal referring expressions and, when those objects do not match the human's intent, the human is able to correct her, also multimodally.

HUMAN: Take that purple block. [*points to two purple blocks near each other and far from Diana*]
DIANA: This one? [*points to a purple block*]
HUMAN: No. [*"thumbs down" gesture*]
DIANA: How about this one? [*points to the other purple block*]
HUMAN: Yes. Put it on the green block you just moved. [*points to a red block that* DIANA *recently put down*]
DIANA: Do you mean the red block I just put down?
HUMAN: [*"thumbs up" gesture*]

Figure 2: Sample dialogue.

We expect to deploy this study on a crowdsourcing platform like Prolific or Amazon Mechanical Turk, and aim to solicit interactions from approximately 250 workers using multimodal referring expressions while interacting with Diana in the task describe above. Each worker will view 10 scenes with different configurations in which to refer to up to 10 distinct target objects, resulting in a total of 25,000 samples. These multimodal referring expressions are expected to fall into three categories; attributive REs, relational REs, and historical REs, as we describe in §3.1.2.

We anticipate taking 3 months to build the web-based version of Diana; 1 month to gather raw data from workers; 1 month to annotate the data; 2 months to perform statistical analysis on the data and investigate good model features; and 3-4 months to design, build, and train our proposed RE generation models.

#### 3.1.1 Input Quality Assurance

For the avatar to respond appropriately, inputs need to be as clean as possible. In our multimodal use case, this includes the speech input, the pointing input, and the parse.

We solicited voice recordings of 30 university graduate students reading scripts containing domain-specific vocabulary. These cover diverse vocal profiles, including accent and timbre, so speech models suitable for these voices should be suitable for a crowd-sourced study. We are using these to assess the quality of speech recognition (e.g., Google Cloud ASR) in the task domain.

Our web-based Diana uses the mouse as a proxy for deixis, instead of CNN-based gesture recognition. We want to avoid participants "gaming the system" by using accurate mouse deixis alone, so we build some variance into this deixis proxy. The purple circle shown in Fig. 1 fluctuates in size proportionally to the variance in pointing location of the aforementioned gesture recognizer. The location of mouse "deixis" is imprecise by design, forcing participants to also use language to properly describe the target object.

Parsers under investigation are Stanford-CoreNLP and Google's SyntaxNet, and are being evaluated for the the syntactic dependencies they provide and the ability to extract entities and constituent relationships between them.

#### 3.1.2 Proposed Generation Models

When an embodied interactive agent is a partner in a dialogue, this provides a layer of exposure not present in end-to-end systems. The agent's responses can be used to probe where in the pipeline errors occur, be it in the speech recognition, the parse, or the interpretation. As discussed in §2, the existence of multiple modal channels allows investigation into which channel, e.g., the language, the gesture, the gaze/attention, etc. is the likely cause.

Assuming maximally correct inputs, as discussed in §3.1, existing NLP technologies, combined with an embodied multimodal agent, creates a mechanism to examine how multiple modalities can combine to signal aspects of an input that the agent can understand, or extract intent from, and reproduce, or communicate its own intent.

The EMRE dataset contains referring expressions generated via a mix of stochastic sampling and slot filling. From our crowd-sourced study, we plan to extract three particular kinds of additional data to train our multimodal referring expression generation (MREG) models:

- **Attributes** used to denote objects (A-MRE);
- **Relations** to other objects used to describe the target object (R-MRE);
- Dialogue **history** invoked when describing objects (H-MRE), which involves modeling when previous introductions into the common ground lose relevancy.

Attributes, relations, and actions in the history are encoded in VoxML, and serve as the *symbolic* inputs to our neurosymbolic architectures.

We intend our approaches to generate multimodal referring expressions in context that can blend modalities at runtime, for instance using demonstratives with gesture and distance of the target object relative to the agent.

Our proposed MREG models are centered around LSTMs (Hochreiter and Schmidhuber, 1997) for their ability to capture sequential information as occurs in a dialogue. MREG model outputs are likely to take the form $\langle M$odality, $U$tterance, $L$ocation, $D$emonstratives$\rangle$, where $M \in [Gesture, Language, Ensemble]$, $U$ is a decoded sentence embedding, $L$ is the location the gesture grounds to, and $D \in [this, that]$. Depending on the value of $M$, some of the other parameters may be empty by default. Fig. 3 shows schematics of the MREG architectures we are currently exploring.

**A-MRE** Object attributes are predicted by training an LSTM (**A-LSTM**) over the attributive terms participants use to describe objects (e.g., constituents tagged as $nmod$ in a parse), tracking how they vary terms for the same object over time. The A-LSTM takes a query representing the target object and outputs a descriptor tuple $\langle M, U, L, D\rangle$.

**R-MRE** Relations are predicted with another LSTM (**R-LSTM**) that takes as input $C$, pairwise permutations of the target object's configuration

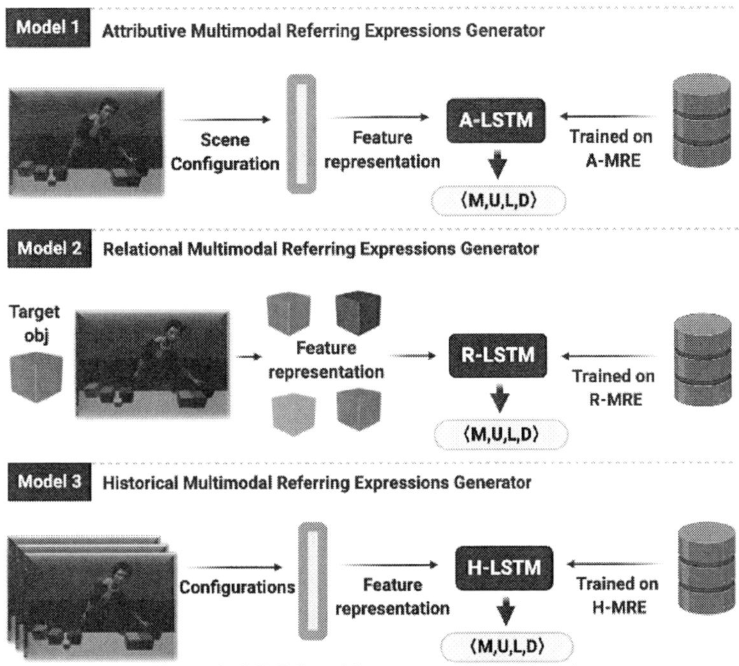


Figure 3: MREG architectures under exploration

relative to objects around it. E.g., in Fig. 3, if the target is "green block," then the proximate objects (orange and red blocks) are used to create binary relation pairs with them and the target (e.g., $left(O, G) \leftrightarrow right(G, O)$). These inputs are then fed to the R-LSTM trained over the R-MRE data with a query consisting of the target, which outputs relational descriptors of the target.

**H-MRE** Instead of features of a single configuration, the **H-LSTM** is trained over the H-MRE data, or sequences of configurations and the moves the agent makes that led to each of them. The job of the H-LSTM is to encode the features of this list and return the decoded multimodal RE expressions compatible with the given list of configurations.

## 4 Conclusion

Clark (1996) casts language as a joint activity. We propose that introducing the interactive element into natural language technology enables a number of opportunities to build systems that go beyond *processing* language to *understanding* it. We focus our experiments on embodied systems because they create a conceit of interacting with another "person." If these systems can interact in a way that suggests understanding of their interlocutor's intents, they will have demonstrated a step toward true computational natural language understanding. We are pursuing experiments in multimodal referring expression generation as an illustrative use case.

## References

Andrei Barbu, David Mayo, Julian Alverio, William Luo, Christopher Wang, Dan Gutfreund, Josh Tenenbaum, and Boris Katz. 2019. Objectnet: A large-scale bias-controlled dataset for pushing the limits of object recognition models. In *Advances in Neural Information Processing Systems*, pages 9448–9458.

Roghayeh Barmaki and Charles E Hughes. 2018. Embodiment analytics of practicing teachers in a virtual immersive environment. *Journal of Computer Assisted Learning*, 34(4):387–396.

Daisuke Bekki and Moe Masuko. 2014. Meta-lambda calculus and linguistic monads. In *Formal Approaches to Semantics and Pragmatics*, pages 31–64. Springer.

Emily M Bender and Alexander Koller. 2020. Climbing towards nlu: On meaning, form, and understanding in the age of data. In *Proc. of ACL*.

Yoshua Bengio. 2017. The consciousness prior. *arXiv preprint arXiv:1709.08568*.

Tarek R Besold, Artur d'Avila Garcez, Sebastian Bader, Howard Bowman, Pedro Domingos, Pascal Hitzler, Kai-Uwe Kühnberger, Luis C Lamb, Daniel Lowd, Priscila Machado Vieira Lima, et al. 2017. Neural-symbolic learning and reasoning: A survey and interpretation. *arXiv preprint arXiv:1711.03902*.

Richard A Bolt. 1980. *"Put-that-there": Voice and gesture at the graphics interface*, volume 14. ACM.

Tom B Brown, Benjamin Mann, Nick Ryder, Melanie Subbiah, Jared Kaplan, Prafulla Dhariwal, Arvind Neelakantan, Pranav Shyam, Girish Sastry, Amanda Askell, et al. 2020. Language models are few-shot learners. *arXiv preprint arXiv:2005.14165*.

Stephanie Carnell, Benjamin Lok, Melva T James, and Jonathan K Su. 2019. Predicting student success in communication skills learning scenarios with virtual humans. In *Proceedings of the 9th International Conference on Learning Analytics & Knowledge*, pages 436–440.

Justine Cassell. 2000. *Embodied conversational agents*. MIT press.

Herbert H Clark. 1996. *Using language*. Cambridge university press.

Bruno Dumas, Denis Lalanne, and Sharon Oviatt. 2009. Multimodal interfaces: A survey of principles, models and frameworks. *Human machine interaction*, pages 3–26.

William Fedus, Barret Zoph, and Noam Shazeer. 2021. Switch transformers: Scaling to trillion parameter models with simple and efficient sparsity.

Artur Garcez, Tarek R Besold, L d Raedt, Peter Földiak, Pascal Hitzler, Thomas Icard, Kai-Uwe Kühnberger, Luis C Lamb, Risto Miikkulainen, and Daniel L Silver. 2015. Neural-symbolic learning and reasoning: contributions and challenges.

Sepp Hochreiter and Jürgen Schmidhuber. 1997. Long short-term memory. *Neural computation*, 9(8):1735–1780.

Adam Kendon. 2004. *Gesture: Visible action as utterance*. Cambridge University Press.

Casey Kennington, Spyridon Kousidis, and David Schlangen. 2013. Interpreting situated dialogue utterances: an update model that uses speech, gaze, and gesture information. *Proceedings of SIGdial 2013*.

Nikhil Krishnaswamy and James Pustejovsky. 2019. Generating a novel dataset of multimodal referring expressions. In *Proceedings of the 13th International Conference on Computational Semantics-Short Papers*, pages 44–51.

Alex Lascarides and Matthew Stone. 2009. A formal semantic analysis of gesture. *Journal of Semantics*, page ffp004.

Tom McCoy, Ellie Pavlick, and Tal Linzen. 2019. Right for the wrong reasons: Diagnosing syntactic heuristics in natural language inference. In *Proceedings of the 57th Annual Meeting of the Association for Computational Linguistics*, pages 3428–3448, Florence, Italy. Association for Computational Linguistics.

David G McNeely-White, Francisco R Ortega, J Ross Beveridge, Bruce A Draper, Rahul Bangar, Dhruva Patil, James Pustejovsky, Nikhil Krishnaswamy, Kyeongmin Rim, Jaime Ruiz, et al. 2019. User-aware shared perception for embodied agents. In *2019 IEEE International Conference on Humanized Computing and Communication (HCC)*, pages 46–51. IEEE.

Johnathan Mell, Jonathan Gratch, Tim Baarslag, Reyhan Aydoğan, and Catholijn M Jonker. 2018. Results of the first annual human-agent league of the automated negotiating agents competition. In *Proceedings of the 18th International Conference on Intelligent Virtual Agents*, pages 23–28.

Timothy Niven and Hung-Yu Kao. 2019. Probing neural network comprehension of natural language arguments. In *Proceedings of the 57th Annual Meeting of the Association for Computational Linguistics*, pages 4658–4664, Florence, Italy. Association for Computational Linguistics.

James Pustejovsky. 2018. From actions to events. *Interaction Studies*, 19(1-2):289–317.

James Pustejovsky and Nikhil Krishnaswamy. 2016. VoxML: A visualization modeling language. In *Proceedings of the Tenth International Conference on Language Resources and Evaluation (LREC 2016)*, Paris, France. European Language Resources Association (ELRA).

Francis Quek, David McNeill, Robert Bryll, Susan Duncan, Xin-Feng Ma, Cemil Kirbas, Karl E McCullough, and Rashid Ansari. 2002. Multimodal human discourse: gesture and speech. *ACM Transactions on Computer-Human Interaction (TOCHI)*, 9(3):171–193.

Matthew Turk. 2014. Multimodal interaction: A review. *Pattern Recognition Letters*, 36:189–195.

Christina Unger. 2011. Dynamic semantics as monadic computation. In *JSAI international symposium on artificial intelligence*, pages 68–81. Springer.

Joseph Weizenbaum. 1966. Eliza—a computer program for the study of natural language communication between man and machine. *Communications of the ACM*, 9(1):36–45.

Terry Winograd. 1972. Shrdlu: A system for dialog.

Zhuotun Zhu, Lingxi Xie, and Alan L Yuille. 2016. Object recognition with and without objects. *arXiv preprint arXiv:1611.06596*.

# Putting Humans in the Natural Language Processing Loop: A Survey

**Zijie J. Wang*** **Dongjin Choi*** **Shenyu Xu*** **Diyi Yang**
College of Computing, Georgia Tech
{jayw, jin.choi, shenyuxu, dyang888}@gatech.edu

## Abstract

How can we design Natural Language Processing (NLP) systems that learn from human feedback? There is a growing research body of Human-in-the-loop (HITL) NLP frameworks that continuously integrate human feedback to improve the model itself. HITL NLP research is nascent but multifarious—solving various NLP problems, collecting diverse feedback from different people, and applying different methods to learn from human feedback. We present a survey of HITL NLP work from both Machine Learning (ML) and Human-computer Interaction (HCI) communities that highlights its short yet inspiring history, and thoroughly summarize recent frameworks focusing on their *tasks*, *goals*, *human interactions*, and *feedback learning methods*. Finally, we discuss future studies for integrating human feedback in the NLP development loop.

## 1 Introduction

Traditionally, Natural Language Processing (NLP) models are trained, fine-tuned, and tested on existing dataset by machine learning experts, and then deployed to solve real-life problems of their users. Model users can often give invaluable feedback that reveals design details overlooked by model developers, and provide data instances that are not represented in the training dataset (Kreutzer et al., 2020). However, the traditional linear NLP development pipeline is not designed to take advantage of human feedback. Advancing on conventional workflow, there is a growing research body of Human-in-the-loop (HITL) NLP frameworks, or sometimes called mixed-initiative NLP, where model developers continuously integrates human feedback into different steps of the model deployment workflow (Figure 1). This continuous feedback loop cultivates a human-AI partnership that enhance model performance and build users' trust in the NLP system.

*denotes equal contribution

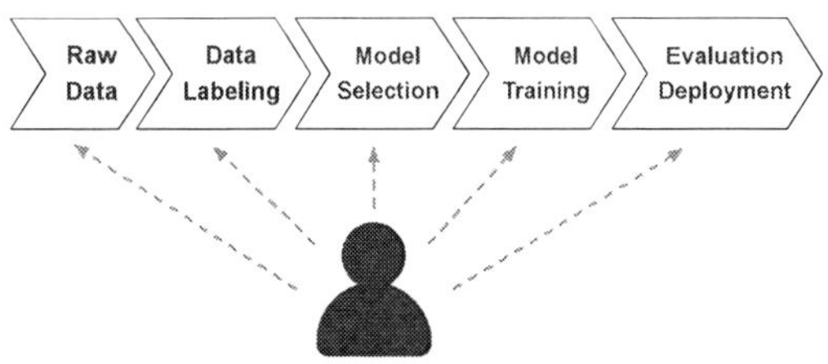


Figure 1: Collaboration between humans and models under a human-in-the-loop Natural Language Processing paradigm. Humans provide various types of feedback in different stages of the workflow to improve the model's performance, interpretability, and usability.

Just like traditional NLP frameworks, there is a high-dimensional design space for HITL NLP systems. For example, human feedback can come from end users (Li et al., 2017) or crowd workers (Wallace et al., 2019), and human can intervene models during training (Stiennon et al., 2020) or deployment (Hancock et al., 2019). Good HITL NLP systems need to clearly *communicate* to humans of what the model needs, provide intuitive *interfaces* to collect feedback, and effectively *learn* from them. Therefore, HITL NLP research spans across not only NLP and Machine Learning (ML) but also Human-computer Interaction (HCI). A meta-analysis on existing HITL NLP work focusing on bridging different research disciplines is vital to help new researchers quickly familiarize with this promising topic and recognize future research directions. To fill this critical research gap, we provide a timely literature review on recent HITL NLP studies from both NLP and HCI communities.

This is the first survey on the HITL NLP topic. We make two main contributions: (1) We summarize recent studies of HITL NLP and position each work with respect to its *task*, *goal*, *human interaction*, and *feedback learning method* (Table 1);



*Proceedings of the First Workshop on Bridging Human–Computer Interaction and Natural Language Processing*, pages 47–52
April 20, 2021. 

(2) We highlight important research directions and open problems that we distilled from the survey.

## 2 Human-in-the-Loop NLP Tasks

In this section, we categorize surveyed HITL paradigms based on their corresponding tasks.

### 2.1 Text Classification

Text classification is a classic NLP task to categorize text into different groups. Many HITL frameworks are developed for this problem, where most of them start with *training* a text classifier, then recruiting humans to *annotate* data based on the current model behavior, and eventually *retraining* the classifier on the larger dataset continuously. For example, Godbole et al. (2004) develop a HITL paradigm where users can interactively edit text features and label new documents. Also, Settles (2011) integrates active learning in their framework—instead of arbitrarily presenting data for users to annotate, samples are selected in a way that maximizes the expected information gain. With active learning, labelers can annotate fewer data to achieve the same model improvement of a framework using random sampling.

### 2.2 Parsing and Entity Linking

Besides classifying documents, recent research shows great potential of HITL approach in enhancing the performance of existing parsing and entity linking models. Advancing traditional Combinatory Categorial Grammars (CCG) parsers, He et al. (2016) crowdsource parsing tasks—a trained parser is uncertain about—to non-expert mechanical turks, by asking them simple what-questions. Also, with more strategic sampling methods to select instances to present to humans, a smaller set of feedback can quickly improve the entity linking model performance (Klie et al., 2020).

### 2.3 Topic Modeling

In addition to use HITL approach to enhancing learning low-level semantic relationships, researcher apply similar framework to topic modeling techniques that are used to analyze large document collections (Lee et al., 2017). For example, Hu et al. (2014)'s systems allow users to refine a trained model through adding, removing, or changing the weights of words within each topic. Recent work also focuses on human-centered HITL topic modeling methods. Kim et al. (2019) develop an intuitive visualization system that allows end users to up-vote or down-vote specific documents to inform their interest to the model. Smith et al. (2018) conduct users studies with non-experts and develop a responsive and predictable user interface that supports a broad range of topic modeling refinement operations. These examples show that NLP HITL systems can benefit from HCI design techniques.

### 2.4 Summarization and Machine Translation

HITL can be used in text summarization and machine translation. For instance, Stiennon et al. (2020) collects human preferences on pairs of summaries generated by two models, then train a reward model to predict the preference. Then, this reward model is used to train a policy to generate summaries using reinforcement learning. Kreutzer et al. (2018) collect both explicit and implicit language human feedback to improve a machine translation model by using the feedback with reinforcement learning. Experiments show that these models have higher accuracy and better generalization.

### 2.5 Dialogue and Question Answering

Recently, many HITL frameworks have been developed for dialogue and Question Answering (QA) systems, where the AI agent can have conversation with users. We can group these systems into two categories: *online feedback loop* and *offline feedback loop*. With online feedback loop, the system continuously uses human feedback to update the model. For example, Liu et al. (2018) collects dialogue corrections from users during deployment, and then use online reinforcement learning to improve the model. With offline feedback loop, model is updated after collecting a large set of human feedback. For instance, Wallace et al. (2019) invites crowd workers to generate adversarial questions that can fool their QA system, and use these questions for adversarial training. Offline feedback loop can be more robust for dialogue systems, because user feedback can be misleading so directly updating the model is risky (Kreutzer et al., 2020).

### 2.6 Human-in-the-Loop Goals

Among surveyed papers, the most abundant motivation for using a HITL approach in NLP tasks is to improve the **model performance**. For example, with a relatively small set of human feedback, HITL can significantly improve the model accuracy (Smith et al., 2018), model robustness

| | TASK | | | | | GOAL | | | INTERACTION | | | | | | | UPDATE | | |
|---|---|---|---|---|---|---|---|---|---|---|---|---|---|---|---|---|---|---|
| **Work** | Text Classification | Parsing and Entity Linking | Topic Modeling | Summarization and Machine Translation | Dialogue and Question Answering System | Model Performance | Model Interpretability | Usability | Mediums – Graphical User Interface | Mediums – Natural Language Interface | User Feedback Type – Binary | User Feedback Type – Scaled | User Feedback Type – Natural Language | User Feedback Type – Counterfactual Example | Intelligent Interaction | Data Augmentation – Offline Model Update | Data Augmentation – Online Model Update | Model Direct Manipulation |
| Godbole et al. (2004) | ● | | | | | ● | | | ● | | ● | | | | ● | ● | | |
| Settles (2011) | ● | | | | | ● | | | ● | | ● | | | | ● | ● | | |
| Simard et al. (2014) | ● | | | | | ● | | | ● | | ● | ● | | | | ● | | |
| Karmakharm et al. (2019) | ● | | | | | ● | | ● | ● | | ● | | | | | ● | | |
| Jandot et al. (2016) | ● | | | | | | ● | | ● | | ● | | | | | ● | | |
| Kaushik et al. (2019) | ● | | | | | ● | | | | ● | | | ● | ● | | ● | | |
| He et al. (2016) | | ● | | | | ● | | | ● | | ● | | | | | ● | | |
| Klie et al. (2020) | | ● | | | | ● | | ● | ● | | ● | | | | | ● | | |
| Lo and Lim (2020) | | ● | | | | ● | | | ● | | ● | | | | ● | ● | | |
| Trivedi et al. (2019) | | ● | | | | ● | | | ● | | ● | | ● | | | ● | | |
| Lawrence and Riezler (2018) | | ● | | | | ● | | | | ● | ● | | ● | ● | | ● | | |
| Kim et al. (2019) | | | ● | | | ● | | ● | ● | | ● | | | | | | ● | |
| Kumar et al. (2019) | | | ● | | | ● | | | ● | | ● | ● | | | | | ● | |
| Smith et al. (2018) | | | ● | | | ● | ● | ● | ● | | ● | ● | | | | | ● | |
| Stiennon et al. (2020) | | | | ● | | ● | | | ● | | | ● | | | ● | ● | | |
| Kreutzer et al. (2018) | | | | ● | | ● | | | ● | | | ● | | | ● | | | ● |
| Hancock et al. (2019) | | | | | ● | ● | | | | ● | | | ● | | | | ● | |
| Liu et al. (2018) | | | | | ● | ● | | | | ● | ● | | ● | | ● | | ● | ● |
| Li et al. (2017) | | | | | ● | ● | | | | ● | ● | | ● | | ● | ● | ● | ● |
| Wallace et al. (2019) | | | | | ● | ● | | | | ● | ● | | ● | ● | | ● | | |

Table 1: Overview of representative works in HITL NLP. Each row represents one work. Works are sorted by their task types. Each column corresponds to a dimension from the four subsections (task, goal, human interaction, and feedback learning methods).

and generalization (Stiennon et al., 2020). Besides model performance, HITL can also improve the **interpretability** and **usability** of NLP models. For instance, Wallace et al. (2019) guides humans to generate adversarial questions that fool the question answering model—these adversarial questions are also used as probes for researchers to study the underlying model behaviors. In Smith et al. (2018)'s topic modeling work, user studies have shown that users gain more trust and confidence through the HITL system.

## 3 Human-machine Interaction

This section discusses the mediums that users use to interact with HITL systems and different types of feedback that the system collect.

### 3.1 Interaction Mediums

**Graphical User Interface** (GUI) provides a user interface that allows users to interact with systems through graphical icons and visual indicators. Some HITL NLP systems allow users to directly label samples in the GUI (Godbole et al., 2004). The GUI also makes feature editing possible for end-users who do not develop the model from initial (Simard et al., 2014). Some work even uses the GUI for users to rate training sentences in the text summarization task (Stiennon et al., 2020) and rank generated topics in the topic modeling task (Kim et al., 2019). One obvious advantage of the GUI is that it helps visualize NLP models, enhancing the interpretability of the model. In addition, the GUI supports *Windows, Icons, Menus, Pointer* (WIMP) interactions, providing users more accurate control for refining the models.

**Natural Language Interface** is an interface where the user interacts with the computer through natural language. As this interface usually simulates having a conversation with a computer, it mostly comes with the purpose of building up a dialogue system (Hancock et al., 2019). The natural language interface not only supports users to provide explicit feedback (Liu et al., 2018), such as positive or negative responses. It also allows users to give implicit feedback with natural language sentences (Li et al., 2017). Compared to the GUI, the natural language interface is more intuitive to use as it simulates the process of human's conversation and thus needs no additional tutorial. In particular, it naturally fits in dialogue systems.

### 3.2 User Feedback Types

**Binary Feedback** has two categories which are usually opposite to each other, such as "like" and "dislike". It can be collected by both the GUI and the natural language interface. GUIs can collect binary user feedback from the user's adding or removing labels (Settles, 2011) and features (Godbole et al., 2004). The natural language interface can also support binary user feedback collection with simple short natural language response, such as "agree" and "reject" (Liu et al., 2018).

**Scaled Feedback** has scaled categories and is usually in numerical formats, such as the 5-point scale rating. It often can only be collected through the GUI as it is difficult to express accurate scaled feedback in natural language. Such user feedback is collected in the GUI when users rate their preferences of training data or model results (Kreutzer et al., 2018) and adjust features on a numerical scale (Simard et al., 2014). Similar to binary user feedback, scaled user feedback can provide explicit feedback for the system to update the models (e.g. adjusting the weight of one feature from 1 to 3 on a scale of 5 points). Besides, the scaled ratings of user preferences can also be used as implicit guidance for improving the model.

**Natural Language Feedback**, comparing to binary user feedback and scaled user feedback, is better for representing users' intention but vague and hard for the machine to interpret. It can only be collected through the natural language interface. Users provide this type of user feedback by directly inputting natural language sentences to the system (Hancock et al., 2019). By analyzing the user input sentences, the system implies the user's intention and accordingly update the model.

**Counterfactual Example Feedback**, similar to the natural language user feedback, are usually collected through the natural language interface. The HITL NLP systems collect and analyze user-modified counterfactual text examples and retrain the model accordingly (Kaushik et al., 2019; Lawrence and Riezler, 2018).

### 3.3 Intelligent Interaction

As discussed in section 2, *active learning* is one commonly used technique we observed in our surveyed systems. Active learning allows the system to interactively query a user to label new data points with the desired outputs (Godbole et al., 2004). By strategically choosing samples to maximize information gain with fewer iterations, active learning not only reduces human efforts on data labeling but also improves the efficiency of the interface.

## 4 How to Use User Feedback

This section summarizes how existing HITL NLP systems utilize different types of feedback.

### 4.1 Data Augmentation

One popular approach is to consider the feedback as a new ground truth data sample. We describe two types of techniques to use augmented data set: *Offline Update* re-trains NLP model from scratch after collecting human feedback, while *Online Update* trains NLP models while collecting feedback.

**Offline Model Update** is usually performed after certain amount of human feedback is collected. Offline update does not need to be immediate, so they are suitable for noisy feedback with complex models which takes extra processing and training time. For example, Simard et al. (2014) and Karmakharm et al. (2019) use human feedback as new class labels and span-level annotations, and retrain their models after collecting enough new data.

**Online Model Update** is applied right after user feedback is given. This is effective for dialogue systems and conversational QA systems where recent input is crucial to machine's reasoning (Li et al., 2017). *Incremental learning* technique is often used to learn augmented data in real-time (Kumar et al., 2019). It focuses on making an incremental change to current system using the newly come feedback information effectively. Interactive topic modeling systems and feature engineering systems widely use this technique. For example,

Kim et al. (2019) incrementally updates topic hierarchy by extending or shrinking topic tree incrementally. Also, some frameworks use Latent Dirichlet Allocation (LDA) to adjust sampling parameters with collected feedback in incremental iterations (Smith et al., 2018).

### 4.2 Model Direct Manipulation

Collected numerical human feedback are usually directly used to adjust model's objective function. For example, Li et al. (2017) collect binary feedback as rewards for reinforcement learning of a dialogue agent. Similarly, Kreutzer et al. (2018) uses a 5-point scale rating as reward function of reinforcement and bandit learning for machine translation. Existing works have focused more on numerical feedback than natural language feedback. Numerical feedback is easier to be incorporated into models, but provides limited information than natural language. For future research, incorporating more types of feedback (e.g., speech, log data) will be an interesting direction to gain more useful insights from humans. With more complex feedback type, it is critical to design both quantitative and qualitative methods to evaluate collected feedback, as they can be noisy just like any other data.

## 5 Conclusion and Future Directions

In this paper, we summarize recent literature on HITL NLP from both NLP and HCI communities, and position each work with respect to its task, goal, human interaction, and feedback learning method. The field of HITL NLP is still relatively nascent and we see many different design choices. We find improving model performance is the most popular goal among surveyed NLP HITL frameworks. However, researchers have found HITL method also enhances NLP model interpretability (Jandot et al., 2016) and usability (Lee et al., 2017). we encourage future NLP researchers to explore HITL as a mean to better understand their models and improve the experience of end users. One way is to design systems that take feedback from model engineers and end users beyond crowd workers.

Most of the HITL NLP systems are designed by NLP researchers. As human feedback is the core for HITL design, we believe that this field will be greatly benefited from a deeper involvement of the HCI community. For example, with a poorly designed human-machine interface, the collected human feedback are more likely to be inconsistent, incorrect, or even misleading. Therefore, better interface design and rigorous user study to evaluate interfaces can greatly enhance the quality of feedback collection, which in turn improve the downstream task performance.

To shed light on HITL NLP research from a HCI perspective, Wallace et al. (2019) explore the effect of adding model interpretation cues in the HITL interface on the quality of collected feedback; Schoch et al. (2020) investigate the impacts of question framing imposed on humans; similarly, Rao and Daumé III (2018) study how to ask good questions to which humans are more likely to give helpful feedback. In particular, we recommend future researchers to (1) consider integrating interactive visualization techniques into human-machine interfaces; (2) conduct user study to evaluate the effectiveness of their HITL system in addition to model performance; (3) share collected human feedback data and user study protocols with the community.

## References

Shantanu Godbole, Abhay Harpale, Sunita Sarawagi, and Soumen Chakrabarti. 2004. Document Classification Through Interactive Supervision of Document and Term Labels. In *Knowledge Discovery in Databases: PKDD 2004*, volume 3202, pages 185–196. Springer Berlin Heidelberg, Berlin, Heidelberg.

Braden Hancock, Antoine Bordes, Pierre-Emmanuel Mazaré, and Jason Weston. 2019. Learning from Dialogue after Deployment: Feed Yourself, Chatbot! *arXiv:1901.05415 [cs, stat]*.

Luheng He, Julian Michael, Mike Lewis, and Luke Zettlemoyer. 2016. Human-in-the-Loop Parsing. In *Proceedings of the 2016 Conference on Empirical Methods in Natural Language Processing*, pages 2337–2342, Austin, Texas. Association for Computational Linguistics.

Yuening Hu, Jordan Boyd-Graber, Brianna Satinoff, and Alison Smith. 2014. Interactive topic modeling. *Machine Learning*, 95(3):423–469.

Camille Jandot, Patrice Simard, Max Chickering, David Grangier, and Jina Suh. 2016. Interactive Semantic Featuring for Text Classification. *arXiv:1606.07545 [cs, stat]*.

Twin Karmakharm, Nikolaos Aletras, and Kalina Bontcheva. 2019. Journalist-in-the-Loop: Continuous Learning as a Service for Rumour Analysis. In *Proceedings of the 2019 Conference on Empirical Methods in Natural Language Processing and the 9th International Joint Conference on Natural Language Processing (EMNLP-IJCNLP): System Demonstrations*, pages 115–120, Hong Kong, China. Association for Computational Linguistics.

Divyansh Kaushik, Eduard Hovy, and Zachary C Lipton. 2019. Learning the difference that makes a difference with counterfactually-augmented data. *arXiv preprint arXiv:1909.12434*.

Hannah Kim, Dongjin Choi, Barry Drake, Alex Endert, and Haesun Park. 2019. TopicSifter: Interactive Search Space Reduction through Targeted Topic Modeling. In *2019 IEEE Conference on Visual Analytics Science and Technology (VAST)*, pages 35–45, Vancouver, BC, Canada. IEEE.

Jan-Christoph Klie, Richard Eckart de Castilho, and Iryna Gurevych. 2020. From Zero to Hero: Human-In-The-Loop Entity Linking in Low Resource Domains. In *Proceedings of the 58th Annual Meeting of the Association for Computational Linguistics*, pages 6982–6993, Online. Association for Computational Linguistics.

Julia Kreutzer, Shahram Khadivi, Evgeny Matusov, and Stefan Riezler. 2018. Can Neural Machine Translation be Improved with User Feedback? *arXiv:1804.05958 [cs, stat]*.

Julia Kreutzer, Stefan Riezler, and Carolin Lawrence. 2020. Learning from Human Feedback: Challenges for Real-World Reinforcement Learning in NLP. *arXiv:2011.02511 [cs]*.

Varun Kumar, Alison Smith-Renner, Leah Findlater, Kevin Seppi, and Jordan Boyd-Graber. 2019. Why Didn't You Listen to Me? Comparing User Control of Human-in-the-Loop Topic Models. In *Proceedings of the 57th Annual Meeting of the Association for Computational Linguistics*, pages 6323–6330, Florence, Italy. Association for Computational Linguistics.

Carolin Lawrence and Stefan Riezler. 2018. Counterfactual learning from human proofreading feedback for semantic parsing. *arXiv preprint arXiv:1811.12239*.

Tak Yeon Lee, Alison Smith, Kevin Seppi, Niklas Elmqvist, Jordan Boyd-Graber, and Leah Findlater. 2017. The human touch: How non-expert users perceive, interpret, and fix topic models. *International Journal of Human-Computer Studies*, 105:28–42.

Jiwei Li, Alexander H. Miller, Sumit Chopra, Marc'Aurelio Ranzato, and Jason Weston. 2017. Dialogue Learning With Human-In-The-Loop. *arXiv:1611.09823 [cs]*.

Bing Liu, Gokhan Tur, Dilek Hakkani-Tur, Pararth Shah, and Larry Heck. 2018. Dialogue Learning with Human Teaching and Feedback in End-to-End Trainable Task-Oriented Dialogue Systems. *arXiv:1804.06512 [cs]*.

Pei-Chi Lo and Ee-Peng Lim. 2020. Interactive Entity Linking Using Entity-Word Representations. In *Proceedings of the 43rd International ACM SIGIR Conference on Research and Development in Information Retrieval*, pages 1801–1804, Virtual Event China. ACM.

Sudha Rao and Hal Daumé III. 2018. Learning to Ask Good Questions: Ranking Clarification Questions using Neural Expected Value of Perfect Information. *arXiv:1805.04655 [cs]*.

Stephanie Schoch, Diyi Yang, and Yangfeng Ji. 2020. This is a Problem, Don't You Agree?" Framing and Bias in Human Evaluation for Natural Language Generation.

Burr Settles. 2011. Closing the loop: Fast, interactive semi-supervised annotation with queries on features and instances. In *Proceedings of the 2011 Conference on Empirical Methods in Natural Language Processing*, pages 1467–1478, Edinburgh, Scotland, UK. Association for Computational Linguistics.

Patrice Y. Simard, David Maxwell Chickering, Aparna Lakshmiratan, Denis Xavier Charles, Léon Bottou, Carlos Garcia Jurado Suarez, David Grangier, Saleema Amershi, Johan Verwey, and Jina Suh. 2014. ICE: enabling non-experts to build models interactively for large-scale lopsided problems. *CoRR*, abs/1409.4814.

Alison Smith, Varun Kumar, Jordan Boyd-Graber, Kevin Seppi, and Leah Findlater. 2018. Closing the Loop: User-Centered Design and Evaluation of a Human-in-the-Loop Topic Modeling System. In *Proceedings of the 2018 Conference on Human Information Interaction&Retrieval - IUI 18*, pages 293–304, Tokyo, Japan. ACM Press.

Nisan Stiennon, Long Ouyang, Jeff Wu, Daniel M. Ziegler, Ryan Lowe, Chelsea Voss, Alec Radford, Dario Amodei, and Paul Christiano. 2020. Learning to summarize from human feedback. *arXiv:2009.01325 [cs]*.

Gaurav Trivedi, Esmaeel R Dadashzadeh, Robert M Handzel, Wendy W Chapman, Shyam Visweswaran, and Harry Hochheiser. 2019. Interactive nlp in clinical care: Identifying incidental findings in radiology reports. *Applied clinical informatics*, 10(4):655.

Eric Wallace, Pedro Rodriguez, Shi Feng, Ikuya Yamada, and Jordan Boyd-Graber. 2019. Trick Me If You Can: Human-in-the-Loop Generation of Adversarial Examples for Question Answering. *Transactions of the Association for Computational Linguistics*, 7:387–401.

# Can You Distinguish Truthful from Fake Reviews? User Analysis and Assistance Tool for Fake Review Detection

**Jeonghwan Kim*** **Junmo Kang*** **Suwon Shin*** **Sung-Hyon Myaeng**
School of Computing, KAIST
Daejeon, Republic of Korea
{jeonghwankim123, junmo.kang, ssw0093, myaeng}@kaist.ac.kr

## Abstract

Customer reviews are useful in providing an indirect, secondhand experience of a product. People often use reviews written by other customers as a guideline prior to purchasing a product/service or as a basis for acquiring information directly or through question answering. Such behavior signifies the authenticity of reviews in e-commerce platforms. However, fake reviews are increasingly becoming a hassle for both consumers and product owners. To address this issue, we propose *You Only Need Gold (YONG)*, an assistance tool for detecting fake reviews and augmenting user discretion. Our experimental results show the poor human performance on fake review detection, substantially improved user capability given our tool, and the ultimate need for user reliance on the tool.

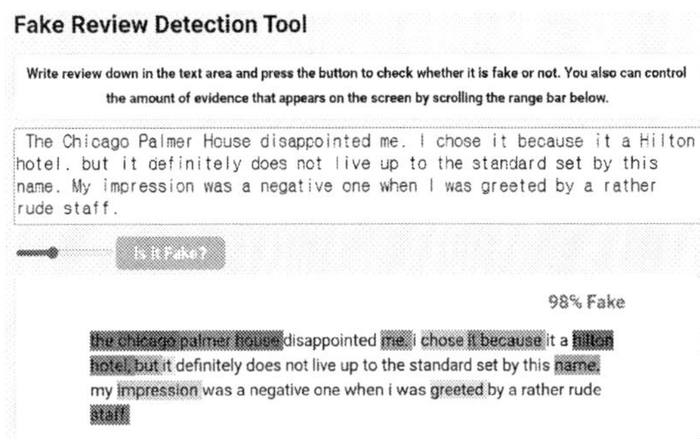


Figure 1: YONG - a prototype interface. Given the review input by user, YONG shows 1) whether it is gold or fake with 2) the probability (%), and 3) evidence that shows how much each word contributes to model's final decision. The highlighted evidences show the top $p\%$ proportion of the contributors, where the proportion can be adjusted using the horizontal slider bar.

## 1 Introduction

The increasing prominence of e-commerce platforms gave rise to numerous customer-written reviews. The reviews, given their authenticity, provide important secondhand experience to other potential customers or to information-seeking functions such as search and question answering. Meanwhile, fake reviews are increasingly becoming a social problem in e-commerce platforms (Chakraborty et al., 2016; Rout et al., 2018; Ellson, 2018). Such deceptive reviews are either incentivized by the beneficiaries (i.e., sellers, marketers) or motivated by those with malicious intention to damage the reputation of the target product.

To date, there have been many studies (Kim et al., 2015; Wang et al., 2017; Aghakhani et al., 2018; You et al., 2018; Kennedy et al., 2019) that address fake review detection in the field of natural language processing (NLP). The use of high-performance deep neural networks such as BERT (Devlin et al., 2018), fast and scalable anomaly detection algorithms like DenseAlert (Shin et al., 2017) have made effective and promising contributions in detection of fraudulent reviews. Despite such contributions, these approaches only focus on better modeling to improve the accuracy in fake review detection, instead of its practical applications such as assisting users to distinguish fake reviews (i.e., an assistance tool) or filtering out deceptive texts for review-based question answering (QA) (Gupta et al., 2019).

In the line of Human-Computer interaction (HCI), there have been a variety of studies on customer reviews (Wu et al., 2010; Alper et al., 2011; Yatani et al., 2011; Zhang et al., 2020). While there are *gold* reviews, which are authentic, real-user written reviews, there are *fake*, deceptive reviews as well. All of the previous works on review visualization and interaction implicitly assume the authenticity of collected reviews. Furthermore, the previous works mentioned above confine the scope

*Equal contribution.



*Proceedings of the First Workshop on Bridging Human–Computer Interaction and Natural Language Processing*, pages 53–59
April 20, 2021. 

of research on reviews to interaction and visualization.

We claim that user capabilities of distinguishing fake reviews are seriously unreliable as suggested in (Lee et al., 2016), and this motivates our work as practical research for helping humans discern fake reviews. While the two lines of research in NLP and HCI have focused on improving the fake review detection models and developing effective visualization of reviews, respectively, the actual victims (the users) of fake reviews are being neglected. The challenges of carefully curated deceptive reviews on the Web necessitate the need for an assistance tool that helps users avoid fraudulent information.

In this work, we propose *You Only Need Gold (YONG)* (Figure 1), a simple assistance tool that augments user discretion in fake review detection. YONG is built upon the body of previous studies by fine-tuning BERT and providing a self-explanatory *gold indicator* to assist users in exploring customer reviews. Through a series of user evaluations, we reveal the over-confident nature of people despite their poor performance in distinguishing fake reviews from real ones and the need to implement an explainable, human-understandable features to guide user decisions in fake review detection. We also demonstrate that the application of YONG effectively augments user performance.

Our contributions is two-fold, the tool and an extensive user understanding, as follows:

- An easy-to-use tool for fake review detection with the intuitive *gold indicator*, which consists of the following three features: (i) Model Decision, (ii) Percentage Indicator (%), and (iii) Evidence.
- User analysis on fake review detection. Our work sheds a light on how susceptible human judgment is to deceptive text. Understanding human decisions and behaviors in discerning fake reviews provides an insight into the design considerations of a system or tool for fake reviews.

## 2 Related Work

### 2.1 Fake Review Detection Using Deep Neural Networks

Fake review detection is an extensively researched topic among deep learning researchers. (Kennedy et al., 2019) provide a list of analytic comparison of non-neural and neural network models. In their work, a fine-tuned BERT performs the best on crowd sourced *Deceptive Opinion Spam* (Ott et al., 2013, 2011) data set and automatically obtained Yelp (Rayana and Akoglu, 2015) data set. Another work proposes a generative framework for fake review generation (Adelani et al., 2020). It proposes a pipeline of GPT-2 (Radford et al., 2019) and BERT to generate fake reviews. Due to the remarkable fluency of these reviews, its participants failed to identify fake reviews, and surprisingly, gave higher fluency score to the generated reviews than to the gold reviews. Similar result is evidenced in (Donahue et al., 2020), where humans have difficulty identifying machine-generated sentences. Other related works (Lee et al., 2016) use probabilistic methods such as Latent Dirichlet Analysis (LDA) to discover word choice patterns and linguistic characteristics of fake reviews.

### 2.2 Review Interaction and Visualization

The growth of customer reviews sparked research on its interaction and visualization. Visualization tools like OpinionBlocks (Alper et al., 2011) provide an interactive visualization for better organization of the reviews in bi-polar sentiments. Similar works like OpinionSeer (Wu et al., 2010) and Review Spotlight (Yatani et al., 2011) are also focused on providing an accessible and interactive visualization of reviews. The major drawback of these works is that they naively assume the *authenticity* of the reviews. From the previous lines of work, we argue the threat of fake reviews and their imminence with the rise of generative models (e.g., GPT-2) necessitate the use of our tool.

## 3 Method

We build a tool that provides straightforward, intuitive features to guide user decision in fake review detection. The tool is built upon a state-of-the-art NLP model fine-tuned on the OpSpam data set.

### 3.1 You Only Need Gold (YONG)

The tool we propose is a prototype for receiving a review text as an input and returns whether it is "Gold" or "Fake". YONG is an easy-to-use tool with three features collectively referred to as the *gold indicator* - namely, (i) Model Decision, (ii) Probability (%) and (iii) Evidence. Model Decision is the model output on the top right corner of Figure 1 as either Gold or Fake. The Probability (%) is the softmax output, which is also the model

| *Models* | *Accuracy* |
|---|---|
| SVM | 0.864 |
| FFN | 0.888 |
| CNN | 0.669 |
| LSTM | 0.876 |
| BERT (Kennedy et al., 2019) | 0.891 |
| **BERT (Ours)** | **0.896** |

Table 1: Accuracy performance comparison of conventional classification models against BERT on OpSpam.

confidence for its decision. The word highlights, which we also define as the Evidence, is a visualization of the attention weights from the last layer of BERT to provide an interpretable medium to model's decision for its users.

### 3.2 Fake Review Detection Model

To validate the claim made by a previous work (Kennedy et al., 2019) that BERT outperforms other baselines in fake review detection and to employ the most effective existing approach to fake review detection in our tool, we compare the performance of BERT against other classification models on the OpSpam (Ott et al., 2011, 2013) data set. In Table 1, we report the results of non-neural and neural network models under the 5-fold cross validation setting from (Kennedy et al., 2019). Our implementation of BERT outperforms all the other baseline models, reaching a 90% accuracy. Based on the model performances on OpSpam data set in Table 1 and the renowned language understanding capability of BERT (Devlin et al., 2018), we decide to employ BERT in our tool. We also fine-tune our BERT with the HuggingFace (Wolf et al., 2020) version of `bert-base-uncased`, where the `[CLS]` embedding is used for binary sequence classification.

### 3.3 Training & Dataset

To fine-tune BERT and to choose carefully curated data on fake review detection, we use the Deceptive Opinion Spam corpus, also known as the OpSpam data set (Ott et al., 2011, 2013). This data set consists of a total of 1,600 review instances, which is divided into truthful (i.e., gold) and deceptive reviews. The gold reviews are extracted from the 20 most popular hotels in Chicago (800 gold reviews) and the set of fake reviews are built using Amazon Mechanical Turk (AMT) (800 fake reviews). The gold reviews are not artificially generated, but are carefully chosen based on the criteria of determining deception as an effort to ensure truthfulness in (Ott et al., 2011). The data set is divided into a training and test set ratio of 8:2 in this work.

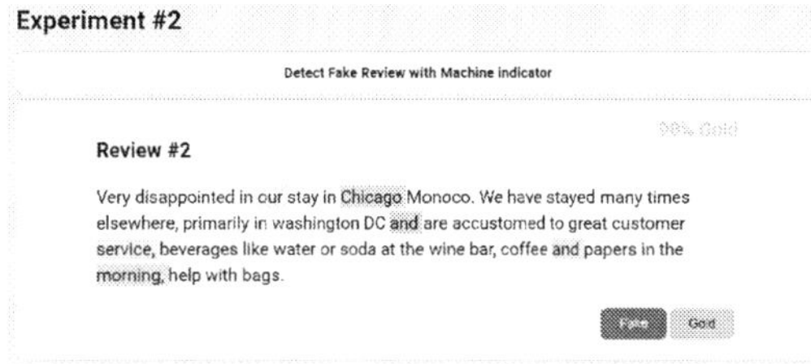


Figure 2: Experiment Test Bed for YONG - Experiment #2

## 4 Experiment and Result

### 4.1 Research Question

To validate the usefulness of our tool and further the understanding of users in the application of our tool, we define the following research questions (RQ):

**RQ1.** "How do humans fare against machines on fake review detection?"

**RQ2.** "Does YONG augment human performance on the task?"

**RQ3.** "Can we increase the level of human trust on YONG by injecting prior knowledge about human and model performance?"

**RQ4.** "How much influence does each feature of the gold indicator have on human trust?"

Here, we define the term "trust" as the level of human reliance on the tool's decision. To be specific, as we evaluate in Section 4.5, the level of trust is calculated on the participant-machine agreement (regardless of the ground-truth label). Through the experiments that correspond to the RQs, we build a concrete understanding of user behaviors in the presence of customer-generated reviews and the gold indicator through human performance evaluation on fake review detection.

### 4.2 Experimental Design

We provided 10 reviews from the data set to a total of 24 participants. The 10 reviews were randomly sampled, resulting in correct-to-wrong ratio of the model prediction to 7:3 (i.e., 7 correct and 3 wrong model predictions; score = 0.70), and the Gold-to-Fake ratio to 5:5. From Experiment 1 to 4 we assess the following criteria: human discretion, tool

| *Experiment* | *Condition* | *Score* | *Trust (low / high group)* |
|---|---|---|---|
| Exp. 1 | w/o tool | 0.41 | - |
| Exp. 2 | w/ tool | 0.54 | 0.81 / 0.79 |
| Exp. 3 | w/ tool & score | 0.56 | 0.83 / 0.71 |
| - | Model | 0.70 | - |

Table 2: Average scores (i.e., the number of correct decision w.r.t. the ground truth) of participants and the model, and the level of trust (i.e., participant-model agreement). Here, *low* and *high* groups are those with below and above average scores in Exp. 1, respectively.

helpfulness, trust level on the tool, and feature-level influence on decisions made:

**Experiment 1.** Users are required to classify fake reviews given 10 reviews without our tool.

**Experiment 2.** Users conduct the same task provided our tool (i.e. gold indicator).

**Experiment 3.** Users are shown their score and the model score for Experiment 1, and conduct the same task as in Experiment 2.

**Experiment 4.** Users are asked to score how each of the three features in our tool influences their decision.

We designed and built a separate Experiment test bed (Figure 2) using React [1] and FastAPI [2] to conduct an extensive quantitative and qualitative experiments on the participants of our study. To alleviate the learning effect, the participants are made unaware of the ground-truth answers and stay oblivious to both their and model scores (until Experiment 3).

### 4.3 Human Discretion Assessment

In Experiment 1, we assess the human performance on fake review detection. The participants are not given any hint - only the raw text. At the end of Experiment 1, we ask the participants enter their expected score. Here, the "score" corresponds to the number of correct decisions with respect to the ground-truth. In Table 2, we see that the average score of the participants are at 0.41. This result contrasts with the high accuracy score of our model (Table 1). An interesting observation made from Experiment 1 is the level of confidence participants had. Their expected score was 0.65 while their actual score was, on average, 0.41. They assumed that they got on average of 2.4 more problems (out of 10) correct than their actual score.

[1]https://reactjs.org

[2]https://fastapi.tiangolo.com

### 4.4 Helpfulness Assessment

To evaluate the helpfulness of our tool in augmenting user performance on fake review detection, we provide the gold indicator as in Figure 2. For a fair comparison, the participants were given the same reviews as in Experiment 1. In Table 2, the accuracy increases substantially from 0.41 to 0.54 by simply providing the gold indicator with the review text. Before proceeding to Experiment 3 - *trust level assessment*, we provide the participants their own scores on Experiment 1 and the model score to see if the injection of prior bias (i.e., being aware of the performance gap) could influence the participants to more align their answers with those of the model.

### 4.5 Trust Level Assessment

As previously stated, the participant is shown both scores prior to entering the experiment. The result shows an increase in the average score in Experiment 3 compared to that in Experiment 1. With the user awareness of their and model scores shown to improve the average participant score on the task, we decide calculate the change in the level of user trust on our tool. The trust level is calculated based on the proportion of overlapping answers (Table 2). The analysis on the trust level reveals two disparate groups: (i) Those who earned lower score than average in Experiment 1 and (ii) those who earned higher score than average in the same experiment. While the latter shows a drop in trust level from Experiment 2 to 3 ($0.79 \rightarrow 0.71$), the former shows an increase in the trust level ($0.81 \rightarrow 0.83$).

From Experiment 1, 2 to 3, we see the increase in average accuracy from 0.41 to 0.54, and to 0.56, respectively. To evaluate the statistical significance of the changes, we apply one-way repeated ANOVA with a post-hoc test to see that there are significant differences between Experiments 1 and 2 *($p < 0.005$)* and Experiments 1 and 3 *($p < 0.005$)*, and no statistically significant difference between Experiments 2 and 3. The result suggests that there is a large gap between human reasoning and data-driven model decision, and thus providing YONG contributes to an augmented human performance on fake review detection.

### 4.6 Feature-Level Influence Assessment

Aside from evaluating performance, we also measure the *feature-wise influence* on decision. We ask each participant to rate the three features in a

| *Feature* | *Decision* | *Probability* | *Evidence* |
|---|---|---|---|
| ***Influence*** | 3.69 | 3.91 | 1.87 |

Table 3: Influence score for each feature of the gold indicator.

1-to-5 scale for how much influence did each feature have on their decision. Here, the scale at 1 represents "No Influence", while scale at 5 means "Major Influence". In Table 3, we show the average rating per gold indicator feature. This result shows that the Probability (%) plays the primary role in convincing users that model prediction is correct. In other words, the higher the probability score, the more "trustworthy" the model decision becomes.

## 5 Discussion

There are three major findings in this work. In a fake review detection setting, (i) human capability is unreliable and needs machine assistance, (ii) the interpretable hidden weights are hardly explicable, and (ii) for DNN-powered assistive tools like YONG, it is essential to provide faith-gaining features for its users.

A notable finding is the difference between *interpretability* and *explainability*. In this work, we distinguish the two terms to ease their equivocal use. Interpretability refers to the property of being able to describe the cause and effect of the model through observation, whereas explainability refers to the human-understandable qualities that can be accepted on the terms of human logic and intuition. Although numerous existing works (Lee et al., 2017; Vig, 2019; Kumar et al., 2020) have repeatedly provided an interpretable look into the model's decision making process through layer-wise hidden vector or attention weight visualization, most stop at showing the colored vectors and matrices. In Figure 2, we can see how the model places much attention on proper and common nouns like "Chicago," and "morning," that fail to disambiguate and explain the reasoning process of our model for a human to understand. We can also observe in Table 3, where the evidence (i.e., highlighted words based on the attention weights) shows the lowest influence score on the users of our tool. This result implies that users found the feature either obsolete or inexplicable, leading to the low reference to the respective feature. These findings are also supported by a number of previous works on attention weights' explainability (Jain and Wallace, 2019; Kobayashi et al., 2020). (Jain and Wallace, 2019) show that the much touted attention weights' transparency for model decision is unaccounted for and do not provide meaningful explanations. (Kobayashi et al., 2020), furthermore, shows that focusing only on the parallels between the attention weights and linguistic phenomena within the model is insufficient and thus requires a norm-based analysis. Based on such observation, a possible addition to our tool can be generating textual explanations (Liu et al., 2018) or providing not only the token-level highlights as in Figure 2, but also more high-level (e.g., sentence-, paragraph-level information) highlights that show a comprehensible process to model decision.

## 6 Conclusion

Our work proposed You Only Need Gold (YONG), an assistant tool for fake review detection. From a series of experiments, we deepened our understanding of human capability in fake review detection. We observed that people were generally overconfident with their ability to discern fake reviews from real ones, and we discovered that the model far outperforms its human counterparts, suggesting the need for effective design to convince users to trust the model decision. Furthermore, our work reveals the need to develop more "explainable" tools and promotes collaboration of users and the machine for fake review detection. For future work, expanding the scope of our tool to other fields such as products and restaurants would likely contribute to its generalizability.


## Acknowledgments

This work was supported by Institute for Information & communications Technology Planning & Evaluation(IITP) grant funded by the Korea government(MSIT) (No. 2013-2-00131, Development of Knowledge Evolutionary WiseQA Platform Technology for Human Knowledge Augmented Services).


## References


David Ifeoluwa Adelani, Haotian Mai, Fuming Fang, Huy H Nguyen, Junichi Yamagishi, and Isao Echizen. 2020. Generating sentiment-preserving fake online reviews using neural language models and their human-and machine-based detection. In *International Conference on Advanced Information Networking and Applications*, pages 1341–1354. Springer.

Hojjat Aghakhani, Aravind Machiry, Shirin Nilizadeh, Christopher Kruegel, and Giovanni Vigna. 2018. Detecting deceptive reviews using generative adversarial networks. In *2018 IEEE Security and Privacy Workshops (SPW)*, pages 89–95. IEEE.

Basak Alper, Huahai Yang, Eben Haber, and Eser Kandogan. 2011. Opinionblocks: Visualizing consumer reviews. In *IEEE VisWeek 2011 Workshop on Interactive Visual Text Analytics for Decision Making*.

Manajit Chakraborty, Sukomal Pal, Rahul Pramanik, and C. Ravindranath Chowdary. 2016. Recent developments in social spam detection and combating techniques: A survey. *Information Processing Management*, 52(6):1053–1073.

Jacob Devlin, Ming-Wei Chang, Kenton Lee, and Kristina Toutanova. 2018. Bert: Pre-training of deep bidirectional transformers for language understanding. *arXiv preprint arXiv:1810.04805*.

Chris Donahue, Mina Lee, and Percy Liang. 2020. Enabling language models to fill in the blanks. In *Proceedings of the 58th Annual Meeting of the Association for Computational Linguistics*, pages 2492–2501, Online. Association for Computational Linguistics.

Andrew Ellson. 2018. 'a third of tripadvisor reviews are fake' as cheats buy five stars.

Mansi Gupta, Nitish Kulkarni, Raghuveer Chanda, Anirudha Rayasam, and Zachary C. Lipton. 2019. Amazonqa: A review-based question answering task. In *Proceedings of the Twenty-Eighth International Joint Conference on Artificial Intelligence, IJCAI-19*, pages 4996–5002. International Joint Conferences on Artificial Intelligence Organization.

Sarthak Jain and Byron C Wallace. 2019. Attention is not explanation. *arXiv preprint arXiv:1902.10186*.

Stefan Kennedy, Niall Walsh, Kirils Sloka, Andrew McCarren, and Jennifer Foster. 2019. Fact or factitious? contextualized opinion spam detection. In *Proceedings of the 57th Annual Meeting of the Association for Computational Linguistics: Student Research Workshop*, pages 344–350, Florence, Italy. Association for Computational Linguistics.

Seongsoon Kim, Hyeokyoon Chang, Seongwoon Lee, Minhwan Yu, and Jaewoo Kang. 2015. Deep semantic frame-based deceptive opinion spam analysis. In *Proceedings of the 24th ACM International on Conference on Information and Knowledge Management*, pages 1131–1140.

Goro Kobayashi, Tatsuki Kuribayashi, Sho Yokoi, and Kentaro Inui. 2020. Attention is not only a weight: Analyzing transformers with vector norms. In *Proceedings of the 2020 Conference on Empirical Methods in Natural Language Processing (EMNLP)*, pages 7057–7075.

Avinash Kumar, Vishnu Teja Narapareddy, Veerubhotla Aditya Srikanth, Aruna Malapati, and Lalita Bhanu Murthy Neti. 2020. Sarcasm detection using multi-head attention based bidirectional lstm. *IEEE Access*, 8:6388–6397.

Jaesong Lee, Joong-Hwi Shin, and Jun-Seok Kim. 2017. Interactive visualization and manipulation of attention-based neural machine translation. In *Proceedings of the 2017 Conference on Empirical Methods in Natural Language Processing: System Demonstrations*, pages 121–126.

Kyungyup Daniel Lee, Kyungah Han, and Sung-Hyon Myaeng. 2016. Capturing word choice patterns with LDA for fake review detection in sentiment analysis. In *Proceedings of the 6th International Conference on Web Intelligence, Mining and Semantics*, pages 1–7.

Hui Liu, Qingyu Yin, and William Yang Wang. 2018. Towards explainable nlp: A generative explanation framework for text classification. *arXiv preprint arXiv:1811.00196*.

Myle Ott, Claire Cardie, and Jeffrey T Hancock. 2013. Negative deceptive opinion spam. In *Proceedings of the 2013 conference of the north american chapter of the association for computational linguistics: human language technologies*, pages 497–501.

Myle Ott, Yejin Choi, Claire Cardie, and Jeffrey T. Hancock. 2011. Finding deceptive opinion spam by any stretch of the imagination. In *Proceedings of the 49th Annual Meeting of the Association for Computational Linguistics: Human Language Technologies*, pages 309–319, Portland, Oregon, USA. Association for Computational Linguistics.

Alec Radford, Jeffrey Wu, Rewon Child, David Luan, Dario Amodei, and Ilya Sutskever. 2019. Language models are unsupervised multitask learners. *OpenAI blog*, 1(8):9.

Shebuti Rayana and Leman Akoglu. 2015. Collective opinion spam detection: Bridging review networks and metadata. In *Proceedings of the 21th acm sigkdd international conference on knowledge discovery and data mining*, pages 985–994.

Jitendra Kumar Rout, Amiya Kumar Dash, and Niranjan Kumar Ray. 2018. A framework for fake review detection: issues and challenges. In *2018 International Conference on Information Technology (ICIT)*, pages 7–10. IEEE.

Kijung Shin, Bryan Hooi, Jisu Kim, and Christos Faloutsos. 2017. Densealert: Incremental densesubtensor detection in tensor streams. In *Proceedings of the 23rd ACM SIGKDD International Conference on Knowledge Discovery and Data Mining*, pages 1057–1066.

Jesse Vig. 2019. A multiscale visualization of attention in the transformer model. *arXiv preprint arXiv:1906.05714*.

Xuepeng Wang, Kang Liu, and Jun Zhao. 2017. Handling cold-start problem in review spam detection by jointly embedding texts and behaviors. In *Proceedings of the 55th Annual Meeting of the Association for Computational Linguistics (Volume 1: Long Papers)*, pages 366–376.

Thomas Wolf, Lysandre Debut, Victor Sanh, Julien Chaumond, Clement Delangue, Anthony Moi, Pierric Cistac, Tim Rault, Rémi Louf, Morgan Funtowicz, Joe Davison, Sam Shleifer, Patrick von Platen, Clara Ma, Yacine Jernite, Julien Plu, Canwen Xu, Teven Le Scao, Sylvain Gugger, Mariama Drame, Quentin Lhoest, and Alexander M. Rush. 2020. Transformers: State-of-the-art natural language processing. In *Proceedings of the 2020 Conference on Empirical Methods in Natural Language Processing: System Demonstrations*, pages 38–45, Online. Association for Computational Linguistics.

Yingcai Wu, Furu Wei, Shixia Liu, Norman Au, Weiwei Cui, Hong Zhou, and Huamin Qu. 2010. Opinionseer: interactive visualization of hotel customer feedback. *IEEE transactions on visualization and computer graphics*, 16(6):1109–1118.

Koji Yatani, Michael Novati, Andrew Trusty, and Khai N Truong. 2011. Review spotlight: a user interface for summarizing user-generated reviews using adjective-noun word pairs. In *Proceedings of the SIGCHI Conference on Human Factors in Computing Systems*, pages 1541–1550.

Zhenni You, Tieyun Qian, and Bing Liu. 2018. An attribute enhanced domain adaptive model for cold-start spam review detection. In *Proceedings of the 27th International Conference on Computational Linguistics*, pages 1884–1895.

Xiong Zhang, Jonathan Engel, Sara Evensen, Yuliang Li, Çağatay Demiralp, and Wang-Chiew Tan. 2020. Teddy: A system for interactive review analysis. In *Proceedings of the 2020 CHI Conference on Human Factors in Computing Systems*, pages 1–13.

# Challenges in Designing Games with a Purpose for Abusive Language Annotation

**Federico Bonetti**[1,2] and **Sara Tonelli**[2]
Dept. of Psychology and Cognitive Science, University of Trento, Italy[1]
Fondazione Bruno Kessler, Trento, Italy[2]
{fbonetti,satonelli}@fbk.eu

## Abstract

In this paper we discuss several challenges related to the development of a 3D game, whose goal is to raise awareness on cyberbullying while collecting linguistic annotation on offensive language. The game is meant to be used by teenagers, thus raising a number of issues that need to be tackled during development. For example, the game aesthetics should be appealing for players belonging to this age group, but at the same time all possible solutions should be implemented to meet privacy requirements. Also, the task of linguistic annotation should be possibly hidden, adopting so-called orthogonal game mechanics, without affecting the quality of collected data. While some of these challenges are being tackled in the game development, some others are discussed in this paper but still lack an ultimate solution.

## 1 Introduction

Cyberbullying has been recognised as a ubiquitous public health issue, with severe negative consequences for teenagers. Studies show that victims are more likely to suffer from psychosocial difficulties, affective disorders and lower school performance (Tokunaga, 2010; Kowalski et al., 2014), with consequences that are just as serious as for traditional bullying. Indeed, both bullying and cyberbullying are universal problems which affect all countries to a greater or lesser extent, regardless of the culture and country of origin of victims and aggressors (Zych et al., 2015).

Cyberbullying attacks are frequent in private chats and channels, while only a small fraction of them is visible in public accounts. This makes the analysis of cyberbullying phenomena difficult, since few data of this kind are accessible, making it hard to study the behaviour of adolescents online, especially if they are underage. The few existing works dealing with NLP and cyberbullying resort to simulations (Sprugnoli et al., 2018; Menini et al., 2020), create datasets starting from school bulletin boards (Nitta et al., 2013) or extract data from ask.fm (Hee et al., 2015; Safi Samghabadi et al., 2020), where however users are anonymous, making it difficult to focus only on adolescents.

Novel ways to understand the behaviour of teenagers with respect to verbal abuse online are therefore needed. Also, it is important to understand their perspective on different types of hate messages, so to develop systems that recognise cyberbullying by applying adolescents' point of view. Indeed, adolescents being part of virtual communities may share communication habits and slang that are different from those of adults, making it difficult for people outside these communities to judge the messages' offensiveness.

In order to deal with this lack of resources, we are developing a game called High School Superhero (Bonetti and Tonelli, 2020), whose goal is two-fold: on the one hand, it is meant to be used by young people to raise awareness on cyberbullying and on the use of offensive language, by playing the role of bystander in offensive interactions among peers. On the other hand, it is designed to collect annotations on hate speech texts, in particular whether players consider a message offensive or not, and which text span should be replaced or removed to make it not offensive. Accomodating these two tasks poses a series of challenges that we discuss in the remainder of this paper.

## 2 Related work

To date, there have been several attempts to gamify a wide range of linguistic annotation tasks. These include, among others, *Phrase Detectives* for anaphora resolution (Poesio et al., 2013), *The Knowledge Towers* (Vannella et al., 2014) and *Puzzle Racer* (Jurgens and Navigli, 2014) for concept-



*Proceedings of the First Workshop on Bridging Human–Computer Interaction and Natural Language Processing*, pages 60–65
April 20, 2021. 

image linking, *Infection* (Vannella et al., 2014), *OnToGalaxy* (Krause et al., 2010) and *JeuxDeMots* (Joubert et al., 2018) for semantic linking, *Argotario* (Habernal et al., 2017) for fallacious argumentation identification, *Zombilingo* (Fort et al., 2014) for dependecy syntax annotation, *Sentimentator* (Öhman and Kajava, 2018) for sentiment annotation, *WordClicker* (Madge et al., 2018) for part-of-speech tagging, *Wordrobe* (Venhuizen et al., 2013) and *Ka-Boom!* (Jurgens and Navigli, 2014) for sense annotation. Researchers stress the fact that games with a purpose (GWAPs) should be designed in such a way that they integrate the task without sacrificing their 'gamefulness', otherwise the tasks may be perceived as work (Vannella et al., 2014).

Concerning the use of gamification to raise awareness against cyberbullying, past works showed that increasing empathy is crucial to control cyberbullying (Barreda-Ángeles et al., 2021; Del Rey et al., 2016) and games can help in this sense as shown in Calvo-Morata et al. (2019). They tested *Conectado*, a game where users take the perspective of bullied victims, with school teachers and students aged from 12 to 17. The authors showed that this change of perspective has a positive impact on awareness and empathy, since players can learn more about bullying and what consequences it can have. DeSmet et al. (2018), on the other hand, stress the importance of promoting positive bystander behavior. In particular, they found that after playing their serious game, participants reported an increase in self-efficacy to end cyberbullying and intention to act as a positive bystander.

## 3 High School Superhero

### 3.1 Setting and gameplay

High School Superhero is a role-playing game set in the school of a small fictional town. Both the school and the town are freely explorable, allowing a certain degree of free roaming. The player is a teenager who has been appointed by the school principal and a scientist to limit bullying.

The main activity consists of engaging players in two different tasks: in Task 1 players are instructed to change other people's messages if they consider them offensive, so that they become inoffensive. To do this they can participate in conversations among non-playing characters and activate a special device that allows them to read their minds. The words displayed in the thought bubble can be changed freely, but the game allows for trap gold sentences to be inserted for quality control. Once the thought is changed, the message is displayed with a surprised reaction from the author. In this way we know which tokens are considered offensive and at the same time we can get alternative sentences. Both the original sentence and the changed one are stored and can be exported at the end of the game, so to be used as a sort of minimal pair containing an offensive and a non-offensive sentence. Changing a token consumes one battery bar, which has to be replenished by exchanging collectibles from specific terminals. Task 2 is similar to Task 1

Figure 1: Task 1: Change other people's messages

except messages are displayed on walls and floors in the form of graffiti or writings on blackboards, and players can erase the words they deem abusive. Erasing has a cost in terms of consumable sponges, which can be replenished like the batteries used in Task 1. In this way, we encourage players to delete only the offensive part of a message (an adjective, a slur), while keeping the rest unchanged, easing the identification of the exact offensive span for future linguistic analyses. The collectibles used to replenish the resources employed in the two tasks are scattered around the town, which means that exploration is deeply interconnected with the tasks.

Figure 2: Task 2: Erase abusive words

### 3.2 Platforms and data management

The game is meant to be played either offline or online. It can be installed on Windows, Machintosh and Linux platforms, but it can also be played via browser thanks to Unity Web Player. At the moment, we do not have plans to bring the game to mobile platforms, such as Android and iOS, especially because the game offers a type of interaction that requires a fair degree of accuracy (namely, clicking or tapping words and erasing them) that can be compromised by the different sizes of smartphone and tablet screens. Furthermore, in this particular type of gameplay, where the player is moved via traditional input, i.e. directional keys or a control stick, and where the third person camera is rotated freely, desktop environments, with a keyboard and a mouse or a controller, represent the optimal solution. The data to be loaded into the game can be put in a folder inside the game directory, as long as the format is .txt, .xml, .csv or .json and the sentences are properly tagged or follow a specific pattern. The aim is to make it easy to feed data to the game, which, provided that there are the appropriate tags, automatically sorts the data and assigns it to each task (namely conversations and graffiti) and adapts it accordingly.

## 4 Challenge 1: Appealing aesthetics

The first challenge we identified during the development of High School Superhero is the game aesthetics: the game should not have a poor graphics, but rather be comparable with similar games that teenagers may know. It should also foster identification and involvement.

### 4.1 Graphics style

Since the game is primarily targeted at teens and young teens, the graphics style is cartoonish, with bright colors, and simple, rounded shapes. It was inspired by some of the latest successful commercial games like Fortnite, Animal Crossing: New Horizons, The Legend of Zelda: Breath of the Wild, Immortals: Fenyx Rising. This style allows one to keep the graphics simple when it comes to 3D modeling and shading, and therefore makes it possible to set up a virtual world without employing professional artists.

The game is being developed with Unity3D[1] and the resources, such as meshes and shaders, are both created from scratch using Blender[2] (an extremely powerful open-source 3D modeling and rendering program) and downloaded for free from the Unity Asset Store. The choice of using 3D graphics was also inspired by the fact that, although a vast portion of successful commercial video games is three-dimesional, to our knowledge a 3D game with a purpose for linguistic annotation had not been developed yet.

### 4.2 Avatar customization

We implemented avatar customization for three reasons: first, a custom avatar is the hallmark of any role-playing game and, more generally, this feature is starting to be ubiquitous, with aesthetic modifications and cosmetic collectibles appearing even in games where the avatar has only minimal importance (see Microsoft's Forza Horizon 4, a racing game where the driver can be customized, as an example). Second, character customization proved to increase the perceived agency and foster identification and empathy with one's avatar (Turkay and Kinzer, 2014), which is important for the specific research domain (abusive language). Third, to a higher sense of agency may follow higher intrinsic motivation according to Self-Determination Theory (Ryan and Deci, 2000; Turkay and Adinolf, 2015). Note that for avatars no pre-defined gender categories are given, and the player is free to customize it selecting the preferred physical traits, clothes and colors in any combination. With the purpose of increasing identification and empathy we are also implementing a minimal story line.

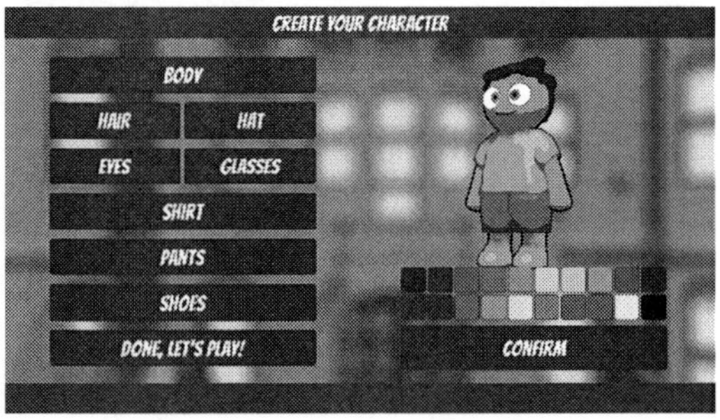


Figure 3: Avatar customization interface

## 5 Challenge 2: Add Orthogonal Mechanics

According to Tuite (2014), orthogonal game mechanics are those mechanics that "do not serve the

[1]https://unity.com/

[2]https://www.blender.org/

purpose". This type of mechanics is functional to a design strategy that Krause et al. (2010) call disjoint design, where "the design and the actual task do not correspond to each other directly". For example, a game where one must aim in order to select a label or an item to be labeled is said to employ orthogonal game mechanics, because aiming requires additional skills that do not strictly pertain to the annotation task. A game with a purpose for linguistic annotation that implements this type of mechanics is *OnToGalaxy* (Krause et al., 2010), where players control a spaceship and, given a concept and a type of semantic relationship, they have to shoot the enemy spaceships accordingly. The goal is to select the spaceships whose label is in relation with the given concept (by ignoring them) and to discard the spaceships whose label is not in relation with the given concept (by shooting them). An example of game with non-orthogonal game mechanics, instead, is *WordClicker* (Madge et al., 2019), where the mechanics directly overlap with those of a clicker game, which is a widespread and quite addictive type of game.

While orthogonal game mechanics may not always the best option, because they require players to have additional skills beside being able to perform the annotation task, they can be useful sometimes to engage players and make the interaction more attractive and interesting, allowing for increased resemblance with mainstream games.

One of the challenges with the development of our game is to introduce a certain degree of orthogonality, thus hiding the task mechanics, while at the same time preserving the overall annotation quality. Task 1 of High-School Superhero does not make use of orthogonal game mechanics, because abusive words are selected by clicking them, as in a non-gamified interface. Task 2, on the other hand, is orthogonal since words are selected by being rubbed with an eraser or a sponge, and one must pay attention not to exceed the boundaries of the abusive words. Although some quality control techniques are used, such as assessing the proportion of the word that has been erased, Task 2 requires the additional ability of erasing with a certain degree of accuracy. Specifically, in the present implementation of orthogonal mechanics, the rate of erased words can be affected by the depletion of resources, while the annotation accuracy can be affected by the sponge size and shape. Comparing the two strategies will be useful to understand whether orthogonal mechanics (potentially more engaging) represent a good alternative to non-orthogonal mechanics in terms of annotation rate and reliability.

## 6 Challenge 3: Respect Users' Privacy and other Ethical Considerations

Since this game aims to collect annotations that can be potentially updated across multiple sessions, and since we want annotations to be linked to specific demographic information, a login system and demographic questionnaires are employed. Indeed, the game will be used in the framework of an international collaboration with schools, and the link to play High School Superhero will be shared only with the schools involved in cyberbullying awareness initiatives. We did not want complex authentication systems to clutter the game interface, so a Google Login system is used where only the email address is read. The address is then converted into a SHA256 string and used as a user ID, while the address is deleted. In this way, we can control how many players have interacted with the game and check basic demographics, without making use or storing any sensitive information. This is particularly relevant in our context, since we involve underage subjects. Providing a completely free access without any kind of login would allow for a fully anonymous use of the game, but we would run the risk to have players producing low-quality data, or losing the possibility to target a specific age group.

Other issues related to having teenagers play our game concern their exposure to offensive language. In order to be aware of cyberbullying and be ready to respond to this phenomenon appropriately it is necessary that players interact with offensive texts. However, this may affect their well-being and have an impact on particularly vulnerable subjects. In order to have access to students, we will have to ask for the approval from the Ethical Committee in our University. Furthermore, we introduced the possibility, when using a local installation of the game, to manually upload the list of texts that will be displayed during the game, so that educators can pre-screen the texts removing extremely hateful messages. This approach is not ideal, since manual filtering is time-consuming and may not work well on a large scale. Alternative approaches will be explored to pre-select texts using NLP or remove messages based on lists of taboo words.

## 7 Conclusions and Future Work

In this paper we have discussed a number of challenges we are addressing in the development of High School Superhero, an online game for teenagers whose goal is two-fold: on the one hand, it can be used to raise awareness on cyberbullying and the use of offensive language among peers. On the other hand, it can serve for collecting instances of offensive and non-offensive language. In the future, we plan to evaluate the game with students in classes along different dimensions, focusing especially on motivation by employing questionnaires based on Self-Determination Theory. We are particularly interested in assessing differences in motivation because it is a key aspect for GWAP dissemination and data collection and can vary a lot across different tasks and different applications.

## Acknowledgments

Part of this work has been funded by the KID_ACTIONS REC-AG project (n. 101005518) on "Kick-off preventIng and responDing to children and AdolesCenT cyberbullyIng through innovative mOnitoring and educatioNal technologieS". We would like to thank Alessia Smeraglia for the help provided in designing the virtual world and the game play of High School Superhero during her internship.

## References

Miguel Barreda-Ángeles, Maria Serra-Blasco, Esther Trepat, Alexandre Pereda-Baños, Montserrat Pàmias, Diego Palao, Ximena Goldberg, and Narcís Cardoner. 2021. Development and experimental validation of a dataset of 360°-videos for facilitating school-based bullying prevention programs. *Computers & Education*, 161:104065.

Federico Bonetti and Sara Tonelli. 2020. A 3D role-playing game for abusive language annotation. In *Workshop on Games and Natural Language Processing*, pages 39–43, Marseille, France. European Language Resources Association.

Antonio Calvo-Morata, Manuel Freire-Moran, Ivan Martinez-Ortiz, and Baltasar Fernandez-Manjon. 2019. Applicability of a Cyberbullying Videogame as a Teacher Tool: Comparing Teachers and Educational Sciences Students. *IEEE Access*, 7:55841–55850.

Rosario Del Rey, Lambros Lazuras, José A. Casas, Vassilis Barkoukis, Rosario Ortega-Ruiz, and Haralambos Tsorbatzoudis. 2016. Does empathy predict (cyber) bullying perpetration, and how do age, gender and nationality affect this relationship? *Learning and Individual Differences*, 45:275–281.

Ann DeSmet, Sara Bastiaensens, Katrien Van Cleemput, Karolien Poels, Heidi Vandebosch, Gie Deboutte, Laura Herrewijn, Steven Malliet, Sara Pabian, Frederik Van Broeckhoven, Olga De Troyer, Gaetan Deglorie, Sofie Van Hoecke, Koen Samyn, and Ilse De Bourdeaudhuij. 2018. The efficacy of the Friendly Attac serious digital game to promote prosocial bystander behavior in cyberbullying among young adolescents: A cluster-randomized controlled trial. *Computers in Human Behavior*, 78:336 – 347.

Karën Fort, Bruno Guillaume, and Hadrien Chastant. 2014. Creating *Zombilingo* , a game with a purpose for dependency syntax annotation. In *Proceedings of the First International Workshop on Gamification for Information Retrieval - GamifIR '14*, pages 2–6, Amsterdam, The Netherlands. ACM Press.

Ivan Habernal, Raffael Hannemann, Christian Pollak, Christopher Klamm, Patrick Pauli, and Iryna Gurevych. 2017. Argotario: Computational Argumentation Meets Serious Games. In *Proceedings of the 2017 Conference on Empirical Methods in Natural Language Processing: System Demonstrations*, pages 7–12, Copenhagen, Denmark. Association for Computational Linguistics.

Cynthia Van Hee, Els Lefever, Ben Verhoeven, Julie Mennes, Bart Desmet, Guy De Pauw, Walter Daelemans, and Véronique Hoste. 2015. Detection and fine-grained classification of cyberbullying events. In *Recent Advances in Natural Language Processing, RANLP 2015, 7-9 September, 2015, Hissar, Bulgaria*, pages 672–680. RANLP 2015 Organising Committee / ACL.

Alain Joubert, Mathieu Lafourcade, and Nathalie Le Brun. 2018. The JeuxDeMots Project is 10 Years Old: What We have Learned. In *Proceedings of the 2018 LREC Workshop "Games and Gamification for Natural Language Processing (Games4NLP)"*, pages 22–26, Miyazaki, Japan.

David Jurgens and Roberto Navigli. 2014. It's All Fun and Games until Someone Annotates: Video Games with a Purpose for Linguistic Annotation. *Transactions of the Association for Computational Linguistics*, 2:449–464.

R. M. Kowalski, Gary W. Giumetti, A. Schroeder, and Micah R. Lattanner. 2014. Bullying in the digital age: a critical review and meta-analysis of cyberbullying research among youth. *Psychological bulletin*, 140 4:1073–137.

Markus Krause, Aneta Takhtamysheva, Marion Wittstock, and Rainer Malaka. 2010. Frontiers of a paradigm: exploring human computation with digital games. In *Proceedings of the ACM SIGKDD Workshop on Human Computation - HCOMP '10*, pages 22–25, Washington DC. ACM Press.

Chris Madge, Richard Bartle, Jon Chamberlain, Udo Kruschwitz, and Massimo Poesio. 2019. Incremental Game Mechanics Applied to Text Annotation. In *Proceedings of the Annual Symposium on Computer-Human Interaction in Play*, pages 545–558, Barcelona Spain. ACM.

Chris Madge, Massimo Poesio, Udo Kruschwitz, and Jon Chamberlain. 2018. Testing TileAttack with Three Key Audiences. In *Proceedings of the 2018 LREC Workshop "Games and Gamification for Natural Language Processing (Games4NLP)"*, pages 6–11, Miyazaki, Japan.

Stefano Menini, Alessio Palmero Aprosio, and Sara Tonelli. 2020. A multimodal dataset of images and text to study abusive language. In *Proceedings of the Seventh Italian Conference on Computational Linguistics, CLiC-it 2020, Bologna, Italy, March 1-3, 2021*, volume 2769 of *CEUR Workshop Proceedings*. CEUR-WS.org.

Taisei Nitta, Fumito Masui, Michal Ptaszynski, Yasutomo Kimura, Rafal Rzepka, and Kenji Araki. 2013. Detecting cyberbullying entries on informal school websites based on category relevance maximization. In *Proceedings of the Sixth International Joint Conference on Natural Language Processing*, pages 579–586, Nagoya, Japan. Asian Federation of Natural Language Processing.

Emily Öhman and Kaisla Kajava. 2018. Sentimentator: Gamifying Fine-grained Sentiment Annotation. In *Proceedings of the Digital Humanities in the Nordic Countries 4th Conference (DHN 2019)*, volume 2084, pages 98–110, Helsinki, Finland.

Massimo Poesio, Jon Chamberlain, Udo Kruschwitz, Livio Robaldo, and Luca Ducceschi. 2013. Phrase detectives: Utilizing collective intelligence for internet-scale language resource creation. *ACM Transactions on Interactive Intelligent Systems*, 3(1):1–44.

Richard M Ryan and Edward L Deci. 2000. Self-Determination Theory and the Facilitation of Intrinsic Motivation, Social Development, and Well-Being. *American Psychologist*, page 11.

Niloofar Safi Samghabadi, Adrián Pastor López Monroy, and Thamar Solorio. 2020. Detecting early signs of cyberbullying in social media. In *Proceedings of the Second Workshop on Trolling, Aggression and Cyberbullying*, pages 144–149, Marseille, France. European Language Resources Association (ELRA).

Rachele Sprugnoli, Stefano Menini, Sara Tonelli, Filippo Oncini, and Enrico Piras. 2018. Creating a WhatsApp dataset to study pre-teen cyberbullying. In *Proceedings of the 2nd Workshop on Abusive Language Online (ALW2)*, pages 51–59, Brussels, Belgium. Association for Computational Linguistics.

Robert S. Tokunaga. 2010. Following you home from school: A critical review and synthesis of research on cyberbullying victimization. *Computers in Human Behavior*, 26(3):277 – 287.

Kathleen Tuite. 2014. GWAPs: Games with a Problem. In *Proceedings of the 9th International Conference on the Foundations of Digital Games*.

Selen Turkay and Sonam Adinolf. 2015. The effects of customization on motivation in an extended study with a massively multiplayer online roleplaying game. *Cyberpsychology: Journal of Psychosocial Research on Cyberspace*, 9(3).

Selen Turkay and Charles K. Kinzer. 2014. The Effects of Avatar-Based Customization on Player Identification:. *International Journal of Gaming and Computer-Mediated Simulations*, 6(1):1–25.

Daniele Vannella, David Jurgens, Daniele Scarfini, Domenico Toscani, and Roberto Navigli. 2014. Validating and Extending Semantic Knowledge Bases using Video Games with a Purpose. In *Proceedings of the 52nd Annual Meeting of the Association for Computational Linguistics (Volume 1: Long Papers)*, pages 1294–1304, Baltimore, Maryland. Association for Computational Linguistics.

Noortje J. Venhuizen, Kilian Evang, Valerio Basile, and Johan Bos. 2013. Gamification for Word Sense Labeling. In *Proceedings of the International Conference on Computational Semantics (IWCS)*, pages 397–403.

Izabela Zych, Rosario Ortega-Ruiz, and Rosario Del Rey. 2015. Systematic review of theoretical studies on bullying and cyberbullying: Facts, knowledge, prevention, and intervention. *Aggression and Violent Behavior*, 23:1–21. Bullying, Cyberbullying, and Youth Violence: Facts, Prevention, and Intervention.

# Challenges in Designing Natural Language Interfaces for Complex Visual Models

**Henrik Voigt[1,2], Monique Meuschke[1], Kai Lawonn[1] and Sina Zarrieß[2]**
[1]University of Jena [2]University of Bielefeld
[1]first.last@uni-jena.de [2]first.last@uni-bielefeld.de

## Abstract

Intuitive interaction with visual models becomes an increasingly important task in the field of Visualization (VIS) and verbal interaction represents a significant aspect of it. Vice versa, modeling verbal interaction in visual environments is a major trend in ongoing research in NLP. To date, research on Language & Vision, however, mostly happens at the intersection of NLP and Computer Vision (CV), and much less at the intersection of NLP and Visualization, which is an important area in Human-Computer Interaction (HCI). This paper presents a brief survey of recent work on interactive tasks and set-ups in NLP and Visualization. We discuss the respective methods, show interesting gaps and conclude by suggesting neural, visually grounded dialogue modeling as a promising potential for NLIs for visual models.

## 1 Introduction

In recent years, research in NLP has become more and more interested in data sets, tasks and models that pair Language and Vision, cf. work on image Captioning (Vinyals et al., 2015; Herdade et al., 2019; He et al., 2020), Visual Question Answering (Antol et al., 2015; Goyal et al., 2017; Kazemi and Elqursh, 2017), or Instruction Following and -Generation in visual domains (Fried et al., 2017, 2018). This new area is generally called Vision & Language (Mogadala et al., 2019), but it is actually based mostly on combining methods from NLP (like e.g. language models) and Computer Vision, e.g. visual analysis and recognition models for encoding visual input like images. Methods and models from the research area of Visualization – which investigates solutions for modelling, exploring, analyzing and communicating data by using visual technologies and can be seen as the field of visual synthesis – are, to the best of our knowledge, less well known in the NLP community.

In the VIS community, interaction with visual models plays an important role and natural language interaction represents a big part of it (Bacci et al., 2020; Kumar et al., 2020; Srinivasan et al., 2020). Natural Language Interfaces (NLIs) that support interactive visualizations based on language queries have found increasing interest in recent research (Narechania et al., 2020; Yu and Silva, 2020; Fu et al., 2020). However, from an NLP point of view, the methods applied in these recent interfaces, mostly rely on established methods for implementing semantic parsers that map natural language instructions to symbolic data base queries, which are consecutively visualized by a visualization pipeline. In this paper, we argue that there is space for further support of intuitive interaction with visual models using state-of-the-art NLP methods that would also pose novel and interesting challenges for both domains.

We focus this brief overview on a selection of methods for modeling interaction in the fields of NLP and VIS based on recent submissions to the top conferences ACL, EACL, VIS and EuroVIS. First, we briefly describe how interaction is understood in the respective fields (Section 2). We provide a short overview of recent, state-of-the-art systems related to interaction with visual models or in visual environments (Section 3). Finally, we discuss potential research gaps and challenges that could be addressed in future work on modelling interaction with visual models (Section 4). As interaction is a major research topic in both NLP and VIS, we do not aim for a complete survey, but we hope to make readers from both communities aware that there could be fruitful directions for collaboration.

## 2 Interaction in NLP and VIS

We refer to *interaction* as the "mutual determination of behaviour" between different entities, like humans, digital agents or interfaces, following



*Proceedings of the First Workshop on Bridging Human–Computer Interaction and Natural Language Processing*, pages 66–73
April 20, 2021. 

Hornbæk and Oulasvirta (2017). Work on interaction in NLP typically investigates verbal communication between human dialogue partners and models dialogue systems that interact with users via natural language, but also recognizes the fact that verbal communication typically happens in combination with other modalities, like touch, movements and gestures in embodied dialogue or gaze and visual stimuli in visual dialogue (Cuayáhuitl et al., 2015). In HCI and VIS, interaction via multiple modalities plays a very prominent role, i.e. involves gestures, movements, different input controllers, screens, gazes, modalities and more. The interaction between a user and a visual model is a key aspect of many VIS tasks and applications and impacts on the user evaluation of a visual model to a significant degree (Yi et al., 2007; Tominski, 2015; Figueiras, 2015).

### 2.1 Interaction in VIS

Generally speaking, the field of VIS is interested in the development of techniques for creating visual models (Brehmer and Munzner, 2013; Liu et al., 2014; Amar et al., 2005). A visual model is data that is mapped into a visually perceivable space by representing concepts in the data through visual concepts to make them easily perceivable and understandable by humans. This supports research and education in many aspects as well as data exploration and understanding of big data sets. Research on interaction in VIS often addresses the design of appropriate human-computer interfaces and the abilities they need to offer for interacting with a visual model. Natural Language Interfaces (NLIs), in this context, can be seen as one possible solution of enabling interaction with a visualization. Dimara and Perin (2019) provide a comprehensive study on how interaction is seen in VIS by defining it as "the interplay between a person and a data interface involving a data-related intent, at least one action from the person and an interface reaction that is perceived as such". The authors deliberately distinguish their view from the HCI definition of interaction as stated in Hornbæk and Oulasvirta (2017), by making the importance of the data related intent of the user the focus in VIS. As a conclusion, the authors observe that approaches towards interaction in VIS currently lack two points, i.e. *flexibility* and a better understanding of the *user goal*. The lack of these currently leads to interfaces that are too predictable, unsatisfying in their capacities to act or risk misdirected interactions with visual models. Despite that, Hornbæk and Oulasvirta (2017) and Dimara and Perin (2019) both argue that interaction foremost represents a form of *dialogue* which the authors evaluate in terms of its "naturalness" and its mutual "strong sense of understanding".

This highlights the point that interaction with a visual model is fundamentally conceived as a multi-modal process that leverages various different interface modalities for communication and information exchange. As discussed below, from an NLP perspective, interactions with systems in VIS can be seen as multi-modal dialogues between a system and a user having data-related goals.

### 2.2 Interaction in NLP

Work in NLP often aims at understanding and modeling how dialogue partners collaborate and achieve common ground by exchanging verbal utterances (potentially in combination with different modalities, like e.g. vision). This typically involves language understanding, dialogue management (reasoning over latent user goals) and language generation (Young et al., 2010, 2013). Recent work on dialogue has turned more and more to so-called neural end-to-end-dialogue systems that do not separate processes of understanding, reasoning and generation, and aim for more flexibility and adaptiveness (Santhanam and Shaikh, 2019). Santhanam and Shaikh (2019) distinguish between goal-driven and open dialogue systems as they address fundamentally different interaction and evaluation set-ups. Goal- or task-oriented systems are typically designed towards helping the user to achieve a very specific goal in a given context. For instance, in instruction-following and -generation (Fried et al., 2017, 2018), a user or system needs to reach a specific position in an environment by following navigation instructions. Here, the interaction is often asymmetric in the sense that the modalities to be used by the partners are very restricted (the instruction follower acts, the giver speaks). Open-domain dialogue systems, like Li et al. (2017); Adiwardana et al. (2020) are not bound to a goal and therefore require a high awareness of context, personality and variety of the dialogue system as Santhanam and Shaikh (2019) point out.

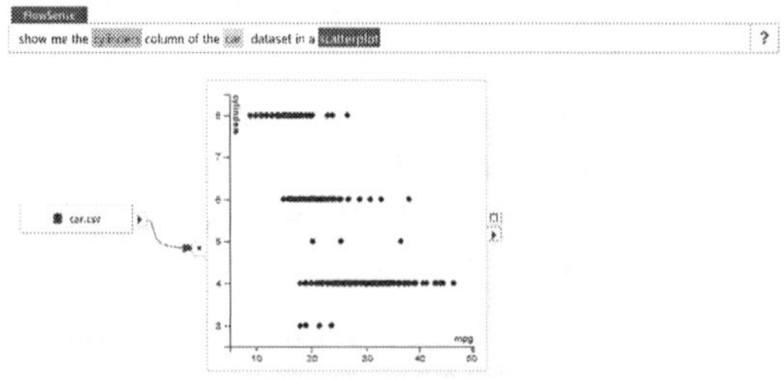

Figure 1: Goal-oriented NLI as used in Yu and Silva (2020), created from: https://visflow.org/demo/

## 3 Existing Work

### 3.1 Natural Language Interfaces in VIS

A range of recent papers have looked into integrating NLP in VIS systems, by implementing NLIs that translate a natural language query to a visualization command in some programming language. This allows users to "talk to some dataset", as illustrated in Figure 1. Existing NLIs are applied in systems that create and manipulate, e.g., chart visualizations (Shao and Nakashole, 2020). Similar interfaces are proposed in Narechania et al. (2020); Huang et al. (2019); Yu and Silva (2020); Fu et al. (2020); Chowdhury et al. (2021); Setlur et al. (2016)

These existing NLIs are mostly applied in the field of visual analytics. Here, the user has a concrete goal in mind, i.e. some manipulation of the underlying data table (e.g. aggregation, filtering). Dimara and Perin (2019) point out that the exact understanding of the users' goal is important in these interfaces and one current approach for improving the inference of the users' intent is to predict it based on activity logs. Setlur and Kumar (2020)'s work suggests that the handling of vague subjective modifiers in utterances can be improved by using sentiment analysis techniques.

In terms of NLP methods, these interfaces are mostly based on manually engineered grammars that parse user input to queries and then generate an appropriate visualization output, as e.g. in (Yu and Silva, 2020). These grammars are relatively easy to set-up even for non-experts (of NLP) and do not require large amounts of training data, as most state-of-the-art dialogue systems developed in NLP. An important limitation of this approach, however, is that such semantic grammars are designed to translate directly between a given user query in natural language and some underlying data query language like e.g. SQL. This means that, in longer multi-turn interactions between a user and a system, users are not able to formulate short, intuitive queries that implicitly refer to the context (e.g. "now, make this a bit bigger" where "this" refers to an aspect of the visual model discussed in the preceding context) or multi-modal queries (e.g. "increase the volume of this particle here" *while user points to a region on the screen*). Finally, and most importantly, they assume that the user can precisely formulate or describe the action or manipulation that is needed to obtain a certain visualization or information from the visual model, as shown for instance in Figure 1.

Beyond NLIs for visual analytics (Narechania et al., 2020; Yu and Silva, 2020), we see further potential for other NLP methods in visualization tasks that require more than plots of data for a specific, precisely formulated goal. In visual exploration, the goal is typically rather vague and developed during the exploration process itself, in an iterative fashion while interacting with the system. Moreover, applications in augmented and virtual reality entail new possibilities of immersive experiences and interaction for supporting performance as in (Butcher et al., 2020) or to enhance retention (Yang et al., 2020), which clearly includes multiple modalities. We argue that users of visual models in such exploratory setups could greatly benefit from natural language interaction, if the NLI would allow for more context-sensitive and situated querying of the model. Moreover, beyond querying, we expect that users would highly appreciate verbal system feedback or suggestions and explanations (see Figure 2). Ideally, this back-and-forth between the user and the system should support the user not only in realizing his goal, but also in establishing his goal or refining his initially vague goal.

Thus, we currently see a lot of interest in systems that enable interaction with an underlying data set via natural language, but the query-based approach used in many NLIs still seems to lack flexibility.

### 3.2 Language & Vision

A lot of recent work in NLP tackles dialogue modelling (Shuster et al., 2020; Qin et al., 2020; Ham et al., 2020; Rameshkumar and Bailey, 2020) or question answering (Baheti et al., 2020; Liu et al., 2020). Goal-based dialogue covers navigation Zhu et al. (2020), manipulation (Jayannavar et al., 2020) or classical information presentation tasks (Andreas et al., 2020). A central problem in these mod-

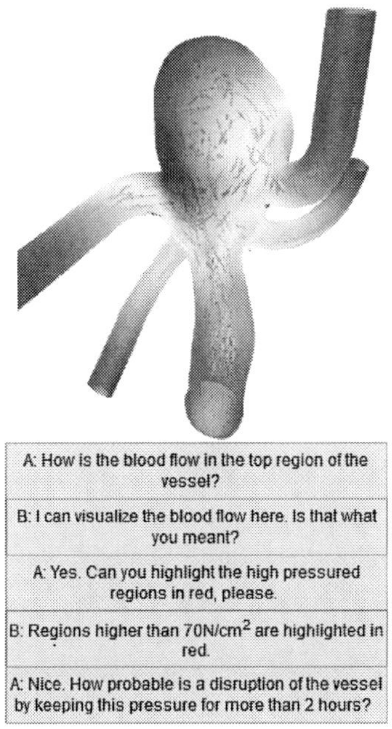


Figure 2: Visual exploration of a visual model of an aneurysm and an exemplary mixed-initiative dialogue

els is the fact that at each point in an interaction, there is uncertainty with respect to the understanding of the user goal. The predominant approach to handle reasoning under uncertainty is (Deep) Reinforcement Learning (RL) where an agent learns a dialogue policy (Jaques et al., 2020; Li et al., 2020, 2016). RL optimizes the utterance understanding and generation in the system with respect to a certain reward function in the given environment.

Next to these improvements on the level of dialogue modeling, recent developments in Language & Vision focus on grounding verbal utterances in visual inputs as, for instance, in visual question answering (Huang et al., 2020; Khademi, 2020). Visual dialogue (Das et al., 2017; Wang et al., 2020) extends the dialogue modelling task to the visual modality. Mixed-initiative visual dialogue, as e.g. in Ilinykh et al. (2019), aims at modeling interactions in which both dialogue partners can talk and act, which could be an interesting setting for visual exploration tasks. We believe that these successes in neural dialogue modelling and the integration of different modalities as in visual dialogue can lead to new possibilities for interactive systems in VIS, as we will discuss below.

## 4 Future Work

**Uncertainty** We believe that a fruitful direction for more flexible NLP-based systems in VIS is to look at scenarios where users might not have a concrete manipulation task or goal in mind, but want to explore a complex visual model. Numerous applications, such as in medicine (Meuschke et al., 2016, 2017) or cultural-technical scenarios (Lawonn et al., 2016), require the visual exploration of complex models. Figure 2 shows an example of a 3D-mesh of an aneurysm and a corresponding, made-up dialogue that would support the user in exploring the model (Meuschke et al., 2018). On the NLP side, this setting involves a high degree of uncertainty. The user investigates a certain region of the model she is interested in, develops an understanding of the visual landscape and/or just learns how to handle it best. Thus, we argue that complex visual models like in Figure 2 probably call for different and more flexible types of interactions, as compared to NLIs discussed in Section 3.1. A user analyzing a barplot might be interested in minima, maxima, trends or outliers, which correspond to fixed goals. In contrast to that, a neurosurgeon inspecting an aneurysm in virtual reality is much more interested in the *how* than in the *what* and the goal might not be precisely formulated beforehand by the surgeon but evolving through the back and forth of the interaction with the visual model.

An important question that arises from that is, if users would really use natural language for exploring a visual model or if they would rather prefer the use of e.g. a controller or touch gesture. For many cases this might indeed be true, but we argue, that certain scenarios in visual exploration especially demand for verbal problem solution: recommendation of possibilities ("show me how to reach the largest vessel from here", "how to achieve a blood pressure increase in this region"), problem-solution-suggestions, tutorial-like action descriptions the user has to mimic, e.g. in educational scenarios or future state simulations that are highly hypothetical ("what would the vessel behave if we changed the blood flow drastically to ..."). These cases are in fact simulations of possible solutions helping the user to visualize and explore the solution space, which are much more convenient and intuitive expressed using natural language which can be supported by strong dialogue models that adapt to the context.

**Visual Grounding** Visual language grounding in these scenarios captures not only the grounding of words into the scene (e.g. "vessel") but also the grounding of movements and gazes like pointer gestures (e.g. "here") which shows that the interplay of context awareness and multi-modal visual grounding are prerequisites for dialogue that humans would describe as "intuitive" and flexible. In contrast to systems like (Narechania et al., 2020) which are restricted to visual output and systems like (Adiwardana et al., 2020) which respond verbally, dialogue systems in visual models should be able to handle multi-modal responses, as illustrated in Figure 2. The highlighting, scaling, coloring or fading of certain visual properties is an important part of the response which not only contains text but rather text and a visual action combined.

**Mixed-Initiative Dialogue** Figure 2 shows an example for a collaborative, mixed-initiative interaction where the the dialogue flow is not entirely centered on user queries. Tang et al. (2020) used dialogue modelling for generating visual story lines in collaboration with a user and obtained promising results in leveraging visual exploration scenarios. In contrast to concise, goal-based visual analytics (see Section 3.1), hard-coded grammars might be too restricted to handle the high uncertainty and the complex underlying reasoning in explorative scenarios. The visual analytics task differs from the visual exploration task considering the fact that it is not driven by a concise goal. Introducing mixed-initiative dialogue in visual exploration enhances the users' ability of communicating uncertainties and supports experimenting and iterative engagement with the environment as applied in active visual problem solving or in educational settings. When no concrete goal can be formulated, a NLI has to adapt to the user and present contextual information like hints, explanations or react to expressed uncertainties (e.g. 'What does this blue region here show me?', 'How can I slice the vessel and investigate the thickness?', 'How does this spot evolve over time?') which is a form of guidance, an evolving field in visual analytics (Ceneda et al., 2020). This interaction also is not bound to text-language interaction, but furthermore accommodates gestures, movements or glances and therefore can be categorized as multi-modal. Here, recent advances in NLP could extend the interface flexibility by providing better context-awareness using visually grounded dialogue techniques and contributing to solve the user goal inference problem by re-framing the task as an iterative goal alignment task executed via mixed-initiative dialogue. We think that especially mixed-initiative dialogue would be a challenging but very promising direction and well-suited for inferring user intentions in complex VIS settings because of the usage of direct user feedback and iterative alignment. Furthermore, mixed-initiative dialogue methods could support the setup of user-centred evaluation of more complex visualization techniques, such as in (Lawonn et al., 2014). In sum, we argue that the role of NLP in interfaces with visual models is to enrich the dialogue between a system and a user (Dimara and Perin, 2019) with more flexible and intuitive ways of dialogue that might include touch-based or controller-based interaction.

## 5 Conclusion

In this paper, we gave a brief introduction on how interaction is understood and modelled in the fields of NLP and VIS. We found that existing work on NLIs in the Visualization domain heavily relies on query-based interactions. We argued that for interacting with highly complex visual models these strict interaction protocols might not be sufficient. Recent developments in Language & Vision investigate dialogue in visual contexts and reach promising results. We believe that this holds interesting research gaps for future work in integrating different variations of NLP-backed dialogue methods into visualizations enabling multi-modal interaction with visual models.

## Acknowledgments

We thank the Michael Stifel Center Jena for the funding of this work, which is part of the "A Virtual Werkstatt for Digitization in the Sciences" project funded by the Carl Zeiss Foundation (062017-02).

## References

D. Adiwardana, Minh-Thang Luong, D. So, J. Hall, Noah Fiedel, R. Thoppilan, Z. Yang, Apoorv Kulshreshtha, G. Nemade, Yifeng Lu, and Quoc V. Le. 2020. Towards a human-like open-domain chatbot. *ArXiv*, abs/2001.09977.

Robert Amar, James Eagan, and John Stasko. 2005. Low-level components of analytic activity in information visualization. In *IEEE Symposium on Information Visualization, 2005. INFOVIS 2005.*, pages 111–117. IEEE.

Jacob Andreas, John Bufe, David Burkett, Charles Chen, Josh Clausman, Jean Crawford, Kate Crim, Jordan DeLoach, Leah Dorner, Jason Eisner, Hao Fang, Alan Guo, David Hall, Kristin Hayes, Kellie Hill, Diana Ho, Wendy Iwaszuk, Smriti Jha, Dan Klein, Jayant Krishnamurthy, Theo Lanman, Percy Liang, Christopher H. Lin, Ilya Lintsbakh, Andy McGovern, Aleksandr Nisnevich, Adam Pauls, Dmitrij Petters, Brent Read, Dan Roth, Subhro Roy, Jesse Rusak, Beth Short, Div Slomin, Ben Snyder, Stephon Striplin, Yu Su, Zachary Tellman, Sam Thomson, Andrei Vorobev, Izabela Witoszko, Jason Wolfe, Abby Wray, Yuchen Zhang, and Alexander Zotov. 2020. Task-oriented dialogue as dataflow synthesis. *Transactions of the Association for Computational Linguistics (TACL)*, 8.

Stanislaw Antol, Aishwarya Agrawal, Jiasen Lu, Margaret Mitchell, Dhruv Batra, C Lawrence Zitnick, and Devi Parikh. 2015. Vqa: Visual question answering. In *Proceedings of the IEEE international conference on computer vision*, pages 2425–2433.

Franscesca Bacci, Federico Maria Cau, and L. D. Spano. 2020. Inspecting data using natural language queries. In *ICCSA*.

Ashutosh Baheti, Alan Ritter, and Kevin Small. 2020. Fluent response generation for conversational question answering. *arXiv preprint arXiv:2005.10464*.

M. Brehmer and T. Munzner. 2013. A multi-level typology of abstract visualization tasks. *IEEE Transactions on Visualization and Computer Graphics*, 19:2376–2385.

Peter William Scott Butcher, Nigel W John, and Panagiotis D Ritsos. 2020. Vria: A web-based framework for creating immersive analytics experiences. *IEEE Transactions on Visualization and Computer Graphics*.

Davide Ceneda, N. Andrienko, G. Andrienko, T. Gschwandtner, S. Miksch, Nikolaus Piccolotto, T. Schreck, M. Streit, Josef Suschnigg, and C. Tominski. 2020. Guide me in analysis: A framework for guidance designers. *Computer Graphics Forum*, 39:269 – 288.

I. Chowdhury, Abdul Moeid, Enamul Hoque, M. Kabir, Md. Sohorab Hossain, and M. M. Islam. 2021. Designing and evaluating multimodal interactions for facilitating visual analysis with dashboards. *IEEE Access*, 9:60–71.

H. Cuayáhuitl, Kazunori Komatani, and Gabriel Skantze. 2015. Introduction for speech and language for interactive robots. *Comput. Speech Lang.*, 34:83–86.

A. Das, S. Kottur, K. Gupta, Avi Singh, Deshraj Yadav, José M. F. Moura, D. Parikh, and Dhruv Batra. 2017. Visual dialog. *2017 IEEE Conference on Computer Vision and Pattern Recognition (CVPR)*, pages 1080–1089.

Evanthia Dimara and Charles Perin. 2019. What is interaction for data visualization? *IEEE transactions on visualization and computer graphics*, 26(1):119–129.

A. Figueiras. 2015. Towards the understanding of interaction in information visualization. *2015 19th International Conference on Information Visualisation*, pages 140–147.

Daniel Fried, Jacob Andreas, and Dan Klein. 2017. Unified pragmatic models for generating and following instructions. *arXiv preprint arXiv:1711.04987*.

Daniel Fried, Ronghang Hu, Volkan Cirik, Anna Rohrbach, Jacob Andreas, Louis-Philippe Morency, Taylor Berg-Kirkpatrick, Kate Saenko, Dan Klein, and Trevor Darrell. 2018. Speaker-follower models for vision-and-language navigation. In *Advances in Neural Information Processing Systems*, pages 3314–3325.

Siwei Fu, Kai Xiong, X. Ge, Y. Wu, Siliang Tang, and W. Chen. 2020. Quda: Natural language queries for visual data analytics. *ArXiv*, abs/2005.03257.

Yash Goyal, Tejas Khot, Douglas Summers-Stay, Dhruv Batra, and D. Parikh. 2017. Making the v in vqa matter: Elevating the role of image understanding in visual question answering. *2017 IEEE Conference on Computer Vision and Pattern Recognition (CVPR)*, pages 6325–6334.

Donghoon Ham, Jeong-Gwan Lee, Youngsoo Jang, and Kee-Eung Kim. 2020. End-to-end neural pipeline for goal-oriented dialogue systems using gpt-2. ACL.

Sen He, Wentong Liao, H. Tavakoli, M. Yang, B. Rosenhahn, and N. Pugeault. 2020. Image captioning through image transformer. *ArXiv*, abs/2004.14231.

Simao Herdade, Armin Kappeler, K. Boakye, and J. Soares. 2019. Image captioning: Transforming objects into words. In *NeurIPS*.

Kasper Hornbæk and Antti Oulasvirta. 2017. *What Is Interaction?*, page 5040–5052. Association for Computing Machinery, New York, NY, USA.

Qingbao Huang, Jielong Wei, Yi Cai, Changmeng Zheng, Junying Chen, Ho-fung Leung, and Qing Li. 2020. Aligned dual channel graph convolutional network for visual question answering. In *Proceedings of the 58th Annual Meeting of the Association for Computational Linguistics*, pages 7166–7176, Online. Association for Computational Linguistics.

Zhaosong Huang, Ye Zhao, Wei Chen, Shengjie Gao, Kejie Yu, Weixia Xu, Mingjie Tang, Minfeng Zhu, and Mingliang Xu. 2019. A natural-language-based visual query approach of uncertain human trajectories. *IEEE Transactions on Visualization and Computer Graphics*, 26(1):1256–1266.

N. Ilinykh, Sina Zarrieß, and D. Schlangen. 2019. Meetup! a corpus of joint activity dialogues in a visual environment. *ArXiv*, abs/1907.05084.

Natasha Jaques, Judy Hanwen Shen, Asma Ghandeharioun, Craig Ferguson, Agata Lapedriza, Noah Jones, Shixiang Gu, and Rosalind Picard. 2020. Human-centric dialog training via offline reinforcement learning. In *Proceedings of the 2020 Conference on Empirical Methods in Natural Language Processing (EMNLP)*, pages 3985–4003, Online. Association for Computational Linguistics.

Prashant Jayannavar, Anjali Narayan-Chen, and Julia Hockenmaier. 2020. Learning to execute instructions in a Minecraft dialogue. In *Proceedings of the 58th Annual Meeting of the Association for Computational Linguistics*, pages 2589–2602, Online. Association for Computational Linguistics.

V. Kazemi and A. Elqursh. 2017. Show, ask, attend, and answer: A strong baseline for visual question answering. *ArXiv*, abs/1704.03162.

Mahmoud Khademi. 2020. Multimodal neural graph memory networks for visual question answering. In *Proceedings of the 58th Annual Meeting of the Association for Computational Linguistics*, pages 7177–7188, Online. Association for Computational Linguistics.

Abhinav Kumar, Jillian Aurisano, B. D. Eugenio, and A. Johnson. 2020. Intelligent assistant for exploring data visualizations. In *FLAIRS Conference*.

Kai Lawonn, Alexandra Baer, Patrick Saalfeld, and Bernhard Preim. 2014. Comparative evaluation of feature line techniques for shape depiction. In *Proc. of Vision, Modeling and Visualization*, pages 31–38, Darmstadt.

Kai Lawonn, Erik Trostmann, Bernhard Preim, and Klaus Hildebrandt. 2016. Visualization and extraction of carvings for heritage conservation. *IEEE transactions on visualization and computer graphics*, 23(1):801–810.

Jiwei Li, Will Monroe, Alan Ritter, Michel Galley, Jianfeng Gao, and Dan Jurafsky. 2016. Deep reinforcement learning for dialogue generation. *arXiv preprint arXiv:1606.01541*.

Jiwei Li, Will Monroe, Tianlin Shi, Sébastien Jean, Alan Ritter, and Dan Jurafsky. 2017. Adversarial learning for neural dialogue generation. *arXiv preprint arXiv:1701.06547*.

Ziming Li, Julia Kiseleva, and Maarten de Rijke. 2020. Rethinking supervised learning and reinforcement learning in task-oriented dialogue systems. In *Findings of the Association for Computational Linguistics: EMNLP 2020*, pages 3537–3546, Online. Association for Computational Linguistics.

Dayiheng Liu, Yeyun Gong, Jie Fu, Yu Yan, Jiusheng Chen, Daxin Jiang, Jiancheng Lv, and Nan Duan. 2020. RikiNet: Reading Wikipedia pages for natural question answering. In *Proceedings of the 58th Annual Meeting of the Association for Computational Linguistics*, pages 6762–6771, Online. Association for Computational Linguistics.

Shixia Liu, Weiwei Cui, Yingcai Wu, and Mengchen Liu. 2014. A survey on information visualization: recent advances and challenges. *The Visual Computer*, 30(12):1373–1393.

Monique Meuschke, Wito Engelke, Oliver Beuing, Bernhard Preim, and Kai Lawonn. 2017. Automatic viewpoint selection for exploration of time-dependent cerebral aneurysm data. In *Bildverarbeitung für die Medizin*, pages 352–357. Springer.

Monique Meuschke, Kai Lawonn, Benjamin Köhler, Uta Preim, and Bernhard Preim. 2016. Clustering of aortic vortex flow in cardiac 4d pc-mri data. In *Bildverarbeitung für die Medizin*, pages 182–187. Springer.

Monique Meuschke, Samuel Voß, Bernhard Preim, and Kai Lawonn. 2018. Exploration of blood flow patterns in cerebral aneurysms during the cardiac cycle. *Computers & Graphics*, 72:12–25.

Aditya Mogadala, Marimuthu Kalimuthu, and Dietrich Klakow. 2019. Trends in integration of vision and language research: A survey of tasks, datasets, and methods. *arXiv preprint arXiv:1907.09358*.

Arpit Narechania, Arjun Srinivasan, and John Stasko. 2020. Nl4dv: A toolkit for generating analytic specifications for data visualization from natural language queries. *IEEE Transactions on Visualization and Computer Graphics*.

Libo Qin, Xiao Xu, Wanxiang Che, Yue Zhang, and Ting Liu. 2020. Dynamic fusion network for multi-domain end-to-end task-oriented dialog. In *Proceedings of the 58th Annual Meeting of the Association for Computational Linguistics*, pages 6344–6354, Online. Association for Computational Linguistics.

Revanth Rameshkumar and Peter Bailey. 2020. Storytelling with dialogue: A Critical Role Dungeons and Dragons Dataset. In *Proceedings of the 58th Annual Meeting of the Association for Computational Linguistics*, pages 5121–5134, Online. Association for Computational Linguistics.

Sashank Santhanam and Samira Shaikh. 2019. A survey of natural language generation techniques with a focus on dialogue systems-past, present and future directions. *arXiv preprint arXiv:1906.00500*.

V. Setlur, S. Battersby, Melanie Tory, R. Gossweiler, and Angel X. Chang. 2016. Eviza: A natural language interface for visual analysis. *Proceedings of the 29th Annual Symposium on User Interface Software and Technology*.

Vidya Setlur and Arathi Kumar. 2020. Sentifiers: Interpreting vague intent modifiers in visual analysis using word co-occurrence and sentiment analysis. *arXiv preprint arXiv:2009.12701*.

Yutong Shao and Ndapa Nakashole. 2020. ChartDialogs: Plotting from Natural Language Instructions. In *Proceedings of the 58th Annual Meeting of the Association for Computational Linguistics*, pages 3559–3574, Online. Association for Computational Linguistics.

Kurt Shuster, Samuel Humeau, Antoine Bordes, and Jason Weston. 2020. Image-chat: Engaging grounded conversations. In *Proceedings of the 58th Annual Meeting of the Association for Computational Linguistics*, pages 2414–2429, Online. Association for Computational Linguistics.

A. Srinivasan, J. Stasko, Daniel F. Keefe, and Melanie Tory. 2020. How to ask what to say?: Strategies for evaluating natural language interfaces for data visualization. *IEEE Computer Graphics and Applications*, 40:96–103.

Tan Tang, Renzhong Li, Xinke Wu, Shuhan Liu, Johannes Knittel, Steffen Koch, Thomas Ertl, Lingyun Yu, Peiran Ren, and Yingcai Wu. 2020. Plotthread: Creating expressive storyline visualizations using reinforcement learning. *IEEE Transactions on Visualization and Computer Graphics*.

C. Tominski. 2015. Interaction for visualization. In *Interaction for Visualization*.

Oriol Vinyals, Alexander Toshev, Samy Bengio, and Dumitru Erhan. 2015. Show and tell: A neural image caption generator. In *Proceedings of the IEEE conference on computer vision and pattern recognition*, pages 3156–3164.

Yue Wang, Shafiq R. Joty, Michael R. Lyu, Irwin King, Caiming Xiong, and S. Hoi. 2020. Vd-bert: A unified vision and dialog transformer with bert. In *EMNLP*.

Fumeng Yang, Jing Qian, Johannes Novotny, David Badre, Cullen Jackson, and David Laidlaw. 2020. A virtual reality memory palace variant aids knowledge retrieval from scholarly articles. *IEEE Transactions on Visualization and Computer Graphics*.

J. S. Yi, Y. Kang, J. Stasko, and J. Jacko. 2007. Toward a deeper understanding of the role of interaction in information visualization. *IEEE Transactions on Visualization and Computer Graphics*, 13:1224–1231.

Steve Young, Milica Gašić, Simon Keizer, François Mairesse, Jost Schatzmann, Blaise Thomson, and Kai Yu. 2010. The hidden information state model: A practical framework for pomdp-based spoken dialogue management. *Computer Speech & Language*, 24(2):150–174.

Steve Young, Milica Gašić, Blaise Thomson, and Jason D Williams. 2013. Pomdp-based statistical spoken dialog systems: A review. *Proceedings of the IEEE*, 101(5):1160–1179.

Bowen Yu and C. T. Silva. 2020. Flowsense: A natural language interface for visual data exploration within a dataflow system. *IEEE Transactions on Visualization and Computer Graphics*, 26:1–11.

Wang Zhu, Hexiang Hu, Jiacheng Chen, Zhiwei Deng, Vihan Jain, Eugene Ie, and Fei Sha. 2020. BabyWalk: Going farther in vision-and-language navigation by taking baby steps. In *Proceedings of the 58th Annual Meeting of the Association for Computational Linguistics*, pages 2539–2556, Online. Association for Computational Linguistics.

# AfriKI: Machine-in-the-Loop Afrikaans Poetry Generation

**Imke van Heerden**
Dept. of Comparative Literature
College of Social Sciences and Humanities
Koç University, Istanbul, Turkey
ivanheerden@ku.edu.tr

**Anil Bas**
Dept. of Computer Engineering
Faculty of Technology
Marmara University, Istanbul, Turkey
anil.bas@marmara.edu.tr

## Abstract

This paper proposes a generative language model called AfriKI. Our approach is based on an LSTM architecture trained on a small corpus of contemporary fiction. With the aim of promoting human creativity, we use the model as an authoring tool to explore machine-in-the-loop Afrikaans poetry generation. To our knowledge, this is the first study to attempt creative text generation in Afrikaans.

## 1 Introduction

Afrikaans[1] is a language spoken largely in South Africa, Namibia, Botswana and Zimbabwe. Masakhane (∀ et al., 2020a,b) draws important attention to the current disproportion of NLP research and resources with respect to African languages. In fact, in the entire ACL Anthology,[2] of the thirteen studies that mention "Afrikaans" in their titles, only four (Sanby et al., 2016; Augustinus et al., 2016; Dirix et al., 2017; Ralethe, 2020) appeared in the last five years. By no means do we ignore studies with inclusive (Eiselen and Puttkammer, 2014) and multilingual approaches (Ziering and Van der Plas, 2016) or those published via other platforms (Van Zaanen and Van Huyssteen, 2003). This is simply an indication that NLP research in Afrikaans is limited, especially in comparison to resource-rich languages, i.e. the so-called "winners" in the taxonomy of Joshi et al. (2020).

In this paper, we present a generative language model called AfriKI, an abbreviation for "Afrikaanse Kunsmatige Intelligensie" (*Afrikaans Artificial Intelligence*). We use this model as an authoring tool to explore machine-in-the-loop poetry generation in Afrikaans. Machine-in-the-loop frameworks promote human creativity through computational assistance, as opposed to human-in-the-loop pipelines, which aim to strengthen machine learning models (Clark et al., 2018). We treat poetry generation as a hybrid system, an experimental approach that enables the generation of high-quality poetic text with very limited data. To our knowledge, this is the first study in creative text generation as well as an initial step towards automatic poetry generation in Afrikaans.

Whereas NLG in its quest for full automation may frown upon human involvement, our human-centred framework does the opposite. According to Lubart (2005),

> one criticism of artificial intelligence programs that claim to be creative is exactly that a human plays a role at some point, which reduces the autonomy of the machine. From the HCI perspective [...] these "failed" AI creativity programs are examples of successful human–computer interactions to facilitate creativity.

This study demonstrates that human-machine collaboration could enhance human creativity. We agree with Shneiderman (2002) that support tools "make more people more creative more often".

## 2 Related Work

Several computational models focus on automatic poetry generation. First approaches follow rule-based, template-based systems (Gervás, 2001; Díaz-Agudo et al., 2002). Levy (2001) and Manurung et al. (2012) apply genetic algorithms while Jiang and Zhou (2008) and He et al. (2012) use statistical machine translation, with Yan et al. (2013) utilising text summarisation to generate poetry.

[1]The Constitution of the Republic of South Africa recognises Afrikaans as one of eleven official languages, alongside Sepedi, Sesotho, Setswana, siSwati, Tshivenda, Xitsonga, English, isiNdebele, isiXhosa and isiZulu (Assembly, 1996). In South Africa, there are approximately 6.9 million first-language speakers of Afrikaans, according to the most recent census (Lehohla, 2012).

[2]https://www.aclweb.org/anthology/



*Proceedings of the First Workshop on Bridging Human–Computer Interaction and Natural Language Processing*, pages 74–80
April 20, 2021. 

Oliveira (2009) provides a clear overview of early systems and presents a comparable method (2012).

Starting with Zhang and Lapata (2014), we have seen great advancements in poetry generation using neural networks. Wang et al. (2016a) extend this using the attention mechanism (Bahdanau et al., 2015). There are many attempts to improve the quality of learning-based generated poetry, by using planning models (Wang et al., 2016b), finite-state machinery (Ghazvininejad et al., 2016), reinforcement learning (Yi et al., 2018) as well as variational autoencoders (Yang et al., 2018).

Conventional recurrent neural networks (RNN) are not suitable for learning long range dependencies (Wang et al., 2016a) due to the vanishing gradient problem (Bengio et al., 1994). Long short-term memory (LSTM) networks (Hochreiter and Schmidhuber, 1997) address this issue and are widely used for language modeling (Sundermeyer et al., 2012). Tikhonov and Yamshchikov (2018) propose word-based LSTM to generate poetry. Potash et al. (2015) adopt a similar technique to produce rap lyrics. Zugarini et al. (2019) apply syllable-based LSTM to generate tercets. Finally, composed of various LSTM models, Deep-speare (Lau et al., 2018) generates Shakespearean sonnets.

The remarkable quality and results of these studies are indisputable. However, they all concentrate on data-rich languages such as English, Chinese, Italian and Russian. For example, the character language model of Hopkins and Kiela (2017) uses a poetry corpus consisting of 7.56 million words and 34.34 million characters. Likewise, a recent study by Liu et al. (2020) trained on over 200 thousand poems and 3 million ancient Chinese prose texts.

We trained an LSTM network for poetic text generation as well. However, our approach differs in significant ways. First, whereas these studies generate verse in a fully automatic manner, we emphasise human creativity, introducing a strong computational component to the creative writing process. Second, the aforementioned studies either trained on comprehensive poetry datasets or model poetic qualities. To illustrate the latter, the recent work of Van de Cruys (2020) focuses on specifically non-poetic text in English and French, however, is able to model the rhyme constraint using phonetic representation of words from Wiktionary. Since there is no publicly available large-scale poetry dataset in Afrikaans, we follow an alternative approach, constructing our model as a text generator that produces individual sentences and phrases instead of stanzas of verse. In other words, the model outputs a set of lines, which we arrange vertically into short poems without modification.

Figure 1: Frequently occurring words in *Die Biblioteek aan die Einde van die Wêreld*. Stop words were removed. Note that Ian and Thuli are the protagonists.

## 3 Model

In this section, we explain the dataset, model architecture as well as the co-creative poetry generation process.

**Corpus:** AfriKI trained on a lengthy (208,616-word) literary novel titled *Die Biblioteek aan die Einde van die Wêreld* (*The Library at the End of the World*) (Van Heerden, 2019) by the South African novelist Etienne van Heerden. In 2020, the book was awarded the University of Johannesburg Prize for Literature (Pienaar, 2020). This work of new journalism combines fictional techniques with documentary language, and is particularly suitable given its use of rich imagery, figurative language as well as different Afrikaans varieties like *Kaaps* (or Cape Afrikaans) and Standard Afrikaans. Figure 1 shows a word cloud of its most commonly used words.

**Model Architecture:** Experimenting with several architectures, including LSTM, Multi-Layer LSTM and Bi-LSTM, we obtain best results with the following two-layer LSTM architecture. We use a vanilla LSTM structure (Hochreiter and Schmidhuber, 1997) and, to avoid repetitiveness, omit to describe the network diagram and equations, similar to Sundermeyer et al. (2012). We start with 100-dimensional word embeddings with a vocabulary size of 23,317 words, where weights are randomly initialised from a normal distribution with zero mean and standard deviation 0.01. Next, we stack two LSTM layers with 50 units in each layer followed by dropout layers with the

| Original (Afrikaans) | Translation (English) |
|---|---|
| *Die konstabel se skiereiland* | *The constable's peninsula* |
| Afrika drink<br>onheil in die water.<br>Die landskap kantel sy rug<br>in sigbewaking en vlam.<br>Ons oopgesnyde sake<br>brandtrappe vir die ander state.<br>Hierdie grond word intimidasie. | Africa drinks<br>disaster in the water.<br>The landscape tilts its back<br>in surveillance and flame.<br>Our cut-open affairs<br>fire escapes for other states.<br>This soil becomes intimidation. |
| *Gedigte, daar by die brul van 'n brander* | *Poetry, there near the roar of a wave* |
| Hier is die oë katvoet vir<br>die spoelrotse onder uitdrukkings<br>die golwe van gister wat<br>getol en woes en water<br>saam met die son skuim in hul woorde | Here the eyes are cautious of<br>the sea rocks under expressions<br>the waves of yesterday that<br>whirled and wild and water<br>froth with the sun in their words |
| die ingedagte see<br>lig die geure en praat<br>'n asemhaal | the introspective sea<br>lifts the scents and utters<br>a breath |
| *Kaapstad* | *Cape Town* |
| Vandag is ons nie net die stad nie<br>maar<br>die vertaler van die son | Today we are not just the city<br>but<br>the translator of the sun |
| Vanaand se gordyne<br>glinster by skuifvensters<br>in die stadsliggies | Tonight's curtains<br>glitter at sliding windows<br>in the city lights |
| Die uur van die winde<br>sorg dat dit rondom klink<br>Sy wil die glasvensters deurkosyn<br>eens iets te beskerm | The hour of the winds<br>takes care it sounds around<br>She wants to doorframe the glass windows<br>to protect something |
| Tafelberg<br>maak 'n vraag waarbinne ons<br>'n duisend name<br>genoem word | Table Mountain<br>creates a question in which we<br>are given<br>a thousand names |

Table 1: Example results of machine-in-the-loop poetry generation.

rate of 0.2. This is followed by a fully connected layer and a softmax layer. We use the Adam optimiser (Kingma and Ba, 2015) with a learning rate = 0.001, batch size = 16, and train for 300 epochs. Although tweaking the parameters did change the model performance, it was not significant.

**Machine-in-the-Loop:** Human-machine collaboration for the enhancement of creative writing has been examined under automated assistance (Roemmele and Gordon, 2015, 2018), co-authorship (Tucker, 2019), co-creativity (Manjavacas et al., 2017; Kantosalo and Riihiaho, 2019; Calderwood et al., 2020), interactive storytelling (Swanson and Gordon, 2012; Brahman et al., 2020) and machine-in-the-loop (Clark et al., 2018; Akoury et al., 2020).

Applying Clark et al. (2018)'s terminology, we employ an iterative interaction structure that follows a push method of initiation with low intrusiveness. To clarify, our process consists of a single loop with two stages. First, the model generates a sizable set of unique individual lines (hundreds). Although memory networks may repeat parts of the training data (Ghazvininejad et al., 2016), the generated phrases are highly distinct from the dataset, with hardly any repetition of word order. Second, the first author responds by choosing phrases at will. To create the final artefact, the author arranges the selected lines vertically. Generated text is used strictly without modification (except for some capitalisation and punctuation). The result of our collaborative writing system is short, compelling works of poetry that draw inspiration from the literary movements Imagism (Hughes, 1972) and Surrealism (Balakian, 1986).

## 4 Results

Table 1 presents three examples of poems produced by means of the co-creative process. Here, we discuss quality from a literary perspective.

Trained on prose, the text is generated as free verse (i.e. free from the restrictions of rhythm and rhyme) which we associate with contemporary poetry. In the lines, various poetic devices can be identified, such as alliteration (e.g. "**g**olwe van **g**ister") and assonance (e.g. "m**aa**k 'n vr**aa**g w**aa**rbinne").

The generated lines abound with figurative language as well. As an instance of an extended metaphor, the first stanza of the second poem suggests sensitivity to the country's turbulent history. Personification is particularly prevalent, lending a visceral quality to the text: Africa drinks, the landscape tilts its back, the sea breathes, and Table Mountain poses a question. The imagery is vivid, portraying sight (*Tonight's curtains / glitter at sliding windows / in the city lights*), smell (*the introspective sea / lifts the scents and utters / a breath*) and sound (*roar of a wave*). The language can be described as minimalist, evocative and abstract, and therefore open to interpretation, resembling Imagist and Surrealist poetry.

Afrikaans has a rich poetic tradition (Brink and Opperman, 2000), and we believe that creative text generation has the potential to enrich poetic language. Alongside Afrikaans varieties, the corpus contains some English as well, which influenced the generated text in interesting ways. As one example, it is grammatically incorrect in Standard Afrikaans to use "sun" as both noun and verb, e.g. "to sun in the garden". The model, however, adopted this and other patterns from the English, generating novel phrases (that do not sound anglicised) such as "sonlig son die promenade" – *sunlight suns the promenade*.

## 5 Conclusion

In this study, we present Afrikaans poetry generation in a machine-in-the-loop setting. Each and every line of poetry is automatically generated by the proposed LSTM network. In order to clearly identify the machine's contribution to the process, the human writer's interaction is limited to the selection and vertical arrangement of the lines – without any modification. We believe this is the first creative text generation study in the Afrikaans language. More broadly, the work encourages human-centred design in low-resource languages. Creative industries would benefit from co-creative tools and methods (Hsu et al., 2019), perhaps more than fully automatic approaches.

## 6 Future Work

There are many ways in which this work can be extended.

First, similar to Yi et al. (2017), we could follow line-to-line poem generation, where the network takes the previous line as prompt and generates a new line which, in turn, is the prompt for the next entry. We could also experiment with different architectures, such as Transformer (Vaswani et al., 2017), as well as training schemes. For example, we could borrow AfriBERT (Ralethe, 2020), the recent BERT (Devlin et al., 2019) adaptation for Afrikaans, to apply transfer learning.

Second, as demonstrated in Van de Cruys (2020), poetry generation is also possible by training on prosaic (non-poetic) text and modeling poetic constraints (e.g. rhyme). This way, we could expand to fully automatic poetry generation. Naturally, this would require an extensive literature corpus.

Third, regarding the unconventional use of some nouns as verbs in Afrikaans, future research could explore how prevalent this type of novel, cross-language variation is. To improve textual quality, we could incorporate Afrikaans datasets such as the NCHLT Annotated Text Corpora (Eiselen and Puttkammer, 2014; Puttkammer et al., 2014) as well as the Afrikaans treebank (Augustinus et al., 2016), which are available via SADiLaR (Roux, 2016) in addition to others.

Finally, a promising direction to pursue would be the involvement of poets and writers to investigate whether this approach could inform and improve their creative writing practices.

## Acknowledgments

This paper has been produced benefiting from the 2232 International Fellowship for Outstanding Researchers Program of TÜBİTAK (Project No: 118C285). However, the entire responsibility of the paper belongs to the owner of the paper. The financial support received from TÜBİTAK does not mean that the content of the publication is approved in a scientific sense by TÜBİTAK.

We would like to thank Etienne van Heerden for providing his manuscript to be used in this study.

## References

Nader Akoury, Shufan Wang, Josh Whiting, Stephen Hood, Nanyun Peng, and Mohit Iyyer. 2020. STORIUM: A dataset and platform for human-in-the-loop story generation. In *Proc EMNLP*, pages 6470–6484.

Constitutional Assembly. 1996. Constitution of the Republic of South Africa. *Cape Town*, 230(38):1241–1331.

Liesbeth Augustinus, Peter Dirix, Daniel Van Niekerk, Ineke Schuurman, Vincent Vandeghinste, Frank Van Eynde, and Gerhard Van Huyssteen. 2016. AfriBooms: An online treebank for Afrikaans. In *Proc LREC*, pages 677–682.

Dzmitry Bahdanau, Kyung Hyun Cho, and Yoshua Bengio. 2015. Neural machine translation by jointly learning to align and translate. In *Proc ICLR*.

Anna Balakian. 1986. *Surrealism: The Road to the Absolute*. University of Chicago Press.

Yoshua Bengio, Patrice Simard, and Paolo Frasconi. 1994. Learning long-term dependencies with gradient descent is difficult. *IEEE transactions on neural networks*, 5(2):157–166.

Faeze Brahman, Alexandru Petrusca, and Snigdha Chaturvedi. 2020. Cue me in: Content-inducing approaches to interactive story generation. In *Proc AACL-IJCNLP*, pages 588–597.

André Philippus Brink and Diederik Johannes Opperman. 2000. *Groot verseboek 2000*. Tafelberg.

Alex Calderwood, Vivian Qiu, Katy Ilonka Gero, and Lydia B Chilton. 2020. How novelists use generative language models: An exploratory user study. In *Proc ACM IUI Workshop*.

Elizabeth Clark, Anne Spencer Ross, Chenhao Tan, Yangfeng Ji, and Noah A Smith. 2018. Creative writing with a machine in the loop: Case studies on slogans and stories. In *Proc ACM IUI*, pages 329–340.

Tim Van de Cruys. 2020. Automatic poetry generation from prosaic text. In *Proc ACL*, pages 2471–2480.

Jacob Devlin, Ming-Wei Chang, Kenton Lee, and Kristina Toutanova. 2019. BERT: Pre-training of deep bidirectional transformers for language understanding. In *Proc NAACL*, pages 4171–4186.

Belén Díaz-Agudo, Pablo Gervás, and Pedro A González-Calero. 2002. Poetry generation in COLIBRI. In *Proc ECCBR*, pages 73–87.

Peter Dirix, Liesbeth Augustinus, Daniel Van Niekerk, and Frank Van Eynde. 2017. Universal dependencies for Afrikaans. In *Proc NoDaLiDa*, pages 38–47.

Roald Eiselen and Martin Puttkammer. 2014. Developing text resources for ten South African languages. In *Proc LREC*, pages 3698–3703.

∀, Wilhelmina Nekoto, Vukosi Marivate, Tshinondiwa Matsila, Timi Fasubaa, Taiwo Fagbohungbe, Solomon Oluwole Akinola, Shamsuddeen Muhammad, Salomon Kabongo Kabenamualu, Salomey Osei, Freshia Sackey, Rubungo Andre Niyongabo, Ricky Macharm, Perez Ogayo, Orevaoghene Ahia, Musie Meressa Berhe, Mofetoluwa Adeyemi, Masabata Mokgesi-Selinga, Lawrence Okegbemi, Laura Martinus, Kolawole Tajudeen, Kevin Degila, Kelechi Ogueji, Kathleen Siminyu, Julia Kreutzer, Jason Webster, Jamiil Toure Ali, Jade Abbott, Iroro Orife, Ignatius Ezeani, Idris Abdulkadir Dangana, Herman Kamper, Hady Elsahar, Goodness Duru, Ghollah Kioko, Murhabazi Espoir, Elan van Biljon, Daniel Whitenack, Christopher Onyefuluchi, Chris Chinenye Emezue, Bonaventure F. P. Dossou, Blessing Sibanda, Blessing Bassey, Ayodele Olabiyi, Arshath Ramkilowan, Alp Öktem, Adewale Akinfaderin, and Abdallah Bashir. 2020a. Participatory research for low-resourced machine translation: A case study in African languages. In *Proc EMNLP*, pages 2144–2160.

∀, Iroro Orife, Julia Kreutzer, Blessing Sibanda, Daniel Whitenack, Kathleen Siminyu, Laura Martinus, Jamiil Toure Ali, Jade Abbott, Vukosi Marivate, Salomon Kabongo, Musie Meressa, Espoir Murhabazi, Orevaoghene Ahia, Elan van Biljon, Arshath Ramkilowan, Adewale Akinfaderin, Alp Öktem, Wole Akin, Ghollah Kioko, Kevin Degila, Herman Kamper, Bonaventure Dossou, Chris Emezue, Kelechi Ogueji, and Abdallah Bashir. 2020b. Masakhane–machine translation for Africa. In *Proc ICLR Workshop*.

Pablo Gervás. 2001. An expert system for the composition of formal Spanish poetry. In *Proc SGES*, pages 19–32.

Marjan Ghazvininejad, Xing Shi, Yejin Choi, and Kevin Knight. 2016. Generating topical poetry. In *Proc EMNLP*, pages 1183–1191.

Jing He, Ming Zhou, and Long Jiang. 2012. Generating Chinese classical poems with statistical machine translation models. In *Proc AAAI*, volume 26.

Sepp Hochreiter and Jürgen Schmidhuber. 1997. Long short-term memory. *Neural computation*, 9(8):1735–1780.

Jack Hopkins and Douwe Kiela. 2017. Automatically generating rhythmic verse with neural networks. In *Proc ACL*, pages 168–178.

Ting-Yao Hsu, Yen-Chia Hsu, and Ting-Hao Huang. 2019. On how users edit computer-generated visual stories. In *Proc ACM CHI*, pages 1–6.

Glenn Hughes. 1972. *Imagism & the Imagists: A Study in Modern Poetry*. Biblo & Tannen Publishers.

Long Jiang and Ming Zhou. 2008. Generating Chinese couplets using a statistical MT approach. In *Proc COLING*, pages 377–384.

Pratik Joshi, Sebastin Santy, Amar Budhiraja, Kalika Bali, and Monojit Choudhury. 2020. The state and fate of linguistic diversity and inclusion in the NLP world. In *Proc ACL*, pages 6282–6293.

Anna Kantosalo and Sirpa Riihiaho. 2019. Experience evaluations for human–computer co-creative processes–planning and conducting an evaluation in practice. *Connection Science*, 31(1):60–81.

Diederik P Kingma and Jimmy Ba. 2015. Adam: A method for stochastic optimization. In *ICLR*.

Jey Han Lau, Trevor Cohn, Timothy Baldwin, Julian Brooke, and Adam Hammond. 2018. Deep-speare: A joint neural model of poetic language, meter and rhyme. In *Proc ACL*, pages 1948–1958.

Pali Lehohla. 2012. *Census in brief 2011*. Statistics South Africa.

Robert P Levy. 2001. A computational model of poetic creativity with neural network as measure of adaptive fitness. In *Proc ICCBR Workshop*.

Yusen Liu, Dayiheng Liu, and Jiancheng Lv. 2020. Deep poetry: A Chinese classical poetry generation system. In *Proc AAAI*, volume 34(09), pages 13626–13627.

Todd Lubart. 2005. How can computers be partners in the creative process: classification and commentary on the special issue. *International Journal of Human-Computer Studies*, 63(4-5):365–369.

Enrique Manjavacas, Folgert Karsdorp, Ben Burtenshaw, and Mike Kestemont. 2017. Synthetic literature: Writing science fiction in a co-creative process. In *Proc CCNLG*, pages 29–37.

Ruli Manurung, Graeme Ritchie, and Henry Thompson. 2012. Using genetic algorithms to create meaningful poetic text. *Journal of Experimental & Theoretical Artificial Intelligence*, 24(1):43–64.

Hugo Oliveira. 2009. Automatic generation of poetry: an overview. *Universidade de Coimbra*.

Hugo Gonçalo Oliveira. 2012. PoeTryMe: a versatile platform for poetry generation. *Computational Creativity, Concept Invention, and General Intelligence*, 1:21.

Hans Pienaar. 2020. *Prize-winning novel on #FeesMustFall is a campus of ideas*. Business Day. https://www.businesslive.co.za/bd/life/books/2020-04-09-book-review-prize-winning-novel-on-feesmustfall-is-a-campus-of-ideas/.

Peter Potash, Alexey Romanov, and Anna Rumshisky. 2015. Ghostwriter: Using an LSTM for automatic rap lyric generation. In *Proc EMNLP*, pages 1919–1924.

Martin Puttkammer, Martin Schlemmer, and Ruan Bekker. 2014. *NCHLT Afrikaans Annotated Text Corpora*. South African Centre for Digital Language Resource. https://hdl.handle.net/20.500.12185/296.

Sello Ralethe. 2020. Adaptation of deep bidirectional transformers for Afrikaans language. In *Proc LREC*, pages 2475–2478.

Melissa Roemmele and Andrew Gordon. 2018. Linguistic features of helpfulness in automated support for creative writing. In *Proc ICIDS*, pages 14–19.

Melissa Roemmele and Andrew S Gordon. 2015. Creative help: A story writing assistant. In *Proc ICIDS*, pages 81–92.

Justus Roux. 2016. South African National Centre for Digital Language Resources. In *Proc LREC*, pages 2467–2470.

Lauren Sanby, Ion Todd, and Maria C Keet. 2016. Comparing the template-based approach to GF: the case of Afrikaans. In *Proc WebNLG*, pages 50–53.

Ben Shneiderman. 2002. Creativity support tools. *Communications of the ACM*, 45(10):116–120.

Martin Sundermeyer, Ralf Schlüter, and Hermann Ney. 2012. LSTM neural networks for language modeling. In *Proc INTERSPEECH*.

Reid Swanson and Andrew S Gordon. 2012. Say anything: Using textual case-based reasoning to enable open-domain interactive storytelling. *ACM Transactions on Interactive Intelligent Systems*, 2(3):1–35.

Aleksey Tikhonov and Ivan Yamshchikov. 2018. Sounds Wilde: Phonetically extended embeddings for author-stylized poetry generation. In *Proc SIGMORPHON*, pages 117–124.

Aaron Tucker. 2019. Machine co-authorship (s) via translative creative writing. *Journal of Creative Writing Studies*, 4(1):7.

Etienne Van Heerden. 2019. *Die Biblioteek aan die Einde van die Wêreld*. NB-Uitgewers.

Menno Van Zaanen and Gerhard Van Huyssteen. 2003. Improving a spelling checker for Afrikaans. In *Proc CLIN*, pages 143–156.

Ashish Vaswani, Noam Shazeer, Niki Parmar, Jakob Uszkoreit, Llion Jones, Aidan N Gomez, Łukasz Kaiser, and Illia Polosukhin. 2017. Attention is all you need. In *Proc NIPS*, pages 6000–6010.

Qixin Wang, Tianyi Luo, Dong Wang, and Chao Xing. 2016a. Chinese song iambics generation with neural attention-based model. In *Proc IJCAI*, pages 2943–2949.

Zhe Wang, Wei He, Hua Wu, Haiyang Wu, Wei Li, Haifeng Wang, and Enhong Chen. 2016b. Chinese poetry generation with planning based neural network. In *Proc COLING*, pages 1051–1060.

Rui Yan, Han Jiang, Mirella Lapata, Shou-De Lin, Xueqiang Lv, and Xiaoming Li. 2013. I, poet: automatic Chinese poetry composition through a generative summarization framework under constrained optimization. In *Proc IJCAI*.

Xiaopeng Yang, Xiaowen Lin, Shunda Suo, and Ming Li. 2018. Generating thematic Chinese poetry using conditional variational autoencoders with hybrid decoders. In *Proc IJCAI*, pages 4539–4545.

Xiaoyuan Yi, Ruoyu Li, and Maosong Sun. 2017. Generating Chinese classical poems with RNN encoder-decoder. In *Proc NLP-NABD*, pages 211–223.

Xiaoyuan Yi, Maosong Sun, Ruoyu Li, and Wenhao Li. 2018. Automatic poetry generation with mutual reinforcement learning. In *Proc EMNLP*, pages 3143–3153.

Xingxing Zhang and Mirella Lapata. 2014. Chinese poetry generation with recurrent neural networks. In *Proc EMNLP*, pages 670–680.

Patrick Ziering and Lonneke Van der Plas. 2016. Towards unsupervised and language-independent compound splitting using inflectional morphological transformations. In *Proc NAACL*, pages 644–653.

Andrea Zugarini, Stefano Melacci, and Marco Maggini. 2019. Neural poetry: Learning to generate poems using syllables. In *Proc ICANN*, pages 313–325.

# Situation-Specific Multimodal Feature Adaptation

**Özge Alaçam**
Language Technology Group, Dept. of Informatics, Universität Hamburg
Hamburg, Germany
alacam@informatik.uni-hamburg.de

## Abstract

Current technological and scientific developments on assistive technologies result in a considerable need for NLP models to successfully grasp the intention of the user in situated settings. Situated language comprehension, where different multimodal cues are inherently present and essential parts of the situations, can not be handled in isolation. In this research proposal, we aim to quantify the influence of each modality including the eye-movements of the speaker as a deictic cue to gain deeper understanding about multimodal interaction. By doing this, we mainly focus on the role of various referential complexities in this interaction. The proposed model encodes the referential complexity of the situated settings in the embedding space during the pre-training phase. This will, in return, implicitly guide the model to adjust to situation-specific properties of an unseen test case.

In this paper, we summarize the challenges of intention extraction and propose a methodological approach to investigate a situation-specific feature adaptation to improve crossmodal mapping and meaning recovery from noisy communication settings.

## 1 Motivation

In recent years, we have witnessed a considerable increase in the use of assistive technologies that can engage in communication and perform tasks. These can come in different forms like smart speakers and mobile devices that you can command with audio, or more specialized task-oriented robots that can actually realize users' command in 3D environments. The steady increase in the use of collaborative robots (IFR, 2018) in daily life brings along another important Human-Computer Interaction theme: the capability of engaging in a natural and smooth spoken dialog with humans, which is a major scientific and technological challenge. Particularly, being able to follow a communication that conveys thoughts and intentions expressed in a flexible manner without the restrictions of a close-set of commands is a crucial component of assistive robots for the handicapped and elderly people and for the education / entertainment purposes.

Spoken and situated communication is composed of various perceptual (e.g. audio, visual) and representational modalities (e.g. language, deictic eye-movements, gestures). Effectiveness and fluency of human communication capabilities inspire us to develop robust language models that can deal with uncertainties by evaluating all the available information from multiple sources and reach *a good-enough decision*. In order to reach this performance, we need to model our situated language understanding systems to incorporate those modalities and let them interact in a meaningful way. This brings forth some important questions; how to integrate different modalities and how to utilize adaptive processing for effective situation-awareness to be able to deal with cases where some of the modalities are restricted due to noise in the communication channels. This capability for cross-modal integration can be a very important feature in resolving references or executing commands for smart speakers or helper robots that aid people in their daily activities.

## 2 Situated Language Understanding

In a task-oriented setting (e.g. helper robots completing a given task), the goal of natural language communication is to extract the intention of the speaker. Such communication usually happens in structurally rich visual environments like the one in Figure 1, which contains several glasses of different types (wine and tea glasses), mice (computer mouse and cat toy), windows (open and closed) etc..



*Proceedings of the First Workshop on Bridging Human–Computer Interaction and Natural Language Processing*, pages 81–87
April 20, 2021. 

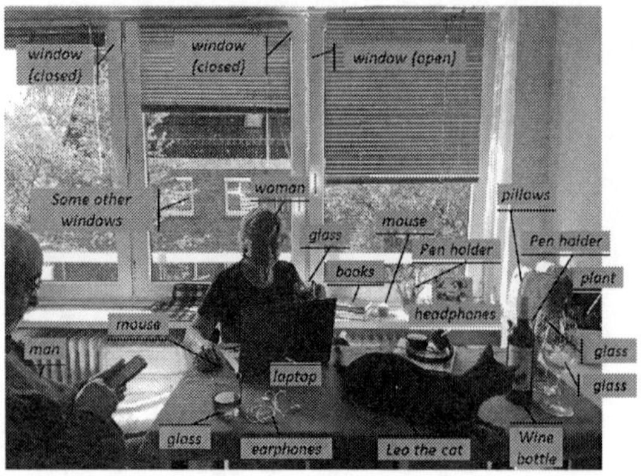


Figure 1: An example image for a living room scenario.

Some of them are even (partially) occluded from the viewer's perspective. The environments usually also include people and their interactions with the objects (actions). Visual information plays a crucial role in determining the referential objects related with the action and to accomplish the task. Thus, computational solutions that incorporate those cues are expected to perform better in grasping the meaning compared to their (text-only) unimodal counterparts (see Alaçam et al. (2020a) for a review).

Determining the correct intention of a user is not always straightforward due to various reasons. Let us take the following sentences as an example:

1. Can you bring me the wine, I want to open it.
2. Can you bring me the wine, I want to drink it.

In both cases, on the syntactic level, the pronoun *it* refers to *the wine*. But in the referential world, the first one clearly refers to *a wine bottle*, while the second (with a lesser degree of certainty) refers to *a glass of wine*.

In many cases, even the object names are verbally omitted in spoken utterances. This kind of implicit commands like *"I prefer red, can you open a bottle and bring it to me?"*, require the hearer to reconstruct the underlying intention *"Open a bottle of red wine, and bring the bottle"* (Gundel et al., 2012). Alternatively, depending on the spatial arrangements of the agents and the objects in the room, the intention of the speaker might be slightly different and more complex. For example, when the empty glasses are closer to the listener than the speaker, the interpretation might be: *"Open a bottle of red wine, pour the wine into one of the empty wine glasses and bring the glass of wine to me"*. Expressing this intention explicitly most often results in unwieldy utterances.

Furthermore, when the environment is noisy, or the communication partner suffers from a motor or cognitive impairment, multimodal integration plays a more critical role. Noise in communication can originate from various sources. It can be linguistic noise (e.g. spelling mistakes, complex attachments), visual ambiguities (e.g. clutter in the environment, occlusions) or an acoustic noise. Instead of waiting for clarification, combining the uncertain information from the linguistic channel with information from the other ones increases the fluency and the effectiveness of the communication (Garay-Vitoria and Abascal, 2004). One of the most well-known examples to this phenomenon is *the cocktail party effect*, that highlights the human ability to focus on one particular source while inhibiting the noisy ones. When the informativeness of one modality is reduced due to environmental conditions, the human language processing system can successfully adjust itself by relying less on the unclear modality and using other cues in the environment. In this specific scenario, other informative cues provide more reliable information compared to the noisy linguistic input. These cues can come from the surrounding environment and from the communicational partners, and include eye-gaze direction or representational gestures combined with their referential link to the entities in the environment.

Eye-tracking is attracting considerable interest in many assistive technologies such as educational VR systems that provide embodied learning environments or driver monitoring systems. The use of eye-tracking in daily technological products such as mobile phones, laptops and virtual reality headsets is increasing day by day (Brousseau et al., 2020; Rogers, 2019; Khamis et al., 2018). Therefore, incorporating eye-movements in our language comprehension models is an inevitable outcome of these latest developments, and this makes the systematic research on the combination of this modality with others very crucial.

## 3 Dataset Collection

The success of a situation-aware language comprehension model is highly dependent on the representativeness of the modalities under various conditions. This kind of coverage requires a richly annotated multimodal corpus that displays the variety of language expressiveness and flexibility. Developing such a corpus is a very costly process. Thus, a dataset that profoundly incorporates a variety of modalities and their various aspects addressing language comprehension tasks is currently not available. Therefore, we plan to train the model on a set of available multimodal datasets (as listed below), by using whichever modality constellations they can offer (including datasets from various domains like psycholinguistics, language technology, computer vision, human-robot interaction etc.) in a stepwise manner; namely starting with simple / few relations, then gradually increasing the complexity of the interactions.

There are general-purpose multimodal datasets that can be used for training:

- MS COCO (Lin et al., 2014) : an object detection and captioning dataset with >200 K labeled images and 5 captions in a sentence form for each image
- Flicker30k (Plummer et al., 2015): 31 K images collected from Flickr, together with 5 reference sentences
- ImageNET (Deng et al., 2009): 14 M annotated images, hierarchically organized (w.r.t. WordNet)
- MVSO (Jou et al., 2015): 15 K visual concepts across 12 languages, 7.36 M images

Additionally, there are multimodal datasets that were created for a specific task:

- HuRIC 2.0 (Bastianelli et al., 2014): audio files (656 sentences) paired with their transcriptions referring to commands for a robot
- LAVA (Berzak et al., 2016): 237 sentences, with 2 to 3 interpretations per sentence, and a total of 1679 videos that depict visual variations of each interpretation
- CLEVR-Ref+ (Liu et al., 2019): 100 K synthetic images with several referring expressions
- Eye4Ref (Alaçam et al., 2020b): 86 systematically controlled sentence-–image pairs and 2024 eye-movement recordings from various referentially complex situations

Multimodal embeddings will be created from this pool of datasets. Creating embeddings from various data sources will allow us to cover concepts from various aspects such as linguistic, auditory and visual representations. The variety on the visual modality will also help us to capture different visual depictions in a range from synthetic images to photographs. This will increase the representativeness of the concepts in the training dataset that will in return improve the prediction when it comes to unseen environments either in virtual reality or in a real-world setting.

70 % of this collection will be used to create multimodal concept embeddings. The remaining 30 % of the datasets will be included in the test and development sets after semi-automatic and manual annotation of contextual representations, target words, missing words, etc. However, Eye4REF will be used as main testset since it was systematically created to involve referentially complex situations.

## 4 Objectives

One of the main objectives of this research proposal is to quantify the effect of each modality and their interactions by conducting systematic empirical research with computational modeling and human subject studies. Another objective lies in creating multimodal and multilayer embedding spaces in which the layers will be sensitive to various situation complexities, an approach that has not been considered yet. Moreover, eye-movements of the speakers, as a substantial but underrepresented component of face-to-face communication, are incorporated to further improve NLP methods on meaning extraction and crossmodal reference resolution.

**Model.** The proposed method will be able to process several modalities that play a crucial role in communication; (i) Linguistic Information (at syntactic and semantic level), (ii) Situational Information, (iii) Prototypical Knowledge and Relations, and (iv) Speech-accompanying eye-movements of the speaker. The initial base model will focus on the first three capabilities by utilizing data-driven language models such as fasttext (Bojanowski et al., 2017) and commonsense knowledge-bases like ConceptNet (Speer et al., 2017). At the same time, two modules that (i) incorporate eye-movements and (ii) perform situation-specific feature adaptation will be developed from scratch. In brief, vocabulary obtained from the pre-trained embeddings is used as a bridge between the modalities. For each vocabulary item, multimodal embeddings will be created by processing every input channel, see Figure 2. For each modality and their joint training, we will utilize an appropriate encoder, such as Fast-R-CNN (Girshick, 2015) for images and attention-based bi-directional LSTMs (e.g. Song et al. (2019), for text and eye-movement data. A neural network ensemble model will be trained on the embeddings for the task of intended object or action prediction from situated settings with masked information.

**Guided Multi-Modal Data Fusion.** Based on the vast support provided (Qi et al., 2020; Akbari et al., 2019; Niu et al., 2017; Aytar et al., 2017; Kiros et al., 2014), *a guided multilayer data-driven approach* will be utilized instead of fusing all datasets together without any guidance. Despite their impressive success to solve specific tasks so far, deep learning methods are hardly interpretable in understanding which properties of inputs contribute to the final decision to which degree. Besides, the abstraction capabilities, which are crucial for dealing with new cases, are still very limited. However, the more we know about the interactions among the modalities, the more we can extract and focus on relevant features, and the more we can guide those effective deep learning methods to perform better in an explainable way. This will pave the ground to advance current methods for cross-modal interaction in situated language processing with a comprehensive approach to process more modalities, thus to deal with new situations even under uncertainty.

We plan to obtain concept representations step-by-step and build the concepts over each other with increasing complexity, similar to the development of the human cognitive system. One of the key elements here is to encode referential complexity of the each situated setting in the training data. The multimodal embedding space for each concept will consist of several embeddings, which are sensitive to various complexities (as illustrated in Figure 2) and this structure forms the backbone of the situation-specific adaptation. By automatically classifying the complexity of multimodal input based on the predefined complexity factors, each entry in the datasets will contribute to the respective embeddings in the embedding space. This presents a new approach for creating embeddings, taking input complexity into account. Additionally, this configuration also provides a testbed to investigate another interesting question: does restricting the model to use only a complexity embedding that corresponds with input complexity improve the crossmodal mapping task performance? For example, when the multimodal input refers to a highly featured concept representation (a dinner accompanied by red wine), using a representation that is created from coarse-grain samples (a clip-art of a wine bottle) may yield misclassification and vice versa.

**Dynamics among different information sources.** In the second objective, we quantify the contribution of each modality and their aspects given the situation to mimic human heuristic processing capability. Language comprehension involves complex sequential decision making and is affected by both uncertainty about the current input and lack of knowledge about the upcoming material. Thus, people use – to a large extent – fast and frugal heuristics, i.e. choosing a good-enough representation (Ferreira, 2003). The heuristic view provides a valid explanation for scenarios with a conversation inside noisy conditions. Instead of waiting / asking for clarification, the model will reach a good-enough decision based on all information gathered through all available input channels. In order to do that, the set of important features given the situated setting should be chosen automatically.

Structuring the embeddings to have separate slots for each modality and for their combinations will allow us to quantify the contribution of each slot individually given the situation in various complexities. Depending on the communication goal or environmental factors, some modalities would contribute to the solution while others could be simply irrelevant or redundant. Understanding the intention of the user requires understanding of which information provided by the modalities is (more) relevant, complementary, or redundant. The human language processing system does this adjustment quite efficiently. Thus, a model will be designed to pick the most effective perceptual and conceptual cues and to ignore the irrelevant ones depending on the situated context. Then, the attention will be channeled towards the most relevant cue sources.

**Integrating eye-movements of the speaker.** Many eye-tracking technologies in the market employ a sufficient sampling frequency to enable gaze-contingent applications. With advancements in the eye-tracking technology, incorporating eye movements of a speaker or a listener enables us to predict / resolve which entity is being referred to in a complex visual environment (Klerke and Plank, 2019; Mitev et al., 2018; Mishra et al., 2017; Koleva et al., 2015). However, these studies are limited to relatively simple scenes. Situated language understanding in a referentially complex environment or under noisy situations imposes a different level

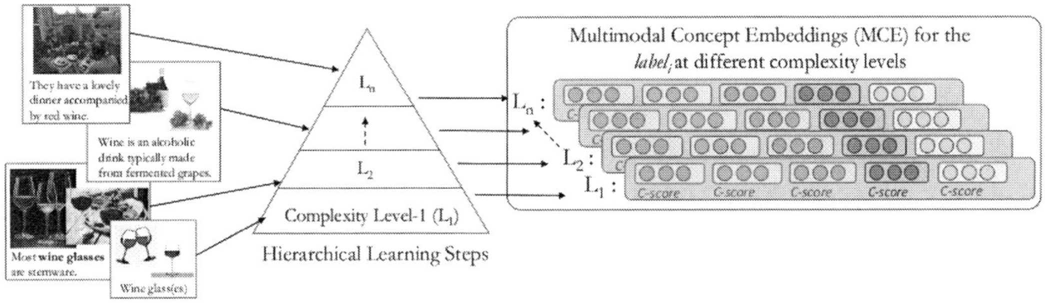


Figure 2: Schematic overview of the hierarchical embeddings.

of challenge that we aim to address. The number of studies that utilize gaze features (Sood et al., 2020; Park et al., 2019; Karessli et al., 2017) is very limited. In this study, we propose to incorporate the eye-movements of the speaker to improve the crossmodal mapping performance. This additional deictic modality may improve the recovery of the intended meaning especially when the communication is noisy (acoustically or visually). The gaze embeddings will be created by using existing eye-movement datasets. However, there are only few big-size eye-movement datasets available (Alaçam et al., 2020b; Wilming et al., 2017; Ehinger et al., 2009). Thus, to enlarge available data, we will conduct a set of experimental studies with increasing referential complexity. There, we will record participants' instructions on a task-oriented scenario and their eye-movements regarding target objects.

**Evaluation of the assistive model.** After all information sources from various modalities are made available and integrated, the contribution of each modality will be investigated by performing systematic manipulations (e.g. removing a modality one-by-one from the input). The standard accuracy and efficiency metrics will be used for evaluating the models' performance, including the overall runtime, modality-specific accuracy parameters (such as PoS-tag or semantic class accuracy), target mapping accuracy, and accuracy in recovering the missing word.

In addition to evaluating how this model improves the task of reference resolution for acoustically and/or visually noisy settings, its role as assistive technology will be investigated by conducting a user study. The experimental setup will be very similar to the one in the data collection phase. However, this time the participant will interact with a demo model that displays all the above-mentioned capabilities. The model will try to extract user intention by predicting the communicationally relevant objects on the fly. The usability study on the demo model will be evaluated based on the efficiency (how long does it take to reach a decision?), effectiveness (how accurate is the system decision?) and the user satisfaction ratings that will be obtained through the same evaluation metrics and a user survey.

## 5 Conclusion

In this research proposal, we focus on three factors that can enhance the communication between humans and assistive technologies. The first one is the encoding of the referential complexity of the situated settings while creating multimodal embeddings. As pointed out in (Singh et al., 2020), pre-trained models, that were created by fusing the modalities without constraints, are expected to be an out-of-the-box solution and work well for a variety of simpler tasks. In this research, we propose to encode referential complexity during the training phase to see whether the complexity-sensitive embeddings will improve the tasks of crossmodal mapping and meaning recovery. We believe that this will implicitly direct the model to focus on various textual and visual forms of the same concepts.

The second factor is the inclusion of eye-movements as an additional modality to enhance meaning recovery from noisy settings where some parts of the sentences or visual labels are masked.

At last, this research will also contribute to a better understanding of the contributions of each individual modality, of amodal and modality-specific features and their interactions.

The proposed method will be beneficial for other task-oriented communication scenarios, where the cognitive systems need to understand the intention and to aid the user in the most efficient and effective way, such as educational video-games, training simulations, and assistive navigation systems.

## References


Hassan Akbari, Svebor Karaman, Surabhi Bhargava, Brian Chen, Carl Vondrick, and Shih-Fu Chang. 2019. Multi-level multimodal common semantic space for image-phrase grounding. In Proceedings of the IEEE Conference on Computer Vision and Pattern Recognition, pages 12476–12486, Long Beach, CA, USA.

Özge Alaçam, Xingshan Li, Wolfgang Menzel, and Tobias Staron. 2020a. Crossmodal language comprehension – psycholinguistic insights and computational approaches. Frontiers in Neurorobotics, 14:2.

Özge Alaçam, Eugen Ruppert, Amr R. Salama, Tobias Staron, and Wolfgang Menzel. 2020b. Eye4Ref: A multimodal eye movement dataset of referentially complex situations. In Proceedings of the12th International Conference on Language Resources and Evaluation (LREC), page 2396–2404, Marseille, France.

Yusuf Aytar, Carl Vondrick, and Antonio Torralba. 2017. See, hear, and read: Deep aligned representations. arXiv preprint arXiv:1706.00932.

Emanuele Bastianelli, Giuseppe Castellucci, Danilo Croce, Luca Iocchi, Roberto Basili, and Daniele Nardi. 2014. Huric: a human robot interaction corpus. In LREC, pages 4519–4526.

Yevgeni Berzak, Andrei Barbu, Daniel Harari, Boris Katz, and Shimon Ullman. 2016. Do you see what i mean? visual resolution of linguistic ambiguities. arXiv preprint arXiv:1603.08079.

Piotr Bojanowski, Edouard Grave, Armand Joulin, and Tomas Mikolov. 2017. Enriching word vectors with subword information. Transactions of the Association for Computational Linguistics, 5:135–146.

Braiden Brousseau, Jonathan Rose, and Moshe Eizenman. 2020. Hybrid eye-tracking on a smartphone with cnn feature extraction and an infrared 3d model. Sensors, 20(2):543.

Jia Deng, Wei Dong, Richard Socher, Li-Jia Li, Kai Li, and Li Fei-Fei. 2009. Imagenet: A large-scale hierarchical image database. In IEEE conference on computer vision and pattern recognition, pages 248–255, Miami, Florida, USA.

Krista A Ehinger, Barbara Hidalgo-Sotelo, Antonio Torralba, and Aude Oliva. 2009. Modelling search for people in 900 scenes: A combined source model of eye guidance. Visual cognition, 17(6-7):945–978.

Fernanda Ferreira. 2003. The misinterpretation of noncanonical sentences. Cognitive Psychology, 47(2):164–203.

Nestor Garay-Vitoria and Julio Abascal. 2004. A comparison of prediction techniques to enhance the communication rate. In ERCIM Workshop on User Interfaces for All, pages 400–417, Vienna, Austria. Springer.

Ross Girshick. 2015. Fast r-cnn. In Proceedings of the IEEE international conference on computer vision, pages 1440–1448, Santiago, Chile.

Jeanette K. Gundel, Nancy Hedberg, and Ron Zacharski. 2012. Underspecification of cognitive status in reference production: Some empirical predictions. Topics in Cognitive Science, 4(2):249–268.

IFR. 2018. Executive summary world robotics 2019 service robots.

Brendan Jou, Tao Chen, Nikolaos Pappas, Miriam Redi, Mercan Topkara, and Shih-Fu Chang. 2015. Visual affect around the world: A large-scale multilingual visual sentiment ontology. In Proceedings of the 23rd ACM international conference on Multimedia, pages 159–168.

Nour Karessli, Zeynep Akata, Bernt Schiele, and Andreas Bulling. 2017. Gaze embeddings for zero-shot image classification. In Proceedings of the IEEE conference on computer vision and pattern recognition, pages 4525–4534, Honolulu, USA.

Mohamed Khamis, Florian Alt, and Andreas Bulling. 2018. The past, present, and future of gaze-enabled handheld mobile devices: survey and lessons learned. In Proceedings of the 20th International Conference on Human-Computer Interaction with Mobile Devices and Services, pages 1–17, Barcelona, Spain.

Ryan Kiros, Ruslan Salakhutdinov, and Richard S. Zemel. 2014. Unifying visual-semantic embeddings with multimodal neural language models. arXiv preprint arXiv:1411.2539.

Sigrid Klerke and Barbara Plank. 2019. At a glance: The impact of gaze aggregation views on syntactic tagging. In Proceedings of the Beyond Vision and LANguage: inTEgrating Real-world kNowledge (LANTERN), pages 51–61, Hong Kong, China.

Nikolina Koleva, Martín Villalba, Maria Staudte, and Alexander Koller. 2015. The impact of listener gaze on predicting reference resolution. In Proceedings of the 53rd Annual Meeting of the Association for Computational Linguistics and the 7th International Joint Conference on Natural Language Processing, volume 2, pages 812–817, Beijing, China.

Tsung-Yi Lin, Michael Maire, Serge Belongie, James Hays, Pietro Perona, Deva Ramanan, Piotr Dollár, and C Lawrence Zitnick. 2014. Microsoft coco: Common objects in context. In European conference on computer vision, pages 740–755, Zurich, Switzerland. Springer.

Runtao Liu, Chenxi Liu, Yutong Bai, and Alan L Yuille. 2019. Clevr-ref+: Diagnosing visual reasoning with referring expressions. In Proceedings of the IEEE/CVF Conference on Computer Vision and Pattern Recognition, pages 4185–4194, Long Beach, CA, USA.

Abhijit Mishra, Kuntal Dey, and Pushpak Bhattacharyya. 2017. Learning cognitive features from gaze data for sentiment and sarcasm classification using convolutional neural network. In Proceedings of the 55th Annual Meeting of the Association for Computational Linguistics, pages 377–387, Vancouver, Canada.

Nikolina Mitev, Patrick Renner, Thies Pfeiffer, and Maria Staudte. 2018. Using listener gaze to refer in installments benefits understanding. In Proceedings of the 40th Annual Meeting of the Cognitive Science Society, pages 2122–2127, Madison, Wisconsin, USA.

Zhenxing Niu, Mo Zhou, Le Wang, Xinbo Gao, and Gang Hua. 2017. Hierarchical multimodal lstm for dense visual-semantic embedding. In The IEEE International Conference on Computer Vision (ICCV), Venice, Italy.

Seonwook Park, Shalini De Mello, Pavlo Molchanov, Umar Iqbal, Otmar Hilliges, and Jan Kautz. 2019. Few-shot adaptive gaze estimation. In Proceedings of the IEEE/CVF International Conference on Computer Vision (ICCV), pages 9368–9377, Seoul, Korea.

Bryan A Plummer, Liwei Wang, Chris M Cervantes, Juan C Caicedo, Julia Hockenmaier, and Svetlana Lazebnik. 2015. Flickr30k entities: Collecting region-to-phrase correspondences for richer image-to-sentence models. In Proceedings of the IEEE international conference on computer vision, pages 2641–2649, Santiago, Chile.

Di Qi, Lin Su, Jia Song, Edward Cui, Taroon Bharti, and Arun Sacheti. 2020. Imagebert: Cross-modal pre-training with large-scale weak-supervised image-text data. arXiv preprint arXiv:2001.07966.

Sol Rogers. 2019. Seven reasons why eye-tracking will fundamentally change vr. https://www.forbes.com/sites/solrogers/2019/02/05/seven-reasons-why-eye-tracking-will-fundamentally-change-vr/. Accessed: 2021-01-05.

Amanpreet Singh, Vedanuj Goswami, and Devi Parikh. 2020. Are we pretraining it right? Digging deeper into visio-linguistic pretraining. arXiv preprint arXiv:2004.08744.

Shengli Song, Haitao Huang, and Tongxiao Ruan. 2019. Abstractive text summarization using lstm-cnn based deep learning. Multimedia Tools and Applications, 78(1):857–875.

Ekta Sood, Simon Tannert, Philipp Müller, and Andreas Bulling. 2020. Improving natural language processing tasks with human gaze-guided neural attention. arXiv preprint arXiv:2010.07891.

Robyn Speer, Joshua Chin, and Catherine Havasi. 2017. Conceptnet 5.5: An open multilingual graph of general knowledge. In Proceedings of the AAAI Conference on Artificial Intelligence, volume 31, San Francisco, CA, USA.

Niklas Wilming, Selim Onat, José P Ossandón, Alper Açık, Tim C Kietzmann, Kai Kaspar, Ricardo R Gameiro, Alexandra Vormberg, and Peter König. 2017. An extensive dataset of eye movements during viewing of complex images. Scientific data, 4(1):1–11.

# Machine Translation Believability

**Marianna J. Martindale† Kevin Duh° Marine Carpuat‡**
†iSchool, ‡Dept. of Computer Science, University of Maryland, College Park, USA
°HLTCOE, Johns Hopkins University, Baltimore, USA
mmartind@umd.edu, kevinduh@cs.jhu.edu, marine@cs.umd.edu

## Abstract

Successful Machine Translation (MT) deployment requires understanding not only the intrinsic qualities of MT output, such as fluency and adequacy, but also user perceptions. Users who do not understand the source language respond to MT output based on their perception of the likelihood that the meaning of the MT output matches the meaning of the source text. We refer to this as *believability*. Output that is not believable may be off-putting to users, but believable MT output with incorrect meaning may mislead them. In this work, we study the relationship of believability to fluency and adequacy by applying traditional MT direct assessment protocols to annotate all three features on the output of neural MT systems. Quantitative analysis of these annotations shows that believability is closely related to but distinct from fluency, and initial qualitative analysis suggests that semantic features may account for the difference.

## 1 Introduction

Past work on evaluating Machine Translation (MT) has focused on the intrinsic quality of the translation product without taking into account how translations are perceived by their users. Yet, some translation errors are more obvious than others, and have different consequences depending on what the translations are used for.

In this work, we take a user-centered view of MT evaluation, exploring one aspect of users' perception of MT: *believability* of the output, defined as a monolingual user's perception of the likelihood that the meaning of the MT output matches the meaning of the input, without understanding the source. Assessing the degree to which MT is believable acknowledges that users play an active role in interpreting its output, informed by their linguistic competence, their common sense reasoning abilities, and their knowledge of the world. What we learn from assessing believability can complement traditional evaluation methods to inform the deployment and even development of MT systems, particularly for gisting and communication use cases.

We first define believability of MT and contextualize it within prior work on credibility and MT evaluation. We apply MT direct assessment (DA) protocols to obtain human judgments of believability, annotating the output of neural machine translation (NMT) systems for three challenging language pairs (Arabic-, Farsi-, and Korean-to-English) with varying translation quality. These annotations show that believability is closely related to, but distinct from fluency. Preliminary qualitative analysis suggests that in addition to fluency features, believability is also influenced by semantic features.

We define *believability* as a user's perception of the likelihood that the meaning of a given MT output matches the meaning of the input, *without understanding the input*. Whether the user accepts the output unquestioningly or finds it unbelievable, their judgment will affect how they act on it, regardless of the true accuracy of the translation. For example, a Facebook user might be dubious of a translation from Chinese with the phrase "blowing a little more cow" and ask the author for clarification and learn that it is a literal translation of an idiom, "吹牛" (meaning to brag). Users may take more consequential action, such as the Israeli police officers who chose not to consult an Arabic speaker before arresting a man based on a believable mistranslation of his "good morning" Facebook post as "attack them" (Berger, 2017).

To illustrate how believability can be independent of adequacy, Table 1 shows examples of different levels of believability for translations at different levels of adequacy, based on our annotations. The translations on the right (More Adequate) convey key information: a named entity (*sputnik*), its



*Proceedings of the First Workshop on Bridging Human–Computer Interaction and Natural Language Processing*, pages 88–95
April 20, 2021. ©2021 Association for Computational Linguistics

| | Less Adequate | More Adequate |
|---|---|---|
| More Believable | "putnik" was an interactive film. | "Sputnik" was in the city center, the negative. It was not affected. |
| Less Believable | spaghetti, the nigerian was in the middle of the city, he didn't touch it. | sputnik was downtown, didn't look, never touched. |

Table 1: Machine Translations of human translations of a line from a TED talk discussing the loss of film negatives in a fire (Hoffman, 2008). One film "Sputnik" was spared from the fire because it was not in the building. Original text: *"Sputnik" was downtown, the negative. It wasn't touched.*

location (*downtown*), and the fact that it was not affected, but a user might not accept the information in the bottom-right translation because it is not believable. The less adequate translations (left) are missing important information and also include incorrect information. The bottom-left translation is not believable so a monolingual user would not be misled by it. However, the more believable top-left translation might mislead a monolingual user.

Because these judgments are based on perception, they may be more subjective than traditional MT DA features. We control for some factors that may affect believability (Section 3), resulting in annotations that are similarly reliable to the DA features (Section 4).

## 2 Related Work

Although believability is an unexplored aspect of MT, there is prior work outside of MT on the general concept of *credibility*. Common elements of credibility include source, media, and message credibility (Rieh and Danielson, 2007). For MT, we can think of the MT provider as the source, the interface through which the MT is viewed as the medium, and the output itself as the message or content. All of these aspects likely affect the credibility of deployed MT systems, but our investigation of MT believability is focused on the content (MT output). Some intrinsic content features addressed in the credibility literature that may affect MT believability include reasonableness (Liu, 2004; Kim and Oh, 2009; Kim, 2010; John et al., 2011) and grammatical errors (Fogg et al., 2001; Everard and Galletta, 2005; Metzger et al., 2010; Chesney and Su, 2010; John et al., 2011).

Reasonableness is a semantic feature encompassing elements of plausibility, logic, and internal consistency. These elements are related to previously studied concepts in the Computational Linguistics literature: semantic plausibility, commonsense reasoning, and discourse coherence. Semantic plausibility can be thought of as, "whether in an ordinary real-life situation (not "fairy-tale" circumstances) the sentence could be reasonably uttered" (Kruszewski et al., 2016). If the source text is expected to reflect "ordinary real-life," the output should be plausible to be believable. MT output may also be unbelievable if it violates commonsense reasoning, a challenging element of Natural Language Understanding (Mostafazadeh et al., 2016). Lack of discourse coherence might likewise signal unbelievable translations. For document generation, improving the consistency of generated documents makes it harder for human subjects to distinguish automatically generated text from real text (Karuna et al., 2018).

Grammatical errors are related to *fluency*, a traditional MT quality evaluation feature. Fluency has been defined as a judgment of "whether the translation reads like good English...without knowing the accuracy of the content," and is typically combined with *adequacy*, an assessment of "the degree to which the information in a professional translation can be found in an MT (or control) output of the same text" (White et al., 1994). A user who cannot understand the source cannot judge adequacy, but may use expectations based on features like fluency and reasonableness to guess. Believability could thus be seen as *predicted adequacy* via a *human cognitive process* with inputs from surface features of the output such as fluency and semantic cues from context.

Two other Computational Linguistics concepts that relate to both reasonableness and grammatical errors may affect believability: acceptability and comprehensibility. In empirical linguistics, acceptability judgments measure users' linguistic competence (Schütze, 2016). While acceptability is primarily used to observe grammatical knowledge, judgments are not limited to grammaticality in practice: "semantic plausibility, various types of processing difficulties, and so on, can individually or jointly cause grammaticality and acceptability to come apart" (Lau et al., 2017). These breakdowns can lead to issues with comprehensibility. Popović (2020) cites comprehensibility as a key factor in misleadingness of MT output: if a user cannot understand the text, they cannot be misled by it. Similarly, if they cannot understand it, the user is unlikely to believe that the translation is correct.

## 3 Annotating Believability

To understand the relationships between believability and traditional MT quality criteria (fluency and adequacy), we hired professionals to annotate MT output for these characteristics in tasks based on the fluency and adequacy DA methods of Graham et al. (2013) and Bojar et al. (2016). The annotated data sets are available at: `https://github.com/mjmartindale/mt_believability`.

**Annotators** Our annotators were salaried translators with proficiency levels of at least Advanced on the ACTFL scale (ACTFL, 2012) rather than MT researchers or crowd workers as in WMT (Barrault et al., 2019). Because they were not paid per item, they were willing to spend significant time on each item, averaging 15 items in 30 minutes. We believe this reflects more attention to detail as indicated by the correlation between annotators (see Section 4). We note that factors such as foreign language proficiency may affect believability judgments. Further work with a wider variety of annotators is needed to identify and quantify those effects.

**Tasks** We followed segment-level DA scoring best practices established by WMT (Barrault et al., 2019). The fluency and adequacy questions were taken directly from WMT16 (Bojar et al., 2016). The believability question uses our definition of believability with an introductory phrase to assure the annotator that we understand that it is not possible to truly evaluate the meaning without the source: "Even without having seen the source text, I believe the *meaning* of this translation is likely to match the *meaning* of the original." Annotations were performed using the Turkle[1] annotation platform. Screenshots of the annotation interface are provided in Appendix B.

Long documents were broken up into salient chunks and segments were annotated in their original order to provide discourse context, as in WMT19 "Segment Rating + Document Context" (Barrault et al., 2019). For each chunk, annotators first scored fluency and believability based only on the MT output. They then scored the same segments for adequacy given both source and output.

**Annotations** For each segment, we calculate a z-score and a label for each feature. We calculate scores following Bojar et al. (2018). Each annotator's raw scores are converted to z-scores based on their own mean and standard deviation, and the z-scores for each segment are averaged across annotators. Segments with positive z-scores are labeled TRUE and negative z-scores are labeled FALSE.

**Test Data** We chose a test set that is comparable across three typologically different languages with different amounts of training data. Our test data comes from The Multi-Target TED Talks Task (MTTT)–a collection of bitexts across 20 languages (Duh, 2018). The test set is fully sentence parallel with original talk transcripts as the English and human translations for the other languages. We use the non-English translations in MTTT as "source" and machine translate into English. In the test set, there are 29 talks totalling 1,982 segments, however, we exclude one talk ("Nellie McKay sings 'Clonie'") that is too poetic for MT. The final set is 1,976 segments.

**MT Systems** Because our goal is to examine *segments* annotated for believability, fluency, and adequacy judgments rather than to *compare* systems, we need MT that will produce outputs across a range of quality. Output that is inadequate but believable is of particular interest, so we rely on estimates of the distribution of "fluently inadequate" translations on MTTT from Martindale et al. (2019) to inform our choice of models. They estimated that fluently inadequate translations were most frequent in the "general" NMT models, trained on out-of-domain data. We use their Arabic, Farsi, and Korean "general" models to capture the range of training data sizes and output quality we believe will provide interesting examples for our analysis. The training data is 49M, 6.2M, and 1.4M segments in Arabic, Farsi, and Korean, respectively. The systems are built in Sockeye (Hieber et al., 2017) using the 'SockeyeNMT rm1' settings from the MTTT leaderboard[2]. The resulting systems achieved BLEU (Papineni et al., 2002) scores of 26.6 for Arabic, 22.2 for Farsi and 11.6 for Korean.

[1]https://github.com/hltcoe/turkle

[2]www.cs.jhu.edu/ kevinduh/a/multitarget-tedtalks/

| | Arabic | | | Farsi | | | Korean | | |
|---|---|---|---|---|---|---|---|---|---|
| | FL | BL | AD | FL | BL | AD | FL | BL | AD |
| Mean Corr. | 0.698 | 0.689 | 0.728 | 0.809 | 0.793 | 0.830 | 0.773 | 0.754 | 0.793 |
| Std dev | 0.137 | 0.122 | 0.129 | 0.087 | 0.099 | 0.083 | 0.112 | 0.120 | 0.076 |

Table 2: Average correlation with the mean for fluency (FL), believability (BL), and adequacy (AD)

| | **Arabic** | **Farsi** | **Korean** | **All** |
|---|---|---|---|---|
| **FL-BL** | 0.89 | 0.96 | 0.97 | 0.94 |
| **BL-AD** | 0.71 | 0.74 | 0.75 | 0.73 |
| **FL-AD** | 0.62 | 0.73 | 0.72 | 0.69 |

Table 3: Pearson correlation between fluency (FL), believability (BL), and adequacy (AD).

| | **%Arabic** | **%Farsi** | **%Korean** | **%All** |
|---|---|---|---|---|
| **Fluent** | 57.9 | 50.4 | 49.4 | 52.5 |
| **Believable** | 61.0 | 51.2 | 49.0 | 53.7 |
| **Adequate** | 59.4 | 52.4 | 44.1 | 52.0 |
| **BL+/AD-** | 25.9 | 19.4 | 21.8 | 22.2 |

Table 4: Percent of segments with each label (rows 1-3) and percent believable but inadequate (BL+/AD-) segments (row 4).

| | **Arabic** | **Farsi** | **Korean** | **All** |
|---|---|---|---|---|
| **BL+/FL+** | 92.1 | 93.8 | 93.8 | 93.1 |
| **BL-/FL+** | 8.0 | 6.2 | 6.3 | 6.9 |
| **BL+/FL-** | 18.3 | 8.0 | 5.4 | 10.1 |
| **BL-/FL-** | 81.7 | 92.1 | 94.6 | 89.9 |

Table 5: Percent of fluent (FL+) and disfluent (FL-) segments that are believable (BL+) or unbelievable (BL-)

## 4 Quantitative Analysis

**Annotation Statistics** 63 translators participated in the annotation process. Korean-to-English and Arabic-to-English had the most annotators (26 and 27) and highest number of annotators per segment (10 for Korean and at least 7 for Arabic). There were three annotators whose annotations were deemed unreliable due to low correlation with the mean (< 0.5). Only 10 annotators were available for Farsi, resulting in fewer annotators per segment (median: 4) but more segments per annotator (median: 802), making the z-score process more reliable. After excluding the questionable annotators, we see strong correlation of individual annotator scores with the mean as shown in Table 2. We see similar average correlation with the mean between fluency and believability and small variance across features. This suggests that among our annotators believability is no more subjective than fluency.

**Label Distribution** Although the distribution of labels is specific to this set of output, it provides context for the other results. The first three rows of Table 4 show the percent of segments with each label. We see that the percent positive examples for each label roughly relates to the system BLEU score, with Arabic having the highest and Korean the lowest.

**Feature Relationships** Table 3 shows the Pearson correlations between the scores for fluency (FL), believability (BL), and adequacy (AD). The BL-AD relationship is important because inadequate believable translations may mislead monolingual users. The BL-AD correlation is higher than the FL-AD correlation across all languages. This may reflect the influence of context: adequate segments may fit the context well enough to be believable even if not fluent. The same trend is reflected in the fourth row of Table 4, BL+/AD-. Most inadequate translations are not believable, but 19-25% are potentially misleading. Arabic has the highest BL+/AD-. The larger training data may improve both translation and generation, improving overall quality but enabling more believable errors. However, the lower quality Korean also has a higher percent potentially misleading than Farsi. This could mean that all results are idiosyncratic to this data or perhaps the relationship is bimodal.

As expected, FL-BL has the strongest correlation. This indicates that the two features are closely linked, but they are not identical. Table 5 illustrates this distinction. The top two rows show the percent of fluent (FL+) translations that are believable (BL+) and unbelievable (BL-) while the bottom two rows show the percent of disfluent (FL-) transla-

| FL | BL | Adequate | Inadequate |
|---|---|---|---|
| ✓ | ✓ | I mean, I'm nervous enough. | this is my lady. |
| ✓ | ✗ | I am the emperor of orange. I am emperor of orange. | we need a human body. we should eat it. |
| ✗ | ✓ | there was a fire on 9 days ago. | three days later, this disappeared, and a week later, there was no complaints. |
| ✗ | ✗ | hoping to attract all peoples' minds and be the first to overcome space. | you can see how hard it is to carry kumin ververbert with a bible in 1455. |

Table 6: Example output for different segments for each combination of fluency, believability, and adequacy.

tions that are (un)believable. If one were to attempt to identify potentially misleading translations using fluency as a proxy for believability, as in Martindale et al. (2019), 6-8% of translations that are fluent but not believable would be incorrectly labeled as misleading, while nearly 20% of segments from the Arabic system that are believable but not fluent would be missed.

## 5 Qualitative Analysis

Based on informal examination of a random sample of segments, we find that those labeled as unbelievable often fail semantically, with strange phrases (e.g., "kidney steel", "iron code"), illogical clauses (e.g., "the only natural thing is that my son is the vending machine"), or unlikely argument structure (e.g., "to prove that it seems impossible", "...a state of treason for a raven, which explains that he's cute"). Unbelievable translations may also be grammatical but unintelligible (e.g., "if you want a long time, I'm actually doing something about it."). By contrast, segments labeled as disfluent may include grammatical errors and/or awkward, non-idiomatic phrases such as "he set me a date" or "in a direct time". These observations support our intuition that believability is more influenced by semantic features than fluency is, but further analysis is needed. Additional examples for each combination of fluency, believability, and adequacy are shown in Table 6.

## 6 Conclusions and Future Work

This work used traditional NLP annotation methods to measure users' perceptions of *believability* of MT output. These methods allow us to identify broad relationships between believability and traditional MT quality metrics, fluency and adequacy, showing that believability is strongly correlated with fluency and somewhat correlated with adequacy. Preliminary qualitative analysis of examples where believability and fluency judgments disagreed suggests that semantic features can overwhelm grammatical features in believability judgments.

A full qualitative analysis of the believability-annotated examples would suggest features that may have influenced annotator's judgments and could indicate approaches that may be effective in automatically predicting believability. Believability used alone could enable an adversarial MT system to deliberately mask errors and produce misleading output, but believability predictions combined with MT quality estimation (Specia et al., 2009) could be used to flag potentially misleading output.

Because believability is a user-centric metric, gaining a complete understanding would require more user-centric methods. The annotator agreement in our results may indicate that believability is less subjective than one might expect, or it may simply indicate that our annotators were fairly homogeneous. A user study could not only tell us exactly what features were most salient in which contexts, but could indicate whether demographic features such as age or education affect perceptions of believability.

## References

ACTFL. 2012. ACTFL Proficiency Guidelines 2012.

Loïc Barrault, Ondrej Bojar, Marta R Costa-jussà, Christian Federmann, Mark Fishel, Yvette Graham, Barry Haddow, Matthias Huck, Philipp Koehn, Shervin Malmasi, et al. 2019. Findings of the 2019 conference on machine translation (wmt19). In *Proceedings of the Fourth Conference on Machine Translation*, volume 2, pages 1–61.

Yotam Berger. 2017. Israel Arrests Palestinian Because Facebook Translated 'Good Morning' to 'Attack Them'. *Haaretz*. [Online; accessed 6-Dec-2017].

Ondřej Bojar, Rajen Chatterjee, Christian Federmann, Yvette Graham, Barry Haddow, Matthias Huck, Antonio Jimeno Yepes, Philipp Koehn, Varvara Logacheva, Christof Monz, Matteo Negri, Aurelie Neveol, Mariana Neves, Martin Popel, Matt Post, Raphael Rubino, Carolina Scarton, Lucia Specia, Marco Turchi, Karin Verspoor, and Marcos Zampieri. 2016. Findings of the 2016 Conference on Machine Translation. In *Proceedings of the First Conference on Machine Translation*, pages 131–198, Berlin, Germany. Association for Computational Linguistics.

Ondřej Bojar, Christian Federmann, Mark Fishel, Yvette Graham, Barry Haddow, Matthias Huck, Philipp Koehn, and Christof Monz. 2018. Findings of the 2018 conference on machine translation (wmt18). In *Proceedings of the Third Conference on Machine Translation*, pages 272–307, Belgium, Brussels. Association for Computational Linguistics.

Thomas Chesney and Daniel K. S. Su. 2010. The impact of anonymity on weblog credibility. *International Journal of Human-Computer Studies*, 68(10):710–718.

Kevin Duh. 2018. The multitarget ted talks task. `http://www.cs.jhu.edu/~kevinduh/a/multitarget-tedtalks/`.

Andrea Everard and Dennis F. Galletta. 2005. How Presentation Flaws Affect Perceived Site Quality, Trust, and Intention to Purchase from an Online Store. *Journal of Management Information Systems*, 22(3):56–95.

B. J. Fogg, Jonathan Marshall, Othman Laraki, Alex Osipovich, Chris Varma, Nicholas Fang, Jyoti Paul, Akshay Rangnekar, John Shon, Preeti Swani, and Marissa Treinen. 2001. What makes Web sites credible? a report on a large quantitative study. In *Proceedings of the SIGCHI Conference on Human Factors in Computing Systems*, CHI '01, pages 61–68, New York, NY, USA. Association for Computing Machinery.

Yvette Graham, Timothy Baldwin, Alistair Moffat, and Justin Zobel. 2013. Continuous measurement scales in human evaluation of machine translation. In *Proceedings of the 7th Linguistic Annotation Workshop & Interoperability with Discourse*, pages 33–41.

Felix Hieber, Tobias Domhan, Michael Denkowski, David Vilar, Artem Sokolov, Ann Clifton, and Matt Post. 2017. Sockeye: A toolkit for neural machine translation. *arXiv preprint arXiv:1712.05690*.

David Hoffman. 2008. David Hoffman: What happens when you lose everything?

Blooma Mohan John, Alton Yeow-Kuan Chua, and Dion Hoe-Lian Goh. 2011. What Makes a High-Quality User-Generated Answer? *IEEE Internet Computing*, 15(1):66–71.

Prakruthi Karuna, Hemant Purohit, Ozlem Uzuner, Sushil Jajodia, and Rajesh Ganesan. 2018. Enhancing cohesion and coherence of fake text to improve believability for deceiving cyber attackers. In *Proceedings of the First International Workshop on Language Cognition and Computational Models*, pages 31–40.

Soojung Kim. 2010. Questioners' credibility judgments of answers in a social question and answer site. *Information Research*, 15(2):15–2.

Soojung Kim and Sanghee Oh. 2009. Users' relevance criteria for evaluating answers in a social Q&A site. *Journal of the American Society for Information Science and Technology*, 60(4):716–727.

Germán Kruszewski, Denis Paperno, Raffaella Bernardi, and Marco Baroni. 2016. There Is No Logical Negation Here, But There Are Alternatives: Modeling Conversational Negation with Distributional Semantics. *Computational Linguistics*, 42(4):637–660.

Jey Han Lau, Alexander Clark, and Shalom Lappin. 2017. Grammaticality, Acceptability, and Probability: A Probabilistic View of Linguistic Knowledge. *Cognitive Science*, 41(5):1202–1241.

Ziming Liu. 2004. Perceptions of credibility of scholarly information on the web. *Information Processing & Management*, 40(6):1027–1038.

Marianna J Martindale, Marine Carpuat, Kevin Duh, and Paul McNamee. 2019. Identifying fluently inadequate output in neural and statistical machine translation. In *Proceedings of Machine Translation Summit XVII Volume 1: Research Track*, pages 233–243.

Miriam J. Metzger, Andrew J. Flanagin, and Ryan B. Medders. 2010. Social and Heuristic Approaches to Credibility Evaluation Online. *Journal of Communication*, 60(3):413–439.

Nasrin Mostafazadeh, Nathanael Chambers, Xiaodong He, Devi Parikh, Dhruv Batra, Lucy Vanderwende, Pushmeet Kohli, and James Allen. 2016. A Corpus and Cloze Evaluation for Deeper Understanding of Commonsense Stories. In *Proceedings of the 2016 Conference of the North American Chapter of the Association for Computational Linguistics: Human Language Technologies*, pages 839–849, San Diego, California. Association for Computational Linguistics.

Kishore Papineni, Salim Roukos, Todd Ward, and Wei-Jing Zhu. 2002. BLEU: A method for automatic evaluation of machine translation. In *Proceedings of the 40th Annual Meeting of the Association for Computational Linguistics*, Philadelphia, PA.

Maja Popović. 2020. Relations between comprehensibility and adequacy errors in machine translation output. In *Proceedings of the 24th Conference on Computational Natural Language Learning*, pages 256–264.

Soo Young Rieh and David R. Danielson. 2007. Credibility: A multidisciplinary framework. *Annual review of information science and technology*, 41(1):307–364.

Carson Schütze. 2016. *The empirical base of linguistics: Grammaticality judgments and linguistic methodology*. Classics in Linguistics. Language Science Press, Berlin.

Lucia Specia, Nicola Cancedda, Marc Dymetman, Marco Turchi, and Nello Cristianini. 2009. Estimating the sentence-level quality of Machine Translation systems. In *In EAMT*, pages 28–35.

John S. White, Theresa O'Connell, and Francis O'Mara. 1994. The ARPA MT Evaluation Methodologies: Evolution, Lessons, and Future Approaches. In *Proceedings of the First Conference of the Association for Machine Translation in the Americas*, pages 193–205, Columbia, Maryland, USA.

## A Additional Annotation Statistics

Statistics on the number of segments per annotator and annotations per segment are provided in tables 7 and 8.

| | Arabic | Farsi | Korean |
|---|---|---|---|
| Annotators | 27 | 10 | 26 |
| Min segs | 9 | 47 | 28 |
| Mean segments | 822 | 760 | |
| Median segs | 525 | 802 | 400 |
| Max segs | 1925 | 1976 | 1976 |

Table 7: Segments annotated per annotator

| Annotators | Arabic | Farsi | Korean |
|---|---|---|---|
| 2+ | 1976 | 1976 | 1976 |
| 4+ | 1976 | 1439 | 1976 |
| 8+ | 1976 | 48 | 1976 |
| 10 | 1713 | 0 | 1976 |
| Mean Annotations | 3 | 4 | 10 |
| Median | 9 | 4 | 10 |
| Max | 10 | 8 | 10 |

Table 8: Annotations per segment

## B Annotation Interface

Figures 1 and 2 are screenshots of the annotation interface for the monolingual fluency and believability task and the bilingual adequacy task.

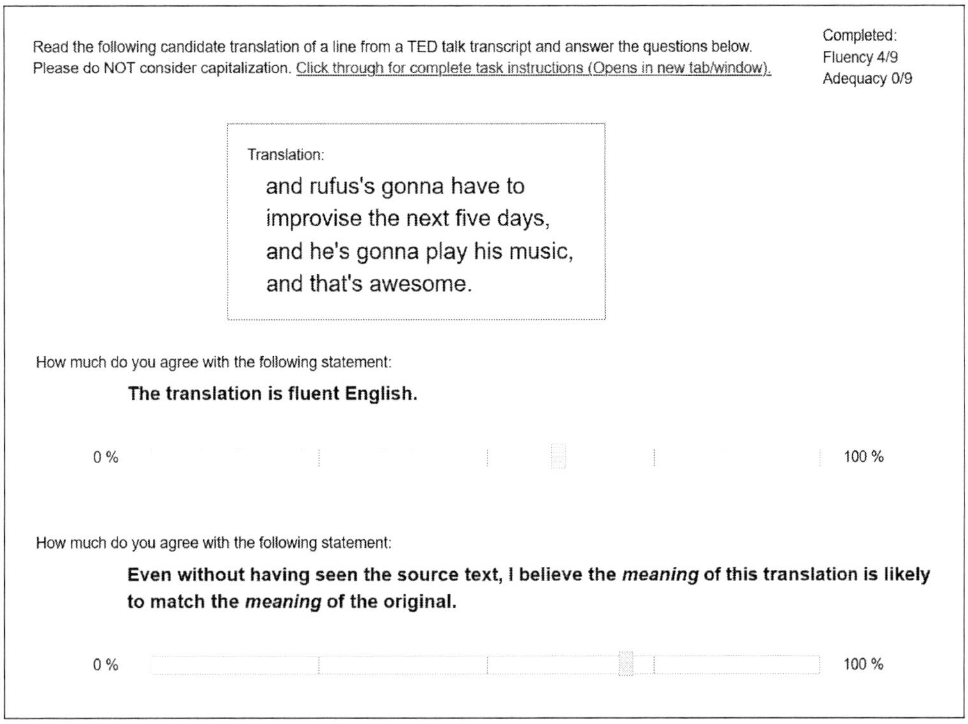


Figure 1: Example question from monolingual annotation phase, fluency and believability

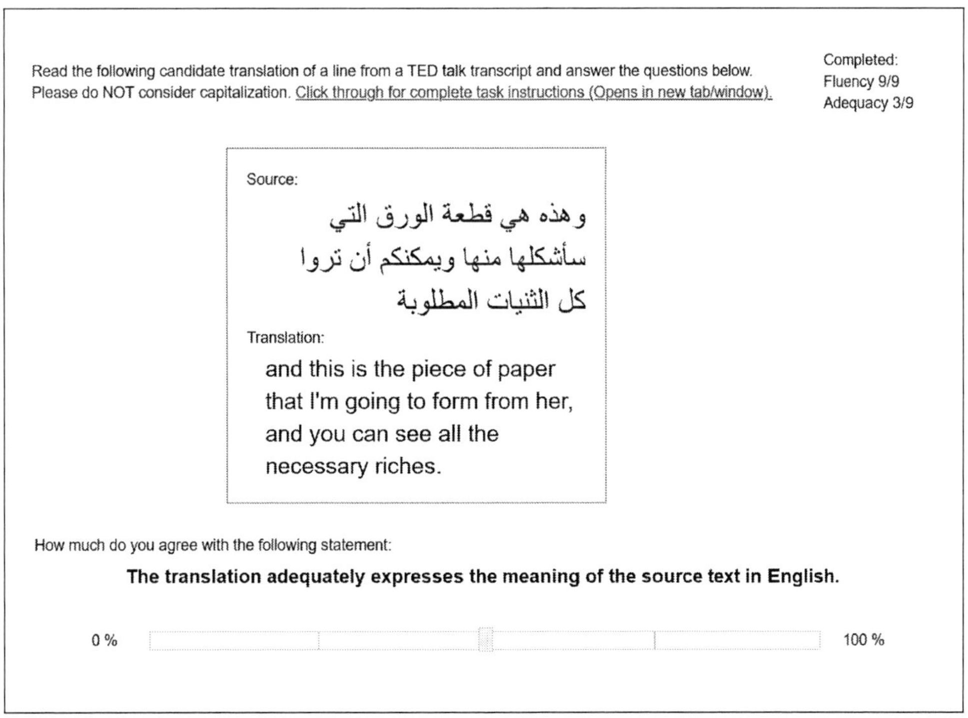


Figure 2: Example question from bilingual annotation phase with adequacy question

# Provocation: Contestability in Large-Scale Interactive NLP Systems

**Tanushree Mitra**
The Information School
University of Washington
tmitra@uw.edu

## 1 Overview

Designing computational systems for language analysis means, increasingly, designing for interactions with natural language processing (NLP) algorithms. For example, sentiment analysis, topic modeling, toxicity classification, and other language modeling techniques have become common in interactive user-facing systems. These developments raise novel, complex challenges, both in terms of designing such systems and user's interactions with them (Baumer et al., 2020). Accordingly researchers have advocated for rethinking interactive ML systems that involve users at every stage of the system (Amershi et al., 2014). For example, Horvitz' principles for effective "mixed-initiative" systems include querying users about goals and preferences and scoping system precision to match users' needs (Horvitz, 1999). Other approaches include value-centered design (Knobel and Bowker, 2011), transparency in design (Ananny and Crawford, 2018) and more recently contestability (Hirsch et al., 2017). Despite these various proposed approaches for ML-based systems, situating the discussion in the context of interactive NLP systems, in particular, has remained elusive. Each of these design principles (mixed-initiative, value-centered, transparency, contestability) can claim it's own spot for a full-day workshop discussion. Hence, to scope the conversation for this workshop, we will primarily focus on **contestability in NLP systems** in this provocation piece.

**Contestability:** The notion of contestability originates from the need for contesting or challenging machine predictions (Hirsch et al., 2017; Kluttz et al., 2018). For example, contestability in recidivism prediction systems or health behavior prediction systems. Here we argue the need for exploring contestability in large-scale online systems and in particular NLP systems. With respect to language-based systems, consider the Perspective API developed by Google's Counter-Abuse Technology team to identify toxic language in text. The technology has now been integrated within the New York Times comment interface to facilitate large-scale moderation of potentially toxic and obscene comments on news stories. However, the same technology has also incorrectly discovered a positive correlation between identity terms containing information on race or sexual orientation (e.g., the phrase "I am a gay black woman" received a high toxicity score) (developers.google.com). But we do not yet have an established way to contest these decisions made by NLP algorithms integrated within large socio-technical systems (in this case a news platforms with widespread readership).

Perhaps the closest form of contestability research in large-scale online systems relates to efforts around auditing algorithmic systems for bias (Bozdag, 2013; Chen et al., 2018), discrimination (Chen et al., 2016; Hannak et al., 2014; Mikians et al., 2012), and fairness (Dwork et al., 2012). While audit studies is a way to detect undesirable behavior in large-scale "black-boxed" Web systems, allowing users to meaningfully *contest* such undesirable behavior will offer ways to help people not only make sense of an algorithm's behavior, but also restore human agency in systems that are intertwining humans and non-human agents (Ananny and Crawford, 2018). *How can we design for contestability in large-scale online NLP systems? What are the goals when designing for contestability in online systems? What are the challenges and limitations of the contestability ideal?*

## 2 Designing Contestability in Large Online NLP Systems

The first step in designing for contestability is to layout the goals we would like to achieve when



*Proceedings of the First Workshop on Bridging Human–Computer Interaction and Natural Language Processing*, pages 96–100
April 20, 2021. ©2021 Association for Computational Linguistics

bringing the ideal of contestability in large-scale online socio-technical systems driven by language technologies. In most predictive systems, the goal is to contest a machine prediction in an attempt to correct a wrong decision. For example, in healthcare systems, contestability strives to improve the accuracy of ML models by deploying the system among expert users and then soliciting feedback from them (Hirsch et al., 2017). However, the goal in large online social systems is more nuanced. For example, in an online ride sharing system a driver might want to contest their ride and route recommendation, a rider might want to contest the tip suggestion or the matched driver, resulting in a multi-stakeholder contestability problem. In this particular case, it is a complex assemblage of the algorithm and the two stake holders (the driver and the rider) who are both using the same instance of the ride sharing platform.

Here I outline two examples of NLP-based online systems along with the phenomenon that could be contested and the contestation goal.

**Contestability in Moderation Systems.** Content moderation is a predominant practice in almost all social media platforms, be it, Twitter, Facebook, Reddit, and is now increasingly common in news platforms (e.g. Perspective APIs usage in NYT comment moderation interface). Most content moderation systems are based on linguistic models (see (Gunasekara and Nejadgholi, 2018) for a review). However, none currently have designs in place where a user can appeal against content removal. If the *goal* is to contest moderation practices, how do we design to meet that goal? Some social media platforms, like Reddit, have a two-tier governance structure, the first tier enforced by the platform's content policy and a 2nd tier rule enforcement set by the human moderators within the community. Such differences in governance structures across online platforms make it almost impossible to come up with a "one size fits all" contestation goal when building a language-based moderation system.

**Contestability in Informatin Retrieval Systems.** Language models are fundamental to driving online information retrieval systems, such as search and recommendation systems (see (Zhai, 2008; Hiemstra, 2001; Liu and Croft, 2004)). For a regular user, online search and recommender systems have become an integral part of their daily lives. Despite their increasingly important role in selecting, presenting, ranking, and recommending what information is considered most relevant for us—a key aspect governing our ability to meaningfully participate in public life (Gillespie, 2014), there is no notion of whether this information is credible or whether the returned results are re-inforcing existing societal biases. Neither do users have any means to contest or challenge to understand *why* they are seeing *what* they are seeing on search platforms and their recommendation feeds. The lack of contestability in search platform coupled with an unwavering trust placed in search engines can together lead to misinformed citizenry. Our goal for including contestability in search systems, would be to contest potential inaccurate results, unreasonable rankings (e.g., a low credible alternative news source ranked higher than a reputed journalistic source), inaccurate recommendations (for e.g., YouTube recommending more pro-conspiracy videos after user watches one anti-vaccine video) or biased results.

### 2.1 *Why, When*, and *How* to Contest

What are the ways in which we can design for contestability in online systems? Does contestability help users improve their understanding and trust of large-scale online systems? One possibility is to draw inspiration from the design of intelligibility in context-aware systems (Lim et al., 2009). Of particular interest are end-user programming systems which allowed users to ask questions when their expectations were not met (Ko and Myers, 2004). Users asked *why did* questions when something unexpected happened and *why not* questions when something expected did not occur (Ko and Myers, 2004, 2009). Another line of work that is relevant is (Kulesza et al., 2011, 2009) *What You See is What You Test* for Machine Learning (WYSIWYT/ML) method for systematic testing of machine learning applications. WYSIWYT/ML offers three key functionalities: 1) *advises* the user about which predictions to test, 2) *contributes* more tests "like" the user's, 3) *measures* how much of the assistant's reasoning has been tested, and 4) continually *monitors* over time whether previous testing still "covers" new behaviors learned. Inspired from these approaches, here I lay a list of intuitive questions that can inform the design of contestability. By no means, this list is exhaustive. The hope is that discussions at the workshop will refine and expand the list.

1. **Why**: Why did the online system do X, where X can be *recommend, suggest, rank, moderate, etc.*?

2. **Why Not**: Why did the system not do Y? For example, in designing contestability for content moderation in social platforms, a user can contest why did the system did not remove this other post?

3. **What if**: What would the system do if Z happens? For example, what would Amazon recommend if I bought the lower ranked product from its ranked product list?

4. **How to**: How can I get the system to do A, given the current context? For example, how can I get this ride sharing service to pair me with a female driver, given that I am a woman and I am traveling in a region notorious for crimes against woman?

## 3 Challenges for Contestability in Large Online NLP Systems

Infusing contestability in complex online systems can lead to unforeseen challenges. The ideal of contestability as a means to provide agency to users can be limited in multiple ways. Here I list a few.

**Contestability can unintentionally occlude.** Ananny and Crawford (Ananny and Crawford, 2018) in their critical interrogation of the ideal of transparency argue that transparency to promote understandibility of black-box ML systems can backfire in various ways, one of them being intentional occlusion—"visibility produces such great quantities of information that important pieces of information become inadvertently hidden in the detritus of the information made visible." Contestability can also result in similar occlusion. For example, an online system that offers too many options for contesting the system's decision may unnecessarily distract the user from the central information that the system intends to offer.

**Contestability can reinforce pre-existing biases.** Considering that most algorithms driving large-scale online systems are personalized—i.e., they serve results based on user's past behavior—such personalization tend to re-enforce pre-existing biases. Imagine a factuality model that sits within an online system and determines the credibility of content based on linguistic features (such models already exist in the literature; see (Soni et al., 2014) and (Mitra et al., 2017). Offering real-time corrections every time the user contests search results that goes against their pre-existing beliefs, often act as mandates and can backfire by inadvertently provoking users into attitude consistent misperceptions (Garrett and Weeks, 2013). Another unforeseen scenario can occur for certain classes of search queries, popularly known as "data voids"—search terms for which the available relevant data is limited or non-existent (Golebiewski and boyd, 2018). Allowing the user to contest and introduce problematic corrections into the system defeats the purpose of contestability in such scenarios.

**Contestability has temporal limitations: When to introduce contestability?** Decisions about when to allow contestability in an online social system can get too complex too quickly to reach any useful design decision. A large-scale social system has multiple stakeholders, each of whose contestability action at any point in time can effect the system and in turn the contestability decision of the next action. For example, a language model working in the moderation interface of a news website has to balance between several stakeholders: the *users* commenting on the news story, the *moderator* managing the commenting system, the *reporter* who wrote the story, and the *editor* who reviewed the story. Moreover online systems are continually changing over time as data are being generated, interacted, and added by users, and as the number of users interacting with the system change. Thus when thinking about designing for contestability in multi-stakeholder online systems, the notion of temporal dimension is key.

I hope that the workshop will provide opportunities to brainstorm on these complex questions and stir new questions in the domain.

## References

Saleema Amershi, Maya Cakmak, William Bradley Knox, and Todd Kulesza. 2014. Power to the people: The role of humans in interactive machine learning. *Ai Magazine*, 35(4):105–120.

Mike Ananny and Kate Crawford. 2018. Seeing without knowing: Limitations of the transparency ideal and its application to algorithmic accountability. *new media & society*, 20(3):973–989.

Eric PS Baumer, Drew Siedel, Lena McDonnell, Jiayun Zhong, Patricia Sittikul, and Micki McGee.

2020. Topicalizer: reframing core concepts in machine learning visualization by co-designing for interpretivist scholarship. *Human–Computer Interaction*, 35(5-6):452–480.

Engin Bozdag. 2013. Bias in algorithmic filtering and personalization. *Ethics and information technology*, 15(3):209–227.

Le Chen, Ruijun Ma, Anikó Hannák, and Christo Wilson. 2018. Investigating the impact of gender on rank in resume search engines. In *Proceedings of the 2018 CHI Conference on Human Factors in Computing Systems*, page 651. ACM.

Le Chen, Alan Mislove, and Christo Wilson. 2016. An empirical analysis of algorithmic pricing on amazon marketplace. In *Proceedings of the 25th International Conference on World Wide Web*, pages 1339–1349. International World Wide Web Conferences Steering Committee.

developers.google.com. Ml practicum: Fairness in perspective api. `https://developers.google.com/machine-learning/practica/fairness-indicators`. [Online; accessed 8-Jan-2021].

Cynthia Dwork, Moritz Hardt, Toniann Pitassi, Omer Reingold, and Richard Zemel. 2012. Fairness through awareness. In *Proceedings of the 3rd innovations in theoretical computer science conference*, pages 214–226. ACM.

R Kelly Garrett and Brian E Weeks. 2013. The promise and peril of real-time corrections to political misperceptions. In *Proc. CSCW*, pages 1047–1058. ACM.

Tarleton Gillespie. 2014. The relevance of algorithms. *Media technologies: Essays on communication, materiality, and society*, 167.

Michael Golebiewski and danah boyd. 2018. Data voids: Where missing data can easily be exploited.

Isuru Gunasekara and Isar Nejadgholi. 2018. A review of standard text classification practices for multi-label toxicity identification of online content. In *Proceedings of the 2nd workshop on abusive language online (ALW2)*, pages 21–25.

Aniko Hannak, Gary Soeller, David Lazer, Alan Mislove, and Christo Wilson. 2014. Measuring price discrimination and steering on e-commerce web sites. In *Proceedings of the 2014 conference on internet measurement conference*, pages 305–318. ACM.

Djoerd Hiemstra. 2001. *Using language models for information retrieval*. Citeseer.

Tad Hirsch, Kritzia Merced, Shrikanth Narayanan, Zac E Imel, and David C Atkins. 2017. Designing contestability: Interaction design, machine learning, and mental health. In *Proceedings of the 2017 Conference on Designing Interactive Systems*, pages 95–99. ACM.

Eric Horvitz. 1999. Principles of mixed-initiative user interfaces. In *Proceedings of the SIGCHI conference on Human Factors in Computing Systems*, pages 159–166.

Daniel Kluttz, Nitin Kohli, and Deirdre K Mulligan. 2018. Contestability and professionals: From explanations to engagement with algorithmic systems. *Available at SSRN 3311894*.

Cory Knobel and Geoffrey C Bowker. 2011. Values in design. *Communications of the ACM*, 54(7):26–28.

Andrew J Ko and Brad A Myers. 2004. Designing the whyline: a debugging interface for asking questions about program behavior. In *Proceedings of the SIGCHI conference on Human factors in computing systems*, pages 151–158. ACM.

Andrew J Ko and Brad A Myers. 2009. Finding causes of program output with the java whyline. In *Proceedings of the SIGCHI Conference on Human Factors in Computing Systems*, pages 1569–1578. ACM.

Todd Kulesza, Margaret Burnett, Simone Stumpf, Weng-Keen Wong, Shubhomoy Das, Alex Groce, Amber Shinsel, Forrest Bice, and Kevin McIntosh. 2011. Where are my intelligent assistant's mistakes? a systematic testing approach. In *International Symposium on End User Development*, pages 171–186. Springer.

Todd Kulesza, Weng-Keen Wong, Simone Stumpf, Stephen Perona, Rachel White, Margaret M Burnett, Ian Oberst, and Andrew J Ko. 2009. Fixing the program my computer learned: Barriers for end users, challenges for the machine. In *Proceedings of the 14th international conference on Intelligent user interfaces*, pages 187–196. ACM.

Brian Y Lim, Anind K Dey, and Daniel Avrahami. 2009. Why and why not explanations improve the intelligibility of context-aware intelligent systems. In *Proceedings of the SIGCHI Conference on Human Factors in Computing Systems*, pages 2119–2128. ACM.

Xiaoyong Liu and W Bruce Croft. 2004. Cluster-based retrieval using language models. In *Proceedings of the 27th annual international ACM SIGIR conference on Research and development in information retrieval*, pages 186–193.

Jakub Mikians, László Gyarmati, Vijay Erramilli, and Nikolaos Laoutaris. 2012. Detecting price and search discrimination on the internet. In *Proceedings of the 11th ACM Workshop on Hot Topics in Networks*, pages 79–84. acm.

Tanushree Mitra, Graham Wright, and Eric Gilbert. 2017. A parsimonious language model of social media credibility across disparate events. In *Proc. CSCW*.

Sandeep Soni, Tanushree Mitra, Eric Gilbert, and Jacob Eisenstein. 2014. Modeling factuality judgments in social media text. In *ACL (2)*, pages 415–420.

ChengXiang Zhai. 2008. Statistical language models for information retrieval. *Synthesis lectures on human language technologies*, 1(1):1–141.

# An IDR Framework of Opportunities and Barriers between HCI and NLP

**Nanna Inie** ✎
IT University of Copenhagen
2300 Denmark
nans@itu.dk

**Leon Derczynski** ✎
IT University of Copenhagen
2300 Denmark
leod@itu.dk

## Abstract

This paper presents a framework of opportunities and barriers/risks between the two research fields Natural Language Processing (NLP) and Human-Computer Interaction (HCI). The framework is constructed by following an interdisciplinary research-model (IDR), combining field-specific knowledge with existing work in the two fields. The resulting framework is intended as a departure point for discussion and inspiration for research collaborations.

## 1 Motivation

Research has long suggested that the fields of Natural Language Processing (NLP) and Human-Computer Interaction (HCI) could both benefit from each other's methods, analyses, and findings, e.g. De Angeli and Petrelli (2000); Ozkan and Paris (2002); Green et al. (2015); Hung (2014). Despite this, it is also regularly pointed out that overlaps between the fields are still rare (Karamanis et al., 2009; Munteanu et al., 2013; Yang, 2017).

Reasons put forward for this gap have included differences of methods and evaluations (Ozkan and Paris, 2002), a perception that language technology is not advanced enough for the processing required in HCI work (Munteanu et al., 2013), as well as lack of programming skills required to work with NLP: *"Deploying an NLP system typically requires a substantial amount of time from an expert NLP developer – normally, applications do not generalize and must be rebuilt, retrained, enhanced, and re-evaluated for each new task"* (Chapman et al., 2011). HCI may even suffer from being perceived as a "soft science", lacking quantitative results allocated merit equal to that in more mathematically founded computer science, e.g. Wang (2013).

✎: These authors contributed to the paper equally.

To better define this interface, this short paper presents a framework of opportunities and barriers/risks for both HCI and NLP in the combination of the two fields. We hope to inspire collaborations between researchers from both fields by presenting some practical gains in cross-pollination, as well as some of the potential pitfalls and challenges researchers might meet.

## 2 An IDR framework

Our interdisciplinary framework is presented in Table 1. It follows the approach described by CohenMiller and Pate (2019). They present a model for developing an interdisciplinary research (IDR) framework founded in two fields by identifying research topics, concepts, disciplines, theory, and terminology from each field. The objective is to create an integrated framework relevant to both.

The authors of this paper have backgrounds in HCI and NLP, respectively, and while we see potential in applying the distinct methods and analyses from both fields in the other field, we have focused especially on identifying common benefits; i.e. research *outputs* that benefit science and research in general, not only in one or the other field.

Our method is to debate and discuss research processes and methods, identifying differences (often in methods) and similarities (often in goals) between the fields. In the following, we attach some words to each of the topics in the framework.

## 3 Opportunities

### 3.1 Methods and analyses

It has been suggested before that NLP and HCI could benefit from applying each others' methods and analyses – by researchers in both fields, e.g. Munteanu et al. (2013); Ozkan and Paris (2002). Collaborations have been exemplified by specific cases, i.e. *applying NLP in clinical research* (Kara-



*Proceedings of the First Workshop on Bridging Human–Computer Interaction and Natural Language Processing*, pages 101–108
April 20, 2021. ©2021 Association for Computational Linguistics

<table>
<tr><th></th><th>Methods and analyses</th><th>Output</th></tr>
<tr><td>Opportunities, NLP</td><td>- Ethnographic methods<br>- Annotation processes<br>- Error analysis<br>- New abstractions<br>- Extra data layers</td><td rowspan="2">- Discoveries<br>- Quality analyses<br>- Artwork<br>- Network</td></tr>
<tr><td>Opportunities, HCI</td><td>- Automatic transcription<br>- Thematic classification and clustering<br>- Novel analysis tools</td></tr>
<tr><td>Barriers/risks, human</td><td>- Coding skills<br>- Detaching from quantitative methods<br>- Terminology<br>- Critical thinking</td><td rowspan="2">- Biases in data</td></tr>
<tr><td>Barriers/risks, technical</td><td>- Limited modalities (speech and text processing)<br>- Data access</td></tr>
</table>

Table 1: An IDR framework of opportunities and barriers/risks in the intersection of NLP and HCI research

manis et al., 2009), *developing language-controlled interfaces* (Munteanu et al., 2013), or *designing interactive documents* (Ozkan and Paris, 2002). In this framework, we have tried to focus on a broad view of methods from NLP which may be useful in HCI research and vice versa. For clarity and overview, we present a brief selection of topics which we found important or obvious. The framework could and should be expanded in use by researchers from both fields.

#### 3.1.1 Opportunities for NLP

**Ethnographic methods.** While NLP studies *natural* language and often reports findings about culture and human interaction, NLP rarely studies the contexts and realities of people. HCI has a strong tradition of researching to understand people and their behaviors and realities through methods of inquiry (Blomberg et al., 2009), as well as viewing behaviors as *situated* in a context which influences and is influenced by human actions (Suchman, 1987). We argue that NLP analyses could gain depth and quality if combined with ethnographic studies of the people whose language are processed.

Understanding how and where to deploy NLP technology in an effective way is a challenge (e.g. Tolmie et al. (2017); Mellinger (2017)) which may be tackled using ethnographic methods. NLP researchers are adept at optimising, so it is important to make sure the right goal is being optimised for. For example, what makes a machine translation output good depends on stakeholder and situation, regardless of the (e.g.) chrF score that indicates "objective" translation performance.

**Annotation processes.** The creation of NLP datasets hinges on quality human annotation. A core challenge in NLP annotation is to develop schemas that allow computation, that model a real-world phenomenon, and that are understandable by annotators (Pustejovsky and Stubbs, 2012; Ferro et al., 2005). These schemas and their description benefit from having a situated understanding the phenomena well and having clear interactions around it. After all, machine learning models tend to learn the behaviours represented their training data – which may not always be desirable (Reidsma and Carletta, 2008; Bender et al., 2021). However, while these schemas are typically developed with both linguistic and computational constraints in mind, the fact that they are to be applied to language by humans in order to generate data is seldom recognised, despite this being the critical part of the process.

Another challenge in annotation processes is assessing quality: annotator disagreement is often a valuable signal, indicating e.g. rich, multi-phenomena instances (Das et al., 2017; Sommerauer et al., 2020) or cases where only an annotator minority has the knowledge to complete the task (Derczynski et al., 2016; Vidgen and Derczynski, 2020). This disagreement, which signals a problem in the interface between human annotator and the dataset goal, should be investigated: its sources are likely to be interesting, and at the least, disagreement can help downstream applications (Plank et al., 2014). HCI offers the tools for exploring and better understanding that interface.

HCI, concerned with assessing qualitative data, offers numerous methods, discussions, and reflections on reliability and when to use (and when *not* to use) inter-rater reliability (IRR) as a measure (McDonald et al., 2019). Analysis work in HCI is often *iterative*, with several steps of testing and inclusion of relevant stakeholders (Zimmerman et al., 2007). In HCI, there is no one correct way to assess reliability – different studies invite different frames and methods. Therefore, HCI research must be *transparent* and *reflective* about its methodology and how analysis is performed, including how analysis categories and schemas are developed (Siegert et al., 2014; Olson and Kellogg, 2014).

We believe methodologies for developing NLP datasets should be discussed and detailed with a similar level of iterativeness and reflection.

**Error analysis.** Understanding and describing how NLP models and systems go wrong requires a different toolkit to the quantitative approaches typically used (e.g. feature ablation, layer freezing, BERTology). NLP has tended to focus more on quantitative rather than qualitative data, leaving potential gaps of understanding, where thorough and methodical qualitative analyses stand to yield new research, especially when combined with existing quantitative methods (e.g. (Bornakke and Due, 2018); also Section 4.1.1).

Qualitative error analysis opens paths to both better understanding of language and to developing new technical results. HCI, building on cognitive and social science, offers many methods and frameworks for establishing such an understanding, e.g. *cognitive modelling* (Olson and Olson, 1995) and *chains of cognitive breakdowns* (Ko and Myers, 2005). These framings and methodologies could readily improve NLP error analyses.

**New abstractions.** HCI is a broad field with many interactions and concepts within its aegis. These can lead to new abstractions regarding the use and structure of NLP technology. For example, the abstract concept of a design material – a conceptual, tangible, or other item used in or by a design process – can be applied to machine learning, improving understanding of how machine learning (or ML-based NLP) can be used or useful (Dove et al., 2017). Similarly, the role played by linguistic actions (e.g. conversation analysis (Norman and Thomas, 1991; Hirst, 1991)) may be differently understood in various HCI frameworks, giving new interfaces that may lead to a deeper problem understanding. A concrete example of such work is VoxML's use of affordances and embodiment for semantic disambiguation (Pustejovsky and Krishnaswamy, 2020).

**Extra data layers.** HCI research produces vast amounts of data, a lot of it transcribed. Interviews, field notes, observations, and video transcripts could all serve as readily accessible data for NLP training datasets and analyses. This novel modality gives an interface for applying NLP to support HCI research while presenting novel NLP tasks and text genres.

#### 3.1.2 Opportunities for HCI

**Automatic transcription.** One of the major potential gains for HCI in the automatic processing of language is automatic transcription of qualitative data, for instance interviews and video recordings. While some tools are already available for this, they are usually substandard to human transcription, and only work for English language.

**Thematic classification and clustering.** Both NLP and HCI analyze text by tagging it with themes or classes. HCI researchers spend years training to identify important themes in qualitative data, in HCI known as *thematic coding* (Gibbs, 2007), *grounded theory development* (Strauss and Corbin, 1997) or *affinity diagramming* (Lucero, 2015). Applying NLP methods to identify themes in qualitative data may reveal themes (or prevalence of themes) that researchers would not have otherwise identified.Concrete examples of successful application of automatic coding of qualitative data is described in Marathe and Toyama (2018) and Crowston et al. (2012)'s work, which both achieved promising IRR scores combining semi-automatic NLP techniques with human coders.

**Novel analysis tools.** NLP offers an array of analysis tools which can be used in HCI to analyze text in a consistent fashion in large quantities of data. This opens up new possibilities for analyzing and comparing language, discovering facets of data which were otherwise not apparent.

Preliminary HCI research has, e.g., explored available NLP tools such as sentiment analysis to explore how frustrated students are while progressing through a design process (Frich et al., 2018).

### 3.2 Output opportunities

New methods and types of analyses are intriguing, but it is valuable to think specifically about the results and outputs one would like to achieve in applying different methods. We believe it is useful to think about these outputs *before* choosing methods from a novel field. Relevant methods may, e.g., vary depending on career stage, and whether one is conducting basic or applied research.

**Discoveries.** The most apparent goal of interdisciplinary research should of course be novel research results. Using the same pen and paper to draw every day will increase one's drawing skills, but it will probably not generate an entirely new artistic expression. Using paint and a canvas may be challenging, but it may produce surprising results. Therefore, the first output topic is *discoveries*, covering any form of novel research output which would not have been otherwise obvious. Examples of research discoveries in the intersection of NLP and HCI include: creating and evaluating automated feedback to psychotherapists (Hirsch et al., 2018); exploring cultural biases in media coverage (El Ali et al., 2018); using NLP to support creative journalism (Maiden et al., 2018); and integrating afforded behaviours with lexical semantics to model motion (Krishnaswamy and Pustejovsky, 2016).

**Quality analyses.** Another clear output of applying NLP and HCI methods to each others' datasets is increasing the quality of analyses. While it is not given that randomly matching methods from two different research fields will produce novel results, we believe NLP and HCI can uniquely augment each other. Both fields are concerned with *communication* as a core concept, and humans' most natural forms of communication, speech and language, are also among the most difficult modalities for machines to process (Ozkan and Paris, 2002; Munteanu et al., 2013).

**Artwork.** HCI conferences have a long-standing history of exhibiting novel technology demonstrations, sometimes in the intersection between utility and art. Traditionally, the realm of computational art has predominantly featured audio and visual works. Language modelling has driven some artwork, such as automatically generated poetry and, with more recent models, a broader range of artworks (e.g. Inie et al. (2020); Rubin (2002)). The range and depth sophistication in NLP is a potentially exciting palette for artists to work with, allowing a novel modality. For example, recent work includes reconsidering storytelling from a generation point of view, which is already leading to new understandings of what constitutes a story (Ammanabrolu et al., 2021). Similarly, artistic ideas for application of NLP may push the boundaries of what is currently computationally possible.

**Network.** Creative thinking requires a combination of field knowledge and conceptually distant inspiration (Chan et al., 2018). Researchers are usually experts in their own domain, and while we can all benefit from learning new skills, interdisciplinary research is strongest when experts from different fields are brought together. By conducting genuinely interdisciplinary research, one tangible outcome is to discover research avenues outside one's core area, as well as hopefully attending events, workshops such as this one, and conferences where experts from other fields are easy to meet and truly novel collaborations become possible.

## 4 Barriers and risks

Interdisciplinary research can be challenging and can carry inherent risks which may be mitigated through thorough reflection and preparation. Here, we present some of the primary barriers for combining NLP and HCI research methods, as well as risks for the resulting research output.

### 4.1 Methods and analyses barriers

#### 4.1.1 Methods barriers, human

**Coding skills.** One of the main barriers for novices to build, adjust, and integrate NLP systems is programming ability. While the level of proficiency required to access the most advanced systems is lower than previously, implementing these systems using even a well-wrapped library (by today's standards) requires a fairly high level of coding aptitude. This creates a barrier to using NLP technology. Providing simple interfaces to this technology helps reduce this barrier. Various programming toolkits have been developed and flourished over time to reduce this barrier (Maynard et al., 2012; Bird et al., 2009; Wolf et al., 2020), but mostly made NLP more accessible only to those with established programming skills.

**Detaching from quantitative methods.** Numbers and code offer the illusion of objectivity and detail. This presents barriers to both use and uptake of qualitative methods. While stable, methodical, and scientific qualitative analysis methods exist, they are not well-established in NLP, creating a risk that NLP researchers and reviewers may have a dimmer view of them due to a lack of familiarity. Establishing excellent qualitative analysis as common practice will require persistence. Frameworks used in HCI applicable to NLP include *thematic analysis*, where themes are identified subjectively by humans based on evidence in results (Castleberry and Nolen, 2018); *in vivo coding*, where attention is placed on participants' use of phrases (Manning, 2017), useful during e.g. annotator debriefing; and *grounded theory method*, that constructs hypotheses through examining data for phenomena where no theory yet exists (Muller, 2014).

**Terminology.** Developing a lingua franca is a necessity for any two research fields to meet and share knowledge. Each research field has its own terminology and assembly of concepts which mean specific things in specific contexts (CohenMiller and Pate, 2019). An obvious example is the term "coding", which means quite different activities in machine learning and qualitative analysis. While embarking on collaborations between NLP and HCI, it may be worth working on research dictionaries or referenced repositories which define concepts like *toolkit*, *codebook*, and *ontololgy* in easily understandable terms from each field's perspective.

**Critical thinking.** From an HCI perspective, quantitative results can seem enchanting in their promise of objective truth. Especially when researchers do not have thorough insight into the algorithms that produce numbers (and the biases built into these algorithms), there is a risk of accepting quantitative results as truthful without reflecting critically (O'Neil, 2016). Using NLP methods therefore requires a level of insight into the methods necessary to afford critical examination and questioning of results.

#### 4.1.2 Methods barriers, technical

**Limited modalities (speech & text processing).** A significant amount of qualitative data from HCI exists first as audio or video recordings. One challenge with such data is that, even if automatic transcription was flawless and available in all languages, NLP focuses on the spoken word, not context or actions. Context, actions, and interactions are often essential information to HCI research. Therefore, valuable NLP transcription/analysis systems might support researchers in annotating actions, interactions, important moments and field notes in relation to spoken and written language.

**Access to data.** Data is stored, processed, and accessed in different ways in NLP and HCI – because the fields traditionally store different kinds of data. NLP datasets are often stored as large .tsv or JSONL files, while HCI datasets may consist of complex field notes and transcriptions in specialized software like ATLAS.ti or NVIVO. These all come with specific technical requirements for storage and access. Data storage significantly influences the way data is *retrieved*, which is crucial to enabling different kinds of analyses by different researchers.

### 4.2 Output risks

**Biases in data.** All data is biased – by the way it is sampled, by the goal behind gathering and annotating it, by the individual implementing its assembly. These biases may present as: class overrepresentation and underrepresentation; missing phenomena, such as languages, entity names, lexical items, or syntactic structures; skew in treatment of borderline cases; and so on (Søgaard et al., 2014). The important part is to label the biases, so they may be addressed and communicated. While NLP researchers and HCI researchers have the expertise and experiential knowledge to be capable of recognising and documenting the biases within their own field, it is harder to properly understand the biases present in data from another discipline. This is a challenge faced by people on both sides of the HCI/NLP interface. We should be each cognisant of our potential lack of insight into the other field, and aware that data from it might be mis-applied, or that assumptions may not port well from one field to another. An example mitigation is the Data Statement for NLP, itself based on an intersection of these two disciplines, a methodological step that documents intent and factors contributing to bias in order to communicate these to data users (Bender and Friedman, 2018).

## 5 Outlook

The topics of the interdisciplinary HCI/NLP framework described in this short paper are the result of the authors' initial dialogue and analysis, and they are focused on being broadly relevant and relatable to researchers in both areas. We invite researchers in both NLP and HCI to expand upon the categories, in detail as well in quantity.

## References


Prithviraj Ammanabrolu, Wesley Cheung, William Broniec, and Mark O Riedl. 2021. Automated storytelling via causal, commonsense plot ordering. In *Proceedings of AAAI*.

Emily M Bender and Batya Friedman. 2018. Data statements for natural language processing: Toward mitigating system bias and enabling better science. *Transactions of the Association for Computational Linguistics*, 6:587–604.

Emily M Bender, Timnit Gebru, Angelina McMillan-Major, and Shmargaret Shmitchell. 2021. On the dangers of stochastic parrots: Can language models be too big? . *Proceedings of FAccT*.

Steven Bird, Ewan Klein, and Edward Loper. 2009. *Natural language processing with Python: analyzing text with the Natural Language Toolkit*. O'Reilly Media, Inc.

Jeanette Blomberg, Mark Burrell, and Greg Guest. 2009. An ethnographic approach to design. *Human-Computer Interaction*, pages 71–94.

Tobias Bornakke and Brian L Due. 2018. Big–thick blending: A method for mixing analytical insights from big and thick data sources. *Big Data & Society*, 5(1):2053951718765026.

Ashley Castleberry and Amanda Nolen. 2018. Thematic analysis of qualitative research data: Is it as easy as it sounds? *Currents in Pharmacy Teaching and Learning*, 10(6):807–815.

Joel Chan, Steven P Dow, and Christian D Schunn. 2018. Do the best design ideas (really) come from conceptually distant sources of inspiration? In *Engineering a Better Future*, pages 111–139. Springer, Cham.

Wendy W Chapman, Prakash M Nadkarni, Lynette Hirschman, Leonard W D'avolio, Guergana K Savova, and Ozlem Uzuner. 2011. Overcoming barriers to nlp for clinical text: the role of shared tasks and the need for additional creative solutions.

AS CohenMiller and P Elizabeth Pate. 2019. A model for developing interdisciplinary research theoretical frameworks. *Qualitative Report*, 24(6).

Kevin Crowston, Eileen E Allen, and Robert Heckman. 2012. Using natural language processing technology for qualitative data analysis. *International Journal of Social Research Methodology*, 15(6):523–543.

Debopam Das, Manfred Stede, and Maite Taboada. 2017. The good, the bad, and the disagreement: Complex ground truth in rhetorical structure analysis. In *Proceedings of the 6th Workshop on Recent Advances in RST and Related Formalisms*, pages 11–19.

Antonella De Angeli and Daniela Petrelli. 2000. Bridging the gap between nlp and hci: A new synergy in the name of the user. In *Proceedings of the CHI 2000 Workshop on Natural Language Interfaces*, volume 4.

Leon Derczynski, Kalina Bontcheva, and Ian Roberts. 2016. Broad Twitter Corpus: A diverse named entity recognition resource. In *Proceedings of COLING 2016, the 26th International Conference on Computational Linguistics: Technical Papers*, pages 1169–1179.

Graham Dove, Kim Halskov, Jodi Forlizzi, and John Zimmerman. 2017. UX design innovation: Challenges for working with machine learning as a design material. In *Proceedings of the 2017 chi conference on human factors in computing systems*, pages 278–288.

Abdallah El Ali, Tim C Stratmann, Souneil Park, Johannes Schöning, Wilko Heuten, and Susanne CJ Boll. 2018. Measuring, understanding, and classifying news media sympathy on twitter after crisis events. In *Proceedings of the 2018 CHI Conference on Human Factors in Computing Systems*, pages 1–13.

Lisa Ferro, L. Gerber, Inderjeet Mani, Beth Sundheim, and Geroge Wilson. 2005. TIDES 2005 standard for the annotation of temporal expressions. Technical report, Mitre Corporation.

Jonas Frich, Nanna Inie, Kim Halskov, and Peter Dalsgaard. 2018. A sentiment analysis of design reflections from design projects. In *Extended Abstracts of the 2018 CHI Conference on Human Factors in Computing Systems*, pages 1–6.

Graham R Gibbs. 2007. Thematic coding and categorizing. *Analyzing qualitative data*, 703:38–56.

Spence Green, Jeffrey Heer, and Christopher D Manning. 2015. Natural language translation at the intersection of ai and hci. *Communications of the ACM*, 58(9):46–53.

Tad Hirsch, Christina Soma, Kritzia Merced, Patty Kuo, Aaron Dembe, Derek D Caperton, David C Atkins, and Zac E Imel. 2018. " it's hard to argue with a computer" investigating psychotherapists' attitudes towards automated evaluation. In *Proceedings of the 2018 Designing Interactive Systems Conference*, pages 559–571.

Graeme Hirst. 1991. Does conversation analysis have a role in computational linguistics? *Computational Linguistics*, 17(2):211–227.

Victor Hung. 2014. Context and NLP. In *Context in Computing*, pages 143–154. Springer.

Nanna Inie, Jeanette Falk Olesen, and Leon Derczynski. 2020. The Rumour Mill: Making the spread of misinformation explicit and tangible. In *Extended Abstracts of the 2020 CHI Conference on Human Factors in Computing Systems*, pages 1–4.

Nikiforos Karamanis, Anne Schneider, Ielka Van Der Sluis, Stephan Schlogl, Gavin Doherty, and Saturnino Luz. 2009. Do hci and nlp interact? In *CHI'09 Extended Abstracts on Human Factors in Computing Systems*, pages 4333–4338. ACM.

Andrew J Ko and Brad A Myers. 2005. A framework and methodology for studying the causes of software errors in programming systems. *Journal of Visual Languages & Computing*, 16(1-2):41–84.

Nikhil Krishnaswamy and James Pustejovsky. 2016. Voxsim: A visual platform for modeling motion language. In *Proceedings of COLING 2016, the 26th International Conference on Computational Linguistics: System Demonstrations*, pages 54–58.

Andrés Lucero. 2015. Using affinity diagrams to evaluate interactive prototypes. In *IFIP Conference on Human-Computer Interaction*, pages 231–248. Springer.

Neil Maiden, Konstantinos Zachos, Amanda Brown, George Brock, Lars Nyre, Aleksander Nygård Tonheim, Dimitris Apsotolou, and Jeremy Evans. 2018. Making the news: Digital creativity support for journalists. In *Proceedings of the 2018 CHI Conference on Human Factors in Computing Systems*, pages 1–11.

Jimmie Manning. 2017. In vivo coding. *The international encyclopedia of communication research methods*, pages 1–2.

Megh Marathe and Kentaro Toyama. 2018. Semi-automated coding for qualitative research: A user-centered inquiry and initial prototypes. In *Proceedings of the 2018 CHI Conference on Human Factors in Computing Systems*, pages 1–12.

Diana Maynard, Kalina Bontcheva, Valentin Tablan, Niraj Aswani, Ian Roberts, Genevieve Gorrell, Adam Funk, Angus Roberts, Danica Damljanovic, Thomas Heitz, Leon Derczynski, et al. 2012. Developing Language Processing Components with GATE Version 7 (a User Guide).

Nora McDonald, Sarita Schoenebeck, and Andrea Forte. 2019. Reliability and inter-rater reliability in qualitative research: Norms and guidelines for cscw and hci practice. *Proceedings of the ACM on Human-Computer Interaction*, 3(CSCW):1–23.

Christopher D Mellinger. 2017. Translators and machine translation: knowledge and skills gaps in translator pedagogy. *The Interpreter and Translator Trainer*, 11(4):280–293.

Michael Muller. 2014. Curiosity, creativity, and surprise as analytic tools: Grounded theory method. In *Ways of Knowing in HCI*, pages 25–48. Springer.

Cosmin Munteanu, Matt Jones, Sharon Oviatt, Stephen Brewster, Gerald Penn, Steve Whittaker, Nitendra Rajput, and Amit Nanavati. 2013. We need to talk: HCI and the delicate topic of spoken language interaction. In *CHI'13 Extended Abstracts on Human Factors in Computing Systems*, pages 2459–2464. ACM.

Michael A. Norman and Peter J. Thomas. 1991. Informing hci design through conversation analysis. *International journal of man-machine studies*, 35(2):235–250.

Judith Reitman Olson and Gary M Olson. 1995. The growth of cognitive modeling in human-computer interaction since goms. In *Readings in Human–Computer Interaction*, pages 603–625. Elsevier.

Judith S Olson and Wendy A Kellogg. 2014. *Ways of Knowing in HCI*, volume 2. Springer.

Cathy O'Neil. 2016. *Weapons of math destruction: How big data increases inequality and threatens democracy*. Crown.

Nadine Ozkan and Cécile Paris. 2002. Cross-fertilization between human computer interaction and natural language processing: Why and how. *International Journal of Speech Technology*, 5(2):135–146.

Barbara Plank, Dirk Hovy, and Anders Søgaard. 2014. Learning part-of-speech taggers with inter-annotator agreement loss. In *Proceedings of the 14th Conference of the European Chapter of the Association for Computational Linguistics*, pages 742–751.

James Pustejovsky and Nikhil Krishnaswamy. 2020. Embodied human-computer interactions through situated grounding. In *Proceedings of the 20th ACM International Conference on Intelligent Virtual Agents*, pages 1–3.

James Pustejovsky and Amber Stubbs. 2012. *Natural Language Annotation for Machine Learning: A guide to corpus-building for applications*. O'Reilly Media, Inc.

Dennis Reidsma and Jean Carletta. 2008. Reliability measurement without limits. *Computational Linguistics*, 34(3):319–326.

Rubin. 2002. Listening post (artwork). https://en.wikipedia.org/wiki/Listening_Post_(artwork).

Ingo Siegert, Ronald Böck, and Andreas Wendemuth. 2014. Inter-rater reliability for emotion annotation in human–computer interaction: comparison and methodological improvements. *Journal on Multimodal User Interfaces*, 8(1):17–28.

Anders Søgaard, Barbara Plank, and Dirk Hovy. 2014. Selection bias, label bias, and bias in ground truth. In *Proceedings of COLING 2014, the 25th International Conference on Computational Linguistics: Tutorial Abstracts*, pages 11–13.

Pia Sommerauer, Antske Fokkens, and Piek Vossen. 2020. Would you describe a leopard as yellow? evaluating crowd-annotations with justified and informative disagreement. In *Proceedings of the 28th International Conference on Computational Linguistics*, pages 4798–4809.

Anselm Strauss and Juliet M Corbin. 1997. *Grounded theory in practice*. Sage.

Lucy A Suchman. 1987. *Plans and situated actions: The problem of human-machine communication*. Cambridge university press.

Peter Tolmie, Rob Procter, David William Randall, Mark Rouncefield, Christian Burger, Geraldine Wong Sak Hoi, Arkaitz Zubiaga, and Maria Liakata. 2017. Supporting the use of user generated content in journalistic practice. In *Proceedings of the 2017 chi conference on human factors in computing systems*, pages 3632–3644.

Bertie Vidgen and Leon Derczynski. 2020. Directions in abusive language training data, a systematic review: Garbage in, garbage out. *PLoS ONE*, 15(12):e0243300.

Tricia Wang. 2013. Big data needs thick data. *Ethnography Matters*, 13.

Thomas Wolf, Julien Chaumond, Lysandre Debut, Victor Sanh, Clement Delangue, Anthony Moi, Pierric Cistac, Morgan Funtowicz, Joe Davison, Sam Shleifer, et al. 2020. Transformers: State-of-the-art natural language processing. In *Proceedings of the EMNLP demos*, pages 38–45.

Qian Yang. 2017. The role of design in creating machine-learning-enhanced user experience. In *2017 AAAI Spring Symposium Series*.

John Zimmerman, Jodi Forlizzi, and Shelley Evenson. 2007. Research through design as a method for interaction design research in hci. In *Proceedings of the SIGCHI conference on Human factors in computing systems*, pages 493–502.

# RE-AIMing Predictive Text

**Matthew Higgs, Claire McCallum, Selina Sutton, and Mark Warner**
Northumbria Social Computing (NorSC) Group, Northumbria University, UK
{matthew.higgs, claire.mccallum, selina.sutton, mark.warner}
@northumbria.ac.uk

## Abstract

Our increasing reliance on mobile applications means much of our communication is mediated with the support of predictive text systems. How do these systems impact interpersonal communication and broader society? In what ways are predictive text systems harmful, to whom, and why? In this paper, we focus on predictive text systems on mobile devices (Figure 1) and attempt to answer these questions. We introduce the concept of a 'text entry intervention' as a way to evaluate predictive text systems through an interventional lens, and consider the **R**each, **E**ffectiveness, **A**doption, **I**mplementation, and **M**aintenance (RE-AIM) of predictive text systems. We finish with a discussion of opportunities for NLP.

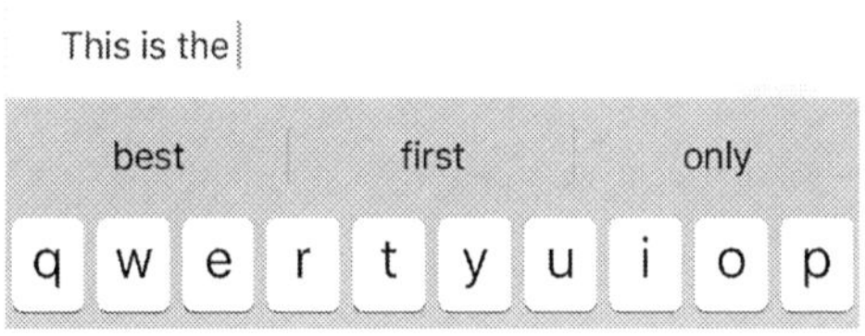


Figure 1: Screenshot of predictive text on an iOS device, with input text above and default keyboard below.

## 1 Introduction

Predictive text systems were born from an engineering paradigm (Church and Mercer, 1993), integrated into user interfaces (Garay-Vitoria and Abascal, 2006), and deployed at scale (Apple, 2014; Samsung, 2021) - with little consideration for their impact on interpersonal communication and broader society. Originally designed to increase the speed and ease of communicating with a computer (Darragh et al., 1990), predictive text systems have been optimised over time towards the goals of accuracy and efficiency on writing tasks (Bi et al., 2014; Quinn and Zhai, 2016), and creators of recent email-based predictive text systems highlight how their system saves users over "one billion characters of typing" (Chen et al., 2019). More recently though, Quinn and Zhai (2016), Arnold et al. (2018, 2020), and Hancock et al. (2020) respectively highlight concerns for the benefits of predictive text on mobile devices, the effects on the content we write, and the impact of predictive text as it mediates our communications.

We aim to begin a discussion on how research priorities and industry practice can change to better our understanding of the benefits and harms of predictive text systems, and to imagine how they might be redesigned. We introduce the concept of a 'text entry intervention' (an intervention delivered as a user enters text) where examples include: an app offering privacy and well-being advice alongside the messages children type (BBC, 2019); a writing assistant intended to influence a writer's grammar, spelling, style and tone (Grammarly, 2019); or an email assistant intended to reduce repetitive writing and the number of keys we type (Chen et al., 2019). We focus on the common 'text suggestion bar' on mobile devices (Figure 1) as an instance of a text entry intervention, and describe a path forward for evaluating its impact. Note that all of these examples of text entry interventions are real products, being used by real people, with little research into the effects they have on the content produced. Once we consider predictive text to be an intervention, we can draw on areas of research focused on the design and evaluation of interventions (Flay, 1986; Glasgow et al., 1999, 2019; Murray et al., 2016). In doing so, a new set of criteria with which to evaluate predictive text systems becomes available; enabling us to examine aspects of their design and potential impact, and encouraging us to consider the relationships between predictive text systems and their downstream effects (Figure 2).



*Proceedings of the First Workshop on Bridging Human–Computer Interaction and Natural Language Processing*, pages 109–115
April 20, 2021. 

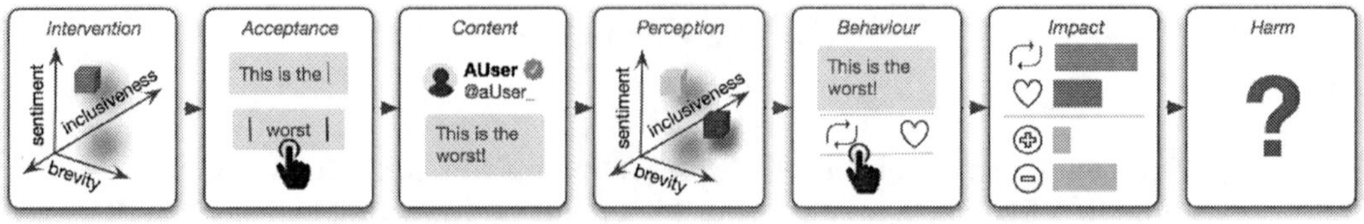


Figure 2: An example connecting a predictive text system to its impact and harms. The *intervention* is represented as a point in a design space, which (when combined with other factors) affects: the user's *acceptance* of the text suggestions and the *content* they post online, the reader's *perception* of the content and their *behaviour* (e.g. like, retweet, or nothing), and (over time) the *impact* and *harm* of the intervention.

We aim to: (i) begin a discussion about the benefits and harms of predictive text systems, (ii) conceptualise predictive text as an intervention, and (iii) highlight opportunities for NLP research.

## 2 Related Work

Predictive text systems have evolved from communication aids designed to benefit novice and reluctant typists (Darragh et al., 1990; Garay-Vitoria and Abascal, 2006) to default features on smartphones (Apple, 2014; Samsung, 2021) and popular email clients (Kannan et al., 2016). While there are some large scale studies of web-based predictive text system for structured transcription tasks (Palin et al., 2019), there is little research into their use in the wild (Buschek et al., 2018) and evidence that lab-based studies might not reflect real world use (Komninos et al., 2020). Recent research into the effects of predictive text on the content we write (Arnold et al., 2020) highlights the need for more studies in-the-wild, but this brings significant challenges (Buschek et al., 2018).

With regards to evaluating predictive text systems, a key challenge for any researcher-developed intervention is ensuring it changes real world practice. To help intervention developers assess real world impact, the RE-AIM framework (Reach, Effectiveness, Adoption, Implementation, Maintenance) was developed (Glasgow et al., 1999, 2019). It asks: does the intervention **R**each those it should? Is it **E**ffective in doing 'more good than harm' in real world contexts? (Flay, 1986)). Is it likely to be **A**dopted and **I**mplemented by those required to deliver it? Will any changes be **M**aintained over time? The RE-AIM framework leads to key questions we need to ask to decide how research priorities and industry practice should change (Murray et al., 2016).

With regards to improving predictive text systems, we propose re-purposing methods for controlling text generation (Ghazvininejad et al., 2017; Holtzman et al., 2018; Tambwekar et al., 2018; Keskar et al., 2019; Sahar et al., 2020) which are being used to control 'bias' in text generation (Sheng et al., 2020; Dinan et al., 2020). With regards to measuring downstream effects, the intersection of causal inference and language provide methods for estimating the causal effects of linguistic properties on downstream outcomes (Pryzant et al., 2020); such as the effect of wording, brevity, and tone on message propagation and impact on Twitter (Tan et al., 2014; Gligorić et al., 2019) and the effects of tone in online debates (Sridhar and Getoor, 2019).

## 3 Evaluating Text Entry Interventions

Conceptualising predictive text systems as a type of text entry intervention, we draw on the RE-AIM framework (Glasgow et al., 1999, 2019) to consider the reach and effects of predictive text systems and how new interventions might be adopted, implemented, and maintained by the industry actors who control their development and deployment. Specifically, application of the RE-AIM framework (and consideration for how research priorities and industry practice could change) forces us to identify significant gaps in our current knowledge regarding the impact of predictive text systems.

### 3.1 Reach

While predictive text systems are available on all mobile devices by default, there exists little evidence on their uptake and the extent to which text suggestions are actually used (Buschek et al., 2018). A recent study of a web-based predictive text system for transcription enrolled 37,000 volunteers, suggesting significant reach, but the study was of a structured task set by researchers (Palin et al., 2019), as opposed to real world use. A significant barrier to assessing the reach of predictive text systems is limited access to usage data, which is often held by industry gatekeepers. Nevertheless, reach must be considered early in the development and redesign of predictive text systems. What is the reach of current predictive text systems? What proportion of smartphone users have predictive text turned on? Which users accept and benefit from text suggestions? In which contexts (e.g. messaging, email, social media) are text suggestions used? How can we ensure new predictive text systems reach intended users? How can we be sure intended users participate and engage? Will reach be limited in some way through, for example, not accounting for various user characteristics or industry gatekeepers?

### 3.2 Effectiveness

To understand effectiveness, we need to consider both benefits and harms (Flay, 1986).

Originally designed to increase the speed and ease of communicating with a computer (Darragh et al., 1990), HCI research has focused on the benefits of predictive text in relation to accuracy and efficiency (Bi et al., 2014; Quinn and Zhai, 2016). However, there are doubts over the benefits of text suggestions on smartphones, and Quinn and Zhai (2016) provided evidence that the costs of attending to and using text suggestions impaired average time performance. So we must ask, who actually benefits from text suggestions on mobile devices, in which contexts, and how?

HCI research into the harms or unintended consequences of predictive text is more limited, though we can connect recent research into the effects of predictive text on content (Arnold et al., 2020) to research into the harms of more general NLP systems (Blodgett et al., 2020). For example, it has been suggested that predictive text may make our writing more predictable (Arnold et al., 2020), and when we consider the scale to which such systems are deployed and the effects of language on society (Blodgett et al., 2020), we must consider the possibility that predictive text on mobile devices is reinforcing social norms and leading to representational harms. Specifically, we can imagine differences in system performance (predictive text benefiting particular social groups more/less than others), stereotyping that propagates through suggestions, and minority languages slowly being rendered invisible through a lack of representation. Currently though, we do not fully understand the unintended consequences and potential harms of predictive text systems, and we need to ask: in what ways are predictive text systems harmful, to whom, and why?

The full extent and variety of downstream consequences and social outcomes can be difficult to anticipate, and capture within a trial (Oliver et al., 2019). As suggested by (Blodgett et al., 2020), qualitative and participatory approaches exploring the lived experiences of those likely to use and be affected by systems, are needed, and in advance of deployment. To understand the benefits and harms of predictive text systems, more evaluations should take place in-the-wild (Buschek et al., 2018). This will help us to understand not only *whether* a predictive text system is effective, but for who, why and in what context.

### 3.3 Adoption, Implementation & Maintenance

Whether new predictive text systems are being introduced, or existing systems are being re-designed, it is imperative that we explore the willingness of industry sectors to deliver them. Consulting and co-designing such interventions with those delivering them will help us understand and mitigate potential barriers to their adoption.

A key challenge to adoption and implementation will be understanding and aligning with the values and goals of the organisations who control delivery. Instances of industry further adapting predictive text interventions (e.g. to meet their own business goals), after they have been tested for their effectiveness, should be monitored. While adaptations and system updates are inevitable, these new versions should be re-tested for their positive and negative effects on users.

Implementation relies on real world user engagement patterns being similar to those found in effectiveness trials. The challenge, however, is assessing real world use outside of trials. Previous research has invested in developing logging systems that can measure typing behaviour (including use of predictive text) in-the-wild (Buschek et al., 2018). However, currently, industry professionals are under little obligation to share this with researchers. So we ask, will such organisations share (in a secure way) the data needed to properly evaluate ongoing implementation and maintenance (i.e. the long term impact) of text systems? And when provided with evidence for the effectiveness of interventions, will they adapt existing systems accordingly?

## 4 Theory to Practice

In this section, we consider how we can involve users and affected communities in the design of improved predictive text systems, and how we can engage with industry players.

### 4.1 Community involvement

Regarding qualitative and participatory approaches involving users and affected communities, we focus on collaborative research through 'co-design' where users and communities would play a large role in knowledge development, idea generation and concept development (Zamenopoulos and Alexiou, 2018). We propose four outputs from such research: 'stakeholder maps' to identify and characterise the communities affected and industry players involved; 'evaluative constructs' (e.g. measures of impact) designed to increase benefits and decrease harms (Metcalf et al., 2021); 'system designs', such as custom keyboards and other text entry interventions (Arnold et al., 2018, 2020); and 'study designs' to evaluate alternative systems with regards to the measures of impact. Additionally, to better understand (and measure) the benefits and harms of predictive text, we need to better understand people's communication goals and use of predictive text in different domains. Focusing on communication through mobile devices, we propose to characterise and compare the benefits and harms of using predictive text when used alongside different types of apps; such as messenger/communication, email, and social.

### 4.2 Industry involvement

Cooperation from industry players is essential for answering many key questions, but industry objectives might be not be in line with the objectives of this work. If this is the case, and the research meets resistance from industry players, we propose a path forward consisting of three (escalating) levels of engagement with industry players.

The first level ('co-design') would involve industry players in the design process, and would attempt to understand the suitability of current predictive text systems in meeting their business needs. Specifically, why are predictive text systems part of their offering? Why it is cost-effective to maintain predictive text? Which objectives are considered when evaluating predictive text? Research would aim to incorporate such objectives into the design process, and work with industry players and affected communities to design new solutions balancing stakeholder needs. The second level ('negotiation') would occur if industry actors refuse to be involved in the design process, and would aim to support the identification and communication of the benefits and harms of predictive text. Specifically, research would aim to develop tools for surfacing and communicating the benefits and harms of predictive text, and building a body of evidence which can be used to negotiate changes in current predictive text systems. Along with this, we might consider establishing a forum to act on the evidence and mandate changes in the implementation of predictive text systems (Metcalf et al., 2021). The third level ('resistance') would occur if efforts relating to the first two levels fail, and would aim to provide affected/concerned communities with the tools to take action themselves. The simplest example of this would be an 'opt out' movement where users (beyond affected communities) are encouraged to turn off predictive text, though it is not clear the impact this would have. An alternative would be to design 'adversarial' text entry interventions to counter the effects of existing predictive text systems. These could take the form of custom keyboards which users install on their devices, though developing and maintaining such systems at scale would come with significant cost and (potentially) need to undergo industry review.

## 5 Opportunities for NLP

In this section, we draw on the literature on controllable text generation (Ghazvininejad et al., 2017; Holtzman et al., 2018; Tambwekar et al., 2018; Keskar et al., 2019; Sahar et al., 2020; Sheng et al., 2020; Dinan et al., 2020) and the intersection of causal inference and language (Tan et al., 2014; Gligorić et al., 2019; Sridhar and Getoor, 2019; Pryzant et al., 2020) to discuss the role NLP can play in the development of improved predictive text systems. Specifically, we focus on: (1) implementing new systems, and (2) measuring downstream effects.

### 5.1 Implementing new systems

To develop improved predictive text systems, we need to be able to align future systems with desired outcomes and communication goals, and we believe existing methods for controlling text generation can be re-purposed for this task.

We believe methods for controlling text gener-

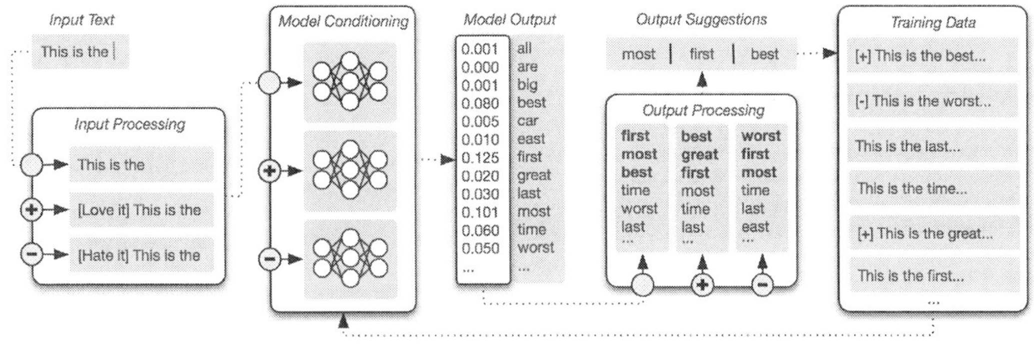


Figure 3: An example text suggestion pipeline showing the three main *control points* for biasing text suggestions: *Input Processing* where the input text is processed before being passed to a language model, *Model Conditioning* where the language model is conditioned during training, and *Output Processing* where the output of the language model is processed before the selection of text suggestions. Each control point can be used to provide different conditions to different groups of participants, and toy examples are shown for generating control ( ), positive (+), and negative (−) sentiment biases at each control point.

ation fall into three main groups, depending on the point in the text processing pipeline at which they exert control (Figure 3). Each have their own advantages and disadvantages with regards to the effort/cost/skills required to implement a new system to achieve a desired outcome, and in how likely the system is to be accepted by users. We highlight: input processing methods such as 'smart prompts' (Sheng et al., 2020), model conditioning methods such as in Tambwekar et al. (2018); Keskar et al. (2019); Dinan et al. (2020), and output processing methods such as 'guided decoding' (Ghazvininejad et al., 2017; Holtzman et al., 2018). Note that input/output processing methods do not require (potentially expensive) data collection/augmentation and/or language model training/fine-tuning.

### 5.2 Measuring downstream effects

To evaluate predictive text, we need to be able to measure its downstream effects (Figure 2).

With regards to measuring the effects of a predictive text system (intervention) on what we write (content), there is evidence that predictive text encourages predictable writing (Arnold et al., 2020) and biased text suggestions leads to biased content (Arnold et al., 2018) for writing tasks, but it's not clear if these results hold in-the-wild. We believe user acceptance is key to successfully delivering a (predictive text) intervention, and studies will need to consider how acceptance will vary for different contexts of use. Indeed, Buschek et al. (2018) observed variation in the use of text suggestions across messenger/communication, email, and social apps. Further downstream, there are opportunities for measuring the effects of content (produced with the support of predictive text) on reader behaviours and perceptions (Pryzant et al., 2020), message propagation (Tan et al., 2014; Gligorić et al., 2019), and online dialogue (Sridhar and Getoor, 2019). With these measurement methods, we hope to co-design and monitor suitable proxies for harms arising from predictive text.

## 6 Conclusion

Through this work, we hope to begin a discussion about the benefits and harms of predictive text systems, and believe the first step is to conceptualise predictive text systems as interventions. We focused on predictive text systems on mobile devices (the 'text suggestion bar'), but believe research opportunities exists for other NLP-driven text entry interventions. We believe research in this area can benefit from evaluation criteria taken from the field of behaviour change, which focuses on taking interventions from research to practice. We believe there are many opportunities for NLP and HCI researchers to improve existing, and design new, predictive text systems. In particular, HCI can center the work around the lived experiences of those affected, and NLP can help implement new systems and measure downstream effects. This will be challenging, and involve conducting studies in-the-wild and negotiating with the organisations who control the delivery of predictive text systems and the collection of user data.

## References


Apple. 2014. ios 8 - quicktype - apple.

Kenneth C. Arnold, Krysta Chauncey, and Krzysztof Z. Gajos. 2018. Sentiment bias in predictive text recommendations results in biased writing. In *Proceedings of the 44th Graphics Interface Conference*, GI '18, page 42–49, Waterloo, CAN. Canadian Human-Computer Communications Society.

Kenneth C. Arnold, Krysta Chauncey, and Krzysztof Z. Gajos. 2020. Predictive text encourages predictable writing. In *Proceedings of the 25th International Conference on Intelligent User Interfaces*, IUI '20, page 128–138, New York, NY, USA. Association for Computing Machinery.

BBC. 2019. Bbc launches 'digital wellbeing' own it app for children.

Xiaojun Bi, Tom Ouyang, and Shumin Zhai. 2014. Both complete and correct? multi-objective optimization of touchscreen keyboard. In *Proceedings of the SIGCHI Conference on Human Factors in Computing Systems*, CHI '14, page 2297–2306, New York, NY, USA. Association for Computing Machinery.

Su Lin Blodgett, Solon Barocas, Hal Daumé III, and Hanna Wallach. 2020. Language (technology) is power: A critical survey of "bias" in NLP. In *Proceedings of the 58th Annual Meeting of the Association for Computational Linguistics*, pages 5454–5476, Online. Association for Computational Linguistics.

Daniel Buschek, Benjamin Bisinger, and Florian Alt. 2018. *ResearchIME: A Mobile Keyboard Application for Studying Free Typing Behaviour in the Wild*, page 1–14. Association for Computing Machinery, New York, NY, USA.

Mia Xu Chen, Benjamin N. Lee, Gagan Bansal, Yuan Cao, Shuyuan Zhang, Justin Lu, Jackie Tsay, Yinan Wang, Andrew M. Dai, Zhifeng Chen, Timothy Sohn, and Yonghui Wu. 2019. *Gmail Smart Compose: Real-Time Assisted Writing*, page 2287–2295. Association for Computing Machinery, New York, NY, USA.

Kenneth W. Church and Robert L. Mercer. 1993. Introduction to the special issue on computational linguistics using large corpora. *Computational Linguistics*, 19(1):1–24.

J. J. Darragh, I. H. Witten, and M. L. James. 1990. The reactive keyboard: a predictive typing aid. *Computer*, 23(11):41–49.

Emily Dinan, Angela Fan, Adina Williams, Jack Urbanek, Douwe Kiela, and Jason Weston. 2020. Queens are powerful too: Mitigating gender bias in dialogue generation. In *Proceedings of the 2020 Conference on Empirical Methods in Natural Language Processing (EMNLP)*, pages 8173–8188, Online. Association for Computational Linguistics.

Brian R. Flay. 1986. Efficacy and effectiveness trials (and other phases of research) in the development of health promotion programs. *Preventive Medicine*, 15(5):451–474.

Nestor Garay-Vitoria and Julio Abascal. 2006. Text prediction systems: a survey. *Universal Access in the Information Society*, 4(3):188–203.

Marjan Ghazvininejad, Xing Shi, Jay Priyadarshi, and Kevin Knight. 2017. Hafez: an interactive poetry generation system. In *Proceedings of ACL 2017, System Demonstrations*, pages 43–48, Vancouver, Canada. Association for Computational Linguistics.

R E Glasgow, T M Vogt, and S M Boles. 1999. Evaluating the public health impact of health promotion interventions: the re-aim framework. *American Journal of Public Health*, 89(9):1322–1327. PMID: 10474547.

Russell E. Glasgow, Samantha M. Harden, Bridget Gaglio, Borsika Rabin, Matthew Lee Smith, Gwendolyn C. Porter, Marcia G. Ory, and Paul A. Estabrooks. 2019. Re-aim planning and evaluation framework: Adapting to new science and practice with a 20-year review. *Frontiers in Public Health*, 7:64.

Kristina Gligorić, Ashton Anderson, and Robert West. 2019. Causal effects of brevity on style and success in social media. *Proc. ACM Hum.-Comput. Interact.*, 3(CSCW).

Grammarly. 2019. Great writing, simplified.

J. Hancock, M. Naaman, and Karen Levy. 2020. Ai-mediated communication: Definition, research agenda, and ethical considerations. *J. Comput. Mediat. Commun.*, 25:89–100.

Ari Holtzman, Jan Buys, Maxwell Forbes, Antoine Bosselut, David Golub, and Yejin Choi. 2018. Learning to write with cooperative discriminators. In *Proceedings of the 56th Annual Meeting of the Association for Computational Linguistics (Volume 1: Long Papers)*, pages 1638–1649, Melbourne, Australia. Association for Computational Linguistics.

Anjuli Kannan, Peter Young, Vivek Ramavajjala, Karol Kurach, Sujith Ravi, Tobias Kaufmann, Andrew Tomkins, Balint Miklos, G.s Corrado, Laszlo Lukacs, and Marina Ganea. 2016. Smart reply: Automated response suggestion for email. pages 955–964.

Nitish Keskar, Bryan McCann, Lav Varshney, Caiming Xiong, and Richard Socher. 2019. Ctrl: A conditional transformer language model for controllable generation.

Andreas Komninos, Kyriakos Katsaris, Emma Nicol, Mark Dunlop, and John Garofalakis. 2020. Mobile text entry behaviour in lab and in-the-wild studies: Is it different?

Jacob Metcalf, Emanuel Moss, Elizabeth Anne Watkins, Ranjit Singh, and Madeleine Clare Elish. 2021. Algorithmic impact assessments and accountability: The co-construction of impacts. *ACM Conference on Fairness, Accountability,and Transparency (FAccT '21)*.

Elizabeth Murray, Eric B Hekler, Gerhard Andersson, Linda M Collins, Aiden Doherty, Chris Hollis, Daniel E Rivera, Robert West, and Jeremy C Wyatt. 2016. Evaluating digital health interventions: Key questions and approaches. *American journal of preventive medicine*, 51(5):843–851.

Kathryn Oliver, Theo Lorenc, Jane Tinkler, and Chris Bonell. 2019. Understanding the unintended consequences of public health policies: the views of policymakers and evaluators. *BMC Public Health*, 19(1):1057.

Kseniia Palin, Anna Maria Feit, Sunjun Kim, Per Ola Kristensson, and Antti Oulasvirta. 2019. How do people type on mobile devices? observations from a study with 37,000 volunteers. In *Proceedings of the 21st International Conference on Human-Computer Interaction with Mobile Devices and Services*, MobileHCI '19, New York, NY, USA. Association for Computing Machinery.

Reid Pryzant, D. Card, Dan Jurafsky, V. Veitch, and D. Sridhar. 2020. Causal effects of linguistic properties. *ArXiv*, abs/2010.12919.

Philip Quinn and Shumin Zhai. 2016. *A Cost-Benefit Study of Text Entry Suggestion Interaction*, page 83–88. Association for Computing Machinery, New York, NY, USA.

Hady El Sahar, Maximin Coavoux, Matthias Gallé, and Jos Rozen. 2020. Self-supervised and controlled multi-document opinion summarization. *ArXiv*, abs/2004.14754.

Samsung. 2021. How can i personalise and turn predictive text on and off on my samsung galaxy device?

Emily Sheng, Kai-Wei Chang, Prem Natarajan, and Nanyun Peng. 2020. Towards Controllable Biases in Language Generation. In *Findings of the Association for Computational Linguistics: EMNLP 2020*, pages 3239–3254, Online. Association for Computational Linguistics.

Dhanya Sridhar and Lise Getoor. 2019. Estimating causal effects of tone in online debates. In *Proceedings of the Twenty-Eighth International Joint Conference on Artificial Intelligence, IJCAI-19*, pages 1872–1878. International Joint Conferences on Artificial Intelligence Organization.

Pradyumna Tambwekar, Murtaza Dhuliawala, Animesh Mehta, Lara Martin, Brent Harrison, and Mark Riedl. 2018. Controllable neural story generation via reinforcement learning.

Chenhao Tan, Lillian Lee, and Bo Pang. 2014. The effect of wording on message propagation: Topic- and author-controlled natural experiments on Twitter. In *Proceedings of the 52nd Annual Meeting of the Association for Computational Linguistics (Volume 1: Long Papers)*, pages 175–185, Baltimore, Maryland. Association for Computational Linguistics.

Theodore Zamenopoulos and Katerina Alexiou. 2018. *Co-design As Collaborative Research*. Connected Communities Foundation Series. Bristol University/AHRC Connected Communities Programme, Bristol.

# How do people interact with biased text prediction models while writing?

**Advait Bhat**
IIT Bombay
advaitmb@gmail.com

**Saaket Agashe**
VJTI, Mumbai
saaket.agashe
@gmail.com

**Anirudha Joshi**
IIT Bombay
anirudha@iitb.ac.in

## Abstract

Recent studies have shown that a bias in the text suggestions system can percolate in the user's writing. In this pilot study, we ask the question: How do people interact with text prediction models, in an inline next phrase suggestion interface and how does introducing sentiment bias in the text prediction model affect their writing? We present a pilot study as a first step to answer this question.

## 1 Introduction

Recent years have seen a great improvement in probabilistic language models and with the advent of transformer based language models, text generation has become sophisticated and viable enough to be used in real time writing interfaces with next phrase suggestions.

Each writer carries a certain opinion that they wish to put forth through the write up. For example a movie review writer may have liked or disliked a certain movie with a certain intensity. Subsequently, they would use a specific vocabulary and style that would display their intent to the readers. Any technology that acts as a mediating interface between people and the world, wold have the potential to influence their writing process and therefore possibly even their writing intent. In our example, a text editor equipped with predictive system, would acts as the mediator and may affect the writing process and intent of the user, thereby making the movie seem better or worse than the writer intended; as well as influencing the quality of the writing itself. This, therefore, becomes an interesting area that needs investigation.

While researchers have quantitatively tried to study the effect of biased text prediction systems on user's final written content, qualitative analysis of a writer's writing process in the presence of text suggestions and furthermore, bias, is not pervasive. Along with that, studies so far have used n-gram based Language Models or Recurrent Neural Networks, but not transformers which are capable of generating much more relevant suggestions.

In this study, we try to understand how people interact with text prediction models in an inline next phrase suggestion interface and how does introducing sentiment bias in the text prediction model affect their writing. We ask people to write movie reviews using an intelligent text prediction interface and try to study their writing process. Movie reviews are particularly useful for such a scenario, as every movie review has a star rating associated with it and this acts as a good and reliable proxy to quantify the writer's original intent. Along with this, writers are encouraged to express their personal opinions through their movie reviews while having to follow a sufficiently standard structure.

We present a pilot study as a first step to answer this question. We present a background of the work in this area, our method, which includes the design of the interface, text generation methods and validation of our language models. We then present qualitative analysis of the same.

## 2 Background

In a recent study (Arnold et al., 2018), introduce sentiment bias in predictive text suggestions on smartphone keyboards for a hotel review writing task. The study demonstrates that if predictive text suggestions are positively sentiment biased for a hotel review writing task, writers tend to write more positive reviews. On the other hand, equivalent effects aren't seen when the system is negatively sentiment biased. Taking these studies as a starting point, we wish to understand how users interact with such a system and how their writing gets affected qualitatively. We also use more updated language models for our study. The larger aim would be to create a model of how users interact with such a system and where this fits into their writing process; similar to cognitive process theory



*Proceedings of the First Workshop on Bridging Human–Computer Interaction and Natural Language Processing*, pages 116–121
April 20, 2021. 

of writing by (Flower and Hayes, 1981). In this paper, we present a pilot study with six users where we qualitatively analyse their writing process.

## 3 Method

### 3.1 Experiment

In this pilot, we ask users to write movie reviews. We also ask them to rate these movies in terms of star rating. In order to compare if the bias in the system affects the user's writing and therefore the perception of the reader who would read it, we randomise these movie reviews and then ask independent readers to read these reviews and guess the rating the movie would've gotten.

Our pilot study had a between and within subject, mixed study design. We assigned two movies to each participant. 3 participants received 2 movies that had low ratings on IMDb and 3 participants received 2 movies that had high ratings on IMDb. We expected that the participants who received movies with low IMDb ratings would also give lower ratings to the movies, as these movies are generally considered bad movies and vice versa for movies with good ratings. We did this to ensure that we get an equal distribution of participants in every condition and so that we covered every condition. Half of the participants were given a pair of below average movies and the other half, above average. Among these individual groups, every participant was given a baseline interface and an interface with suggestions. Within the interfaces with suggestions 2 participants were given a positive biased system, 2 were given a negatively biased system and the remaining 2, neutral.We, therefore had 12 total conditions out of which we could test 6 out leaving out counterbalancing the movie sequence for the pilot.

### 3.2 Interface Design

The experiment includes a simple text editor with word complete and next phrase suggestion capabilities. Figure 1 shows the interface and the distinction between word and phrase complete. Every time a user presses any key; after a delay of 250ms, a word complete suggestion is displayed. The user can then choose to accept the suggestion by pressing tab or right arrow key or can ignore the suggestion by continuing to type. Every time the user pauses for more than 500ms, the next phrase suggestion is displayed. The user can press tab to accept the subsequent word in the phrase. When the user does that, the word gets selected and added to the input field.

Figure 1: The first line shows a "Word Complete" instance, a user can accept the word as they write. The second line shows a combination of "Word Complete" and "Phrase Complete" instance, user can press tab and accept the word suggestion and then as many words from phrase suggestion that they need. Third is a 'Phrase Complete' Instance

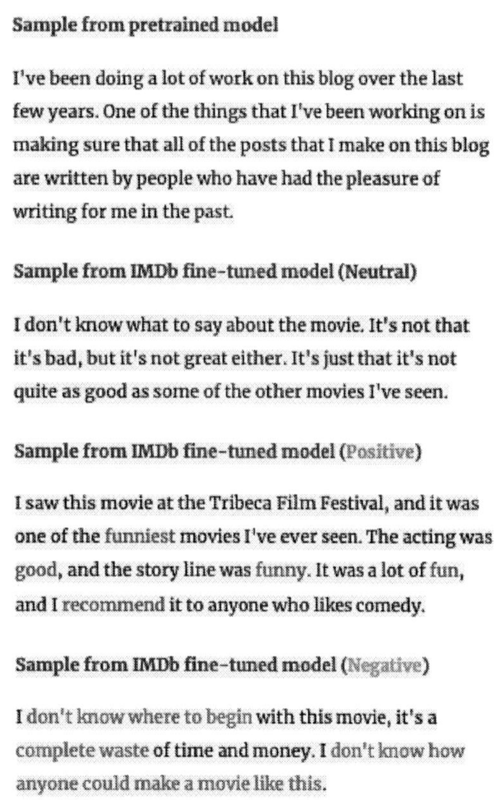


Figure 2: Generated samples from pre-trained, fine-tuned neutral, fine-tuned positive biased and fine-tuned negative biased models

According to the system that users are allotted, users are presented with word complete and next word/phrase suggestions that are either positively or negatively biased or do not have a bias.

### 3.3 Next Phrase Suggestion Model

We have used the GPT-2 (Radford et al., 2019) pretrained model and fine tuned it on the IMDb movie reviews corpus to create the next phrase suggestion model. We have trained one model on positive reviews, one on negative reviews and another general model on both positive and negative reviews. We then use these models to generate next-phrase and word complete suggestions for users. We fine-tuned each model for 3 training epochs and obtained a test perplexity score of 36.9713 for positive model, 34.6978 for negative model and 32.297 for the neutral model. The figure includes sample texts generated by the various fine-tuned models as well as a sample from the original pretrained model for comparison.

### 3.4 Sentiment validation

We performed a validation step to ensure that the models trained in such a way are able to generate sentiment controlled suggestions. We used 500 positive and 500 negative test reviews as prompts and used each of the above models to generate text using said prompts. We then pass the generated text (Just the part of the text that was newly generated leaving out the original prompt as that might affect the performance of sentiment validation process) through a BERT sentiment classifier which had been fine-tuned for the IMDb movies reviews sentiment classification task. Here we see that the text generated by the positive model has a mean sentiment logit score of 2.3 and those generated by the negative model have a mean sentiment logit score of -1.6 (The higher the score, the more positive the sentiment).

### 3.5 Model Usefulness

We describe the model usefulness as the ability of the model to output the same text as the user, given the user's previously typed text. This way of calculating usefulness of the model is inspired by (Arnold et al., 2020). We compute this by running over the sample of user texts which have been written without using text completion. We start with the user's first word and have the model compute the next phrase and we increase the usefulness count by 1 for every consecutive word starting from the first word that the model generates correctly. We then consider both the first and second word typed by the user and generate text using those words, and again update the usefulness count. We continue this process for the entirety of the user's text and finally divide the usefulness count by the total number of words in user input to get the usefulness score. We do this process 5 times for each user and average the scores. We then average the scores for all users to get a usefulness score for the entire model. Higher the score, more relevant suggestions the model gives. We propose this as a way to validate the real-world usefulness of a model in the next phrase suggestion setting. We obtained the following scores from our models and include the score for an AWD-LSTM model fine-tuned on the same IMDb corpus for comparison.

| Model | Usefulness |
|---|---|
| Positive Fine-Tuned GPT-2 | 0.3 |
| Negative Fine-Tuned GPT-2 | 0.29 |
| Neutral Fine-Tuned GPT-2 | 0.29 |
| Neutral Fine-Tuned AWD-LSTM | 0.23 |

Table 1: Usefulness Score Comparison Across different models

### 3.6 Users

The pilot included 6 participants. Participants had a primary and secondary education in an English medium school. None of the participants were native English speakers and all of them considered English to be a second or third language. All the participants were fairly exposed to western cinema in general. We also made sure that the users had previously used next-phrase / word complete interfaces like Google Smart Compose. Most participants did not have experience writing movie reviews before, but almost all of them had read movie reviews at multiple points of time. Participants were recruited through social media platforms.

### 3.7 Analysis Methods

#### 3.7.1 Text Analysis

In order to analyse the text qualitatively, we designed a simple tool to simulate and replay the writer's writing process. The tool had play, pause, rewind and fast-forward functionalities which helped us control the writing process like a video. As seen in Figure 3, we use colours to tag Phrase Completes, Word Completes and Suggestions and replay the entire writing process of the reviewer and analyse the text and user's behaviour. Tagging written content according to user actions gives us an insight into the users writing process and helps us code user behaviour which we can then analyse. We used affinity mapping as a qualitative data analysis approach to analyse these writing processes.

#### 3.7.2 Interviews

After the users wrote their reviews, we conducted a conversational interview. We tried to understand their experience while using the tool and the suggestions, asked them if they remembered any peculiar incidents, and if they had any feedback about the system and the suggestions. We recorded these interview sessions, coded them and analysed them using affinity mapping.

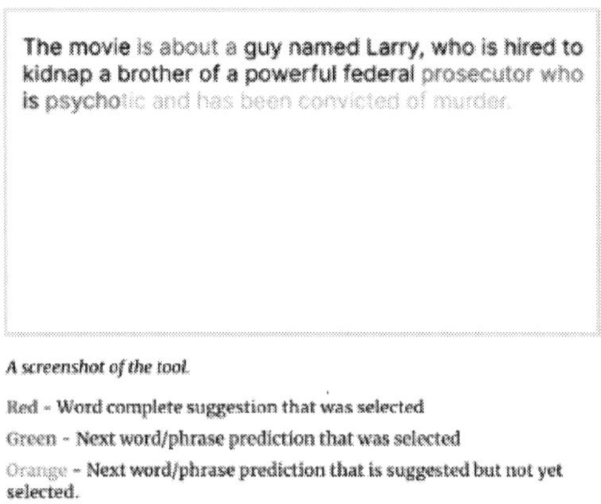


Figure 3: Visualization of the keystroke log with written text tagged with corresponding user actions.

## 4 Results And Analysis

### 4.1 Users used suggestions as prompts for writing.

While traditionally, the aim for having text suggestions in a text editor is to save time and effort while writing, users also used these suggestions as prompts for writing. Users reported that they got ideas about sentence structure, vocabulary, and even content from the suggestions. Almost all users reported that suggestions helped them frame their sentences. Some users also stated that writing reviews were easier with suggestions than without any suggestions because of the same.

### 4.2 Some users considered the suggestions as an authority on how to write movie reviews.

Most users in the study were amateur movie reviewers. Some of them took cues from the suggestions on how to write movie reviews. Users had a notion that the suggestions are 'based on the writing of other (perhaps more experienced) reviewers' while they did not know the exact mechanism through which these suggestions are generated. Users also reported that at times they second-guessed their own writing because of the sentences suggested. As these were inexperienced reviewers, they doubted whether their sentence structure and vocabulary was appropriate for writing a movie review. This could also be a function of users being non-native English speakers.

### 4.3 Influence on writing

Users reported that they selected a suggestion as long as it was 'more or less' similar to what they wanted to write. While this was true for most users, the amount of deviation (from the sentence they had in mind) that they would allow differed between users. There, at times, seemed to be a compromise between being true to what they wanted to write, on one hand, and saving effort by selecting suggestions, on the other. Some users reported that they wrote the 'key words' of a sentence on their own but used suggestions to enter 'filler' or 'generic' words. That being said, users' vocabulary did get influenced by the suggestions. On multiple instances, users took inspiration from previous suggestions and used the vocabulary appearing in those suggestions for composing new sentences.

### 4.4 Users sensed the bias in the system.

Most users could sense that the system was biased towards a particular sentiment. When there was a mismatch in user's intent and system bias, a user rightly pointed out that "The suggestions I got were positive, but the review I was writing was on the negative side." Similarly, users could also sense the extent to which the suggestions were biased. One user mentioned that, "The sentences which i was writing were negative and so were the suggestions, but the words chosen were very different. It changed the meaning of what I wanted to say and made it more extreme." Another user perceived the suggestions to have some form of intention. They said, "When I write something negative, the sug-

| | Model Bias | Writer rating | Guessed Rating | Word Completes (WC) | Phrase Completes (PC) | Mean Words Accepted per PC | Characters Deleted (CD) | Words Deleted (WD) |
|---|---|---|---|---|---|---|---|---|
| 0 | Pos | 7 | 7.7 | 8 | 53 | 3.857143 | 152 | 8 |
| 1 | Neg | 6 | 6.7 | 2 | 17 | 2.428571 | 75 | 8 |
| 2 | Pos | 3 | 2.3 | 19 | 25 | 1.625000 | 274 | 19 |
| 3 | Neu | 10 | 9.3 | 1 | 14 | 5.000000 | 157 | 8 |
| 4 | Pos | 2 | 1.7 | 14 | 33 | 3.888889 | 213 | 20 |
| 5 | Neg | 6 | 5.3 | 6 | 21 | 4.200000 | 293 | 22 |

Table 2: Writer rating is the star rating that the writers gave after watching the movie. Guessed ratings are star ratings which were given only on the basis of the reviews written by corresponding writers by third party readers. We mention the Word Completes and Phrase Completes that were used by each participant. We also mention the characters and words that were deleted by each user. Furthermore, we also show the average words that the user accepted in every phrase complete instance

gestions try to cover it up, most of the time. Not every time."

### 4.5 Users often ended up deleting selected phrase suggestions

When asked whether their writing was influenced because of the bias in the suggestions that they had noticed, users often said it wasn't and that they decided what they wanted to write before they started writing. While this was true, users did select a significant amount of next word/phrase predictions, but they also ended up deleting a considerable chunk of this text and replaced it with their own typed text. It might be that the suggestions felt right in the moment, but did not flow well with the argument they were trying to make and hence on a second glance, users often ended up editing these sentences or straight up deleting them.

### 4.6 Users used the suggestion system creatively with their sentences

Users used the suggestions as tools to anticipate and iterate with different possible sentence constructions to arrive at a desirable final sentence. Similarly, by evaluating how the predicted sentence sounded, users used next phrase prediction to check appropriateness of their sentence's grammar and construction. Users also selected multiple full phrases to see what direction they take and then deleted them but took inspiration from them to write their sentences. Likewise, for word complete, users completed suggested words like 'interesting' and then deleted the last 3 letters to write what the intended to write ie. 'interest'.

### 4.7 Users sometimes ignored suggestions even when the suggestions matched

There were multiple instances for almost every user where users chose to type the full word out even when word complete or next word suggestions matched precisely to what they were typing. According to what the users reported in the interviews, they did not pay much attention to the suggestions when they were exactly sure about what they wanted to write. This could be one explanation for why users typed the whole word even when the same word was suggested.

### 4.8 Suggestions disrupted the user's thought process

When a suggestion was not relevant to what users wanted to write, it disrupted their thought process, often causing them to forget what they originally had planned to write. They were particularly disappointed when the irrelevant suggestions were long, since the effort put into reading them felt like a waste.

## 5 Conclusion

In this pilot study, we qualitatively analysed the writing process of the users while they used an inline next phrase suggestion interface with sentiment bias. This was our first step towards coming up with a theory for how users interact with text prediction models and how introducing sentiment bias in the text prediction model affects users' writing. We conducted the pilot study with 6 users. While we could come up with some interesting themes to describe users' writing process, we are much far away from coming up with a robust theory. We intend to do so in the future.

## References

Kenneth C. Arnold, Krysta Chauncey, and Krzysztof Z. Gajos. 2018. Sentiment bias in predictive text recommendations results in biased writing. In *Proceedings of the 44th Graphics Interface Conference*, GI '18, page 42–49, Waterloo, CAN. Canadian Human-Computer Communications Society.

Kenneth C. Arnold, Krysta Chauncey, and Krzysztof Z. Gajos. 2020. Predictive text encourages predictable writing. In *Proceedings of the 25th International Conference on Intelligent User Interfaces*, IUI '20, page 128–138, New York, NY, USA. Association for Computing Machinery.

Linda Flower and John R. Hayes. 1981. A cognitive process theory of writing. *College Composition and Communication*, 32(4):365–387.

Alec Radford, Jeffrey Wu, Rewon Child, David Luan, Dario Amodei, and Ilya Sutskever. 2019. Language models are unsupervised multitask learners. *OpenAI blog*, 1(8):9.